About the Author

Bill Kresnak is a popular motojournalist with more than 35 years of experience riding all types of motorcycles, from dirt bikes and cruisers to some of the fastest sportbikes on the planet. He currently is the government affairs editor for *American Motorcyclist* magazine, the magazine of the American Motorcyclist Association (AMA), which is the largest motorcycling organization devoted to rights, riding, and racing in the world. Kresnak is intimately familiar with safe motorcycle riding practices through his work at the AMA, but he also has toured many parts of the country by motorcycle and has reported on some of the biggest motorcycling events in the nation. Before becoming a motojournalist, Kresnak worked for almost 20 years as a reporter in Honolulu, where he covered government and politics — first for United Press International and then for *The Honolulu Advertiser.* He earned his journalism degree from Michigan State University in 1978, and he currently lives in Reynoldsburg, Ohio.

Dedication

For my young children, Adrian Samantha and Joshua Enoch Keoki, and their mom, Sheryll, who all still find a remarkable wonder in each day; for Cindy Shultz, my muse who convinced me to sit down and write when I really wanted to go out and ride; and for all my friends, who are also my colleagues, at the American Motorcyclist Association; they are the most knowledgeable, dedicated motorcyclists in the world who do a tremendous job of fostering motorcyclists' rights, riding, and racing.

Author's Acknowledgments

My heartfelt gratitude goes to the following individuals for their help in making this book possible:

Kevin Foley, Yamaha Motor Corporation, USA

Garrett Kai, American Suzuki Motor Corporation

Jan Pressler, Kawasaki Motors Corporation

Mike Morgan, Harley-Davidson Motor Company

Bruce Mullins, Skunkworx Custom Cycles

Jon Row, American Honda Motor Corporation

Publisher's Acknowledgments

We're proud of this book; please send us your comments through our Dummies online registration form located at www.dummies.com/register/.

Some of the people who helped bring this book to market include the following:

Acquisitions, Editorial, and Media Development

Senior Project Editor: Christina Guthrie

Acquisitions Editor: Mike Baker

Copy Editors: Jessica Smith, Krista Hansing

Editorial Program Coordinator: Erin Calligan Mooney

Technical Editor: Grant Parsons

Editorial Manager: Christine Meloy Beck

Editorial Assistants: Joe Niesen, David Lutton, Leeann Harney

Cover Photos:

Cartoons: Rich Tennant (www.the5thwave.com)

Composition Services

Project Coordinator: Katherine Key

Layout and Graphics: Carl Byers, Reuben W. Davis, Alissa D. Ellet, Stephanie D. Jumper, Christine Williams

Proofreaders: Context Editorial Services, John Greenough

Indexer: Christine Spina Karpeles

Special Help: Christy Pingleton, Chad Sievers

Publishing and Editorial for Consumer Dummies

    Diane Graves Steele, Vice President and Publisher, Consumer Dummies

    Joyce Pepple, Acquisitions Director, Consumer Dummies

    Kristin A. Cocks, Product Development Director, Consumer Dummies

    Michael Spring, Vice President and Publisher, Travel

    Kelly Regan, Editorial Director, Travel

Publishing for Technology Dummies

    Andy Cummings, Vice President and Publisher, Dummies Technology/General User

Composition Services

    Gerry Fahey, Vice President of Production Services

    Debbie Stailey, Director of Composition Services

Contents at a Glance

Table of Contents

Part III: You and Your Machine 125

Introduction

You see motorcyclists everywhere: having a good time navigating city streets, enjoying the ocean air while cruising along the beach, or just having fun riding in the countryside. To the outsider, motorcycling is simple. It's just motorcyclists out having fun.

And while it's true that motorcycling is simple, it's also a lot more complex than just a rider, a bike, and a good time. In fact, there are facets to the sport that even many longtime motorcyclists don't understand.

It's easy to have a lot of fun on a motorcycle without knowing a whole lot about motorcycling. But it's even more fun when you do. And it's also a lot safer when you know about the proper riding techniques, the safety gear, the items you should take with you on long trips, and the handling characteristics of different types of motorcycles.

Motorcycling really is a mysterious world to the outsider, to the new rider, and even to some experienced riders. But, really, it isn't that difficult to understand the complexities of motorcycling; it just takes some time to discover them all. In fact, sometimes it takes years — unless, of course, you read this book.

And to be frank, you'll meet a lot of "know-it-alls" in the motorcycling world. But, unlike those folks, I have a lot of knowledge and facts to back up my statements! I began riding when I was 17, and I have been passionate about motorcycles ever since. I've done a little bit of racing, and I've covered all aspects of the sport as a motojournalist for almost a decade.

So, it has taken me about 35 years of being heavily involved in motorcycling to learn everything I know. And with all that knowledge, I wrote this book for new riders, serious riders, and even people who don't ride but want to understand a friend or relative who does.

About This Book

For new riders, this book is full of the useful information that's needed to confidently get started in the wonderful world of motorcycling. I cover everything you need to know. I explain different types of motorcycles, the various motorcycling cultures, how to fit in with other motorcyclists, how to get your motorcycle license, safe riding techniques, and much, much more.

For the experienced rider, this book is just as useful. It's chock-full of information and useful tips to make motorcycling a lot more enjoyable and safer, too. I also delve into topics such as how to keep your bike from getting ripped off both at home and on the ride, what essential items you need to take on a week-long trip, and how to plan a rewarding trip when you have a limited amount of time.

All riders can benefit from the strategies in this book, especially those strategies for buying a new or used bike, selecting the proper safety gear, getting your child involved in motorcycling, and understanding the ins and outs of insurance. Plus, I cover fun stuff like motorcycling movies, major motorcycling events, and customizing your motorcycle.

My goal for this book is to help all riders understand the richness of motorcycling, the camaraderie, and why it's such a passion not only for me but for motorcyclists around the world.

And the greatest thing about this book is that each chapter is written in a simple, understandable way so that even people with zero motorcycling experience (as well as those with many years' experience on the road) can be entertained and benefit. Motorcycling is fun, and the best way to make this motorcycling book fun to read is to simply jump around to the sections and chapters that interest you the most. In fact, even the sections of the chapters are easy to read and digest. Feel free to jump around to different chapters and different sections any time you want.

Conventions Used in This Book

To help you navigate this book with ease, I include the following few conventions:

- **Boldfaced** words highlight the keywords in bulleted lists and numbered steps.
- *Italics* emphasize keywords and important terms.
- `Monofont` indicates Web addresses.

When this book was printed, some Web addresses may have needed to break across two lines of text. If that happens, rest assured that I haven't put in any extra characters (such as hyphens) to indicate the break. So, when using one of these Web addresses, just type in exactly what you see in this book, pretending as though the line break doesn't exist.

What You're Not to Read

As you're going through this book, feel free to skip any text marked with the Technical Stuff icon. This text is interesting, but it isn't essential to your understanding of the topic. The sidebars, which are the gray shaded boxes you see throughout this book, are also skippable (but I highly suggest you read these fun and interesting tidbits!).

Foolish Assumptions

I assume that you have an interest in motorcycling; otherwise, you wouldn't be reading this book. Maybe you think motorcycling looks like a lot of fun but you want to learn more about it before shelling out the big bucks for your very own bike. Or maybe you're an experienced rider looking for good tips to make your riding safer and more fun. Or maybe you just know a motorcyclist and want to find out why he or she is so passionate about motorcycling. No matter why you've picked up this book, you're bound to find the info you need, because I've written it with you in mind.

If you're a new rider or a potential rider, you may have picked up this book to get answers to some of these questions:

- How can I possibly fit in with that tough-looking motorcycling crowd?
- How much is it going to cost me for a bike and safety gear to get started in motorcycling?
- I'm a woman. What special challenges do I face getting into motorcycling?
- What riding techniques do I absolutely need to know to be safe on the road?
- What's a good bike for a beginning motorcyclist?

If you're an experienced rider, you already have a passion for motorcycling and a desire to learn even more. If you fall into this category, you may have questions like this:

- What are some advanced riding techniques I need to master so that I'm prepared for any situation on the road?
- What are some travel tips that ensure I can have a safe and enjoyable long-distance ride?

> ✓ Which of the mega-motorcycling rallies around the country is best for me to attend?
>
> ✓ Which motorcycling organizations should I belong to in order to get the most out of motorcycling?

If you don't ride a motorcycle, but have a loved one or friend who does, maybe you have questions like these:

> ✓ How can anyone in their right mind ride a motorcycle when they're so dangerous? That is, what's the allure of riding one?
>
> ✓ Why do some motorcyclists wear black jackets that make them look so scary while others have colorful jackets (sometimes even with touches of pink)?
>
> ✓ Are motorcyclists lone wolves or social animals?

In *Motorcycling For Dummies,* you get the answers to all these questions and more. This book isn't just Motorcycling 101; it's a fairly complete collection of what every motorcyclist needs to know.

How This Book Is Organized

The six parts of this book are organized so that you can find what you need to know quickly. Each part is centered on a specific topic, so simply determine what it is that you need to know and then check out the corresponding part.

Part 1: The Mysterious World of Motorcycling

If you've never ridden a motorcycle or hung around with motorcycling types, you're probably wondering what the attraction is. Why do bankers, lawyers, movie stars, and factory workers all ride motorcycles? Why are there so many different types of motorcycles? After all, isn't just one style good enough? And why has the media portrayed motorcyclists as thugs? Are they all really bad seeds? Finally, you may wonder how someone learns to ride a motorcycle. In this part, I reveal the answers. If you're more experienced and know the answers, you'll still appreciate this part because I reveal some of the little-known history of motorcycling, and some of the knowledge experienced riders can gain by becoming involved in a track school or getting other advanced riding training.

Part II: Welcome to the Club

So you've decided to get into motorcycling? Great! Remember that there are a lot of different subcultures in motorcycling. But don't worry. This part explains all of the subcultures so you can decide which crowd you want to run with. And if you're in the market for a bike, this is the part for you. Here I reveal the different styles and cultures associated with them. In this part, I also provide some special advice and tips for women, and what everyone needs to know to suit up for the ride. Plus, if your kids want to ride, this part provides the info on how to get them started safely. All in all, this part gives you the information that you need to feel like a veteran rider.

Part III: You and Your Machine

This part is the real nuts-and-bolts part of the book. It explains what makes a good beginner machine, and it shows you what's available out there. I spell out what to look for when buying a new or used motorcycle, and I show you how to maintain your machine to keep it running properly. Plus, because motorcycling is about individuality, I discuss how to customize your bike to make it your own. And, of course, you need insurance for your machine, so I include all the important info. Motorcycle insurance, in some aspects, is different from that which you buy for your car, so don't feel like you can skip this chapter.

Part IV: Let's Ride!

This part has all the really fun stuff that's important for both novice riders and long-time veterans. For instance, what ritual should you follow before taking off on a ride? What are some of the proven techniques for handling obstacles and other dangers while on the road? And how do you deal with potential disasters such as a stuck throttle. How do you ride safely in a large group? Where are some great places to ride, and how does someone plan a dream motorcycle trip? All this, and more, is explored in this part.

Part V: The Part of Tens

Do you need a quick hit to take care of your motorcycling jones? This is the place to look. Here, you find some quick hits in bite-sized morsels that give you a little taste of motorcycling. In these chapters, you get a quick look at some of the best motorcycling events on the planet, some of the greatest motorcycling organizations in the United States, and some of the greatest men and women ever involved in the sport. Plus, there's a rundown of motor-cycling movies, from the great to the, well, not-so-great.

Part VI: Appendixes

Motorcyclists have their own vocabulary, and there are some key words that all motorcyclists must know. What are they? You'll find them in this part. But wait, there's more! If you want to make a cross-country trip — and what motorcyclist doesn't? — there are key motorcycling laws you need to know for every state. Finally, you can never have too much information when it comes to motorcycling, so in the last appendix, I provide a sampling of great motorcycling resources that provide everything from places to buy gear to trip-planning tips.

Icons Used in This Book

In this book, you find icons — little symbols in the margins of the pages — to point out different types of information. The information highlighted by these icons is easy to understand and gives you important time- or money-saving tips. It can also warn you of dangers. Here's a list of the icons I use in this book:

 This icon highlights the technical stuff that motorheads know but that isn't critical for you to know. However, feel free to read these tidbits and then throw them out at biker gatherings. Your riding buddies will be impressed.

 This icon points out pieces of information that are — you guessed it — important to remember.

 When you see this icon you know you're looking at information that will save you time, money, or effort.

 Beware! Read this info carefully because it will keep you from losing money, getting hurt, or being a danger to others.

Where to Go from Here

This book isn't meant to be read from front to back and from cover to cover. However, because you have an interest in motorcycling, you'll probably read the entire book eventually anyway. Just remember that the book is designed so that you can jump around to the parts and chapters that interest you most when you want.

For example, if you're a woman, you may want to read the chapter about women in motorcycling first. If you're an experienced rider, maybe you'll start with the chapter on what to be sure to pack for a long trip. And if you're a new rider undecided about what kind of motorcycle you may want to buy, maybe you'll start by reading the chapters involving different motorcycling cultures or different beginner bikes.

Who knows, maybe you just get bored one Saturday night and want to rent a bunch of motorcycle movies for the evening but don't know which ones. In that case, just turn to Chapter 21 and take your pick. On the other hand, if it's time to get or renew your motorcycle insurance, flip to Chapter 10 to be sure you understand what kind of insurance you need so you don't spend more money than you should.

And if you need to, simply take a look at the table of contents and the index to pick a topic and dive in. After you start down the road of motorcycling, you'll never turn back because motorcycling is all about having fun. And so is this book.

Part I
The Mysterious World of Motorcycling

The 5th Wave   By Rich Tennant

In this part . . .

If you take a look around you see motorcycles every-where. Doctors ride them, and so do lawyers, movie stars, and factory workers. But why? After all, if you want to get from Point A to Point B safely and surrounded by luxury wouldn't you just drive a car? Well, I suppose, but riding a motorcycle isn't just about getting from Point A to Point B. In this part, I explain the allure of motorcycling for so many people.

I also reveal why motorcyclists believe, correctly, that they're part of a special club, not only because of the skills involved in riding but also because of the rich his-tory of the sport. Plus, I give you a heads-up on how to get proper motorcycle safety training, what to expect in class, and what you need to do to get your motorcycle endorse-ment on your car driver's license. Armed with this knowl-edge, you're ready to get started in the wonderful world of motorcycling.

Chapter 1

The Allure of Motorcycling: Six Million Motorcyclists Can't Be Wrong

In This Chapter

▶ Discovering the joy of motorcycling

▶ Understanding the glamorous side of motorcycling

▶ Fitting in as a woman in a traditionally male motorcycling world

▶ Sharing motorcycling with children

▶ Exploring motorcycle safety

"Motorcycles Are Everywhere." That's a popular bumper sticker that bikers like to hand out to car drivers to encourage them to watch for motorcycles on the road. Car drivers aren't trained to look for bikes, so many times they don't see them.

The fact is, motorcycles *are* everywhere. Motorcyclists cruise the highways and byways, ride along city streets, and tackle twisty roads in the mountains. Some 6 million motorcyclists drive in the United States today, including everyone from California Governor Arnold Schwarzenegger to movie stars Brad Pitt and Angelina Jolie; to TV talk show host Jay Leno; to doctors, lawyers, accountants, factory workers, and probably one or more of your neighbors.

Next time you're driving on the road, make a conscious effort to actually look for motorcycles — you'll be surprised by how many you actually see. And you'll wonder why you didn't see them before. Motorcycles *are* everywhere.

In this chapter, you discover why motorcyclists are addicted to motorcycling, why every ride on a motorcycle is an adventure, and why a motorcyclist laughs under his helmet when some hotshot in a Lamborghini pulls up alongside and revs his or her engine. You also get a taste of what it actually feels like to be a motorcyclist, and you get a look at the glamorous world of motorcycle racing. Plus, you discover how women are making inroads into motorcycling, and why a chick who rides her own bike isn't just cool, but supercool. And, of course, you explore motorcycle riding techniques and safety, and how to have great motorcycling fun with your kids.

Are Bikes Better Than Cars? You Bet!

A car driver shouldn't even try to convince a motorcyclist that cars are better than bikes. There's just no comparison. You want basic transportation with a lot of cool factor? A motorcycle has it in spades. You want cheap transportation that's a lot of fun to ride? Yep, that's a motorcycle. You want plush seats, climate control, protection from the rain, and the ability to carry a lot of dogs and stuff? Okay, get a car.

Unless a motorcyclist needs to carry a lot of stuff or it's bitter cold outside with ice on the road, a motorcyclist prefers to ride his or her motorcycle. A motorcycle gives a motorcyclist a true sense of freedom, even when making only a short hop down to the grocery store for a quart of milk. That's true for a lot of reasons, and in this section, I point out a few of the best.

Just in case the reasons I list in this section aren't enough, here's one more: Under federal law, a motorcycle is allowed to use every high-occupancy vehicle (HOV) lane in the United States without having to carry a passenger.

Motorcycling has a certain mystique

One reason motorcyclists prefer their bikes to cars is the long history of motorcyclists being seen as out-of-the-ordinary. They're seen as people who are willing to add a little adventure to their lives and who maybe are a little rough around the edges. Part of this mystique is the thrill of throwing a leg over a motorcycle and feeling the wind rush by as you ride. And part of it is just knowing that you belong to a motorcycling fraternity that includes not only some of the roughest, toughest guys on the planet, but also some of the richest and most glamorous people in the world.

Just about everybody drives a car. But not everybody rides a motorcycle. That alone makes motorcyclists special. Throw in how motorcyclists feel about themselves when they ride, the fact that a motorcycle gets two or even three times the gas mileage that a car does, and the exhilaration of controlling a nimble machine, and you have a combination that adds up to just plain fun.

And really, fun is what motorcycling is all about. How many people have fun when they get in their cars to drive somewhere? For most people, driving the car isn't part of the experience of going somewhere; driving is just transportation. A motorcycle is transportation, but it's also recreation. Motorcyclists are fond of saying that when they have a rough day at work or just want to clear their minds of any troubles, they go for a ride.

Enjoying the outdoors, biker style, is great fun

Imagine that, one sunny day, you decide to take a little trip through farm country into the mountains. Should you take your bike or your car? Decisions, decisions. Not! You hop on your bike, start it up, and hear the motor roar to life. You feel the vibration of the machine, put it in gear, and head out of your driveway toward the countryside.

Cruising along country roads, you feel the warm sun on your face and a soothing, warm breeze rushing past your body, and you smell the sweet fragrance of wildflowers along the road. Cows graze lazily in pastures as you ride by, and you get a strong whiff of, well, cow manure. Okay, so riding in the country isn't always a party for your senses. But most of the time it is, and when you're boxed up in a car riding those country roads, the experience just isn't the same.

Getting off the straight, country roads, you find yourself starting to wind up into the mountains. The road gets steeper, the air cools, and you fall into a rhythm, leaning the bike left, right, left as you climb higher and higher, the strong smell of pine filling your nostrils. You get to a point when the road is just snaking turns with few straights, so you lean the bike over farther to make the turns. On the country roads you were just enjoying the scenery, sights, and sounds, but now you are focused on the road and mastering every corner. It's a challenge, but it's intensely satisfying.

Near the top of the mountain is a lookout, and you see that you aren't alone. Other bikers have also made the trip and have stopped at the lookout to drink in the view. You stop, enjoy the great weather and scenery, and chat. After all, motorcyclists are always instant friends. "Where are you from?" "What are you riding?" "Have you ever been to . . .?"

One by one, the motorcyclists hop on their bikes, click them into gear, and head back down the mountain. You wait, now alone at the lookout, basking in the sun and the silence. Too soon it's time to go. Heading down the mountain, you decide to take a little ride past the beach before you head home.

As you cruise along the beach, heads turn, people smile, and children wave. You slow to a crawl to enjoy the scenery. All is right with the world. Motorcycling really is a sensory experience that you just can't get driving a car.

Every ride is an adventure

Mount up and head out! Today's motorcyclists are modern-day cowboys, seeking adventure wherever they go. And the adventure isn't always the destination. In fact, most times it isn't. The adventure is the ride itself.

Besides feeling alive while riding a bike because all the senses are at work, a motorcyclist enjoys the satisfaction of operating his or her machine. Operating a motorcycle requires a lot of coordination, and operating one *well* takes a lot of skill. Motorcyclists hone their skills every time they hop on a bike, and they get better every day.

So where does the adventure begin? It begins as soon as you stick the key into the bike's ignition switch. You know that this is just the start of a lot of fun, whether the ride is for an hour or a day. Can riding in the city be an adventure? It sure can: You're dodging potholes, navigating traffic, and crossing railroad tracks. Car drivers usually don't think about all these situations, but motorcyclists must in order to stay safe. As a result, motorcyclists have heightened awareness not only of potential road hazards, but also of the traffic around them and the potentials for other danger.

Motorcyclists can have the most fun on twisty roads, even at legal speeds. For a motorcyclist, nirvana is navigating the twists and turns of a curvy road at a spirited pace. Being in total control of the machine, being one with the bike, is almost Zen-like. Having a heightened awareness is much more critical for a motorcyclist than a car driver. After all, if a car goes off the road, the driver has a lot of steel surrounding him or her in a crash. But a motorcyclist? Miss a corner and hit a tree, and the results can be deadly.

To make the ride really special, top it off with a great destination. Maybe you want to ride to the local motorcyclist gathering place to talk about motorcycling and great rides, or maybe you're heading to a giant rally of motorcyclists where you can meet like-minded riders, test-ride the latest offerings of the motorcycle manufacturers, and find deals on that new jacket or helmet you need.

And motorcyclists don't always ride alone. They're social animals; they like to share the adventure. Little is more fun than hooking up with a bunch of riding buddies and heading off to cruise the beach, explore small towns, or test your skills on some of the twistiest roads in the area. Even more fun is the good-natured ribbing that follows every ride when someone makes a mistake, like taking a corner too wide or braking way too early for a turn. Or even getting lost.

Car drivers might get annoyed when they get lost, but bike riders generally don't seem to mind it. After all, getting lost is part of the adventure of motorcycling — exploring new roads and new towns. Who would have thought that getting lost could be fun? A motorcyclist.

Can you say C-H-E-A-P?

Motorcycles attract a lot of riders because they're a lot of fun packed into a small, nimble, inexpensive package. After all, you can get a great new motorcycle for $7,000. And how much is a new car? You want state-of-the-art technology? Okay, maybe you'll have to spend around $10,000 for a new bike. How much is a new car, again? If you just want cheap, reliable transportation, you can get a good bike for around $1,000. What kind of car can you get for a grand? Probably not much more than a junker.

Plus, with gas hovering around the $3-per-gallon mark, a motorcycle is the way to go. Maybe your car gets 25 miles to the gallon. A gas-guzzling motorcycle gets about 45 miles per gallon, and other motorcycles get even better gas mileage. Motorcyclists do the math and know how to keep money in their pockets.

Riding a motorcycle brings other cost-saving benefits as well. Annual registration is cheaper because registration is usually based on vehicle weight — and, of course, motorcycles weigh a lot less than cars. Some cities have free motorcycle parking to encourage the use of motorcycles to reduce traffic congestion. Road tolls are also usually cheaper as well. Plus, depending on your age, locale, and the type of bike you ride, you'll shell out a lot less cash for a motorcycle than you would for a car.

Performance: What car drivers don't want you to know

Maybe you have a bud who likes to take his car to the dragstrip now and then, and he brags about his 13-second quarter-mile times or about how his car can go from 0 to 60 mph in 7 seconds. Well, as a motorcyclist, you can just nod your head knowingly and smile smugly. You can smoke him at that track on your bike.

Even the most high-performance car on the planet (which probably costs hundreds of thousands of dollars) can't match the performance of today's high-performance motorcycles (which, incidentally, cost around $12,000).

High-performance motorcycles can do the quarter-mile in a little more than nine or ten seconds. You want 0-to-60-mph performance? Put another way, you want to get from stoplight to stoplight quickly? Well, you can get bikes that do 0 to 60 mph in 2.8 seconds. No bragging — just fact. And a car can't match the acceleration of a motorcycle from 60 mph to 80 mph, which is great for passing on the freeway.

Want proof? Consider a 2007–2008 limited production (only 20 built) Lamborghini Reventon high-performance sports car, and a 2008 Suzuki Hayabusa mass-produced high-performance motorcycle:

Category	*Reventon*	*Hayabusa*
MSRP	$1,485,100	$11,999
0 to 60 mph	3.3 seconds	2.8 seconds
Top speed	211 mph	186 mph (factory-set limit)

If you really think about it, these stats make sense. After all, the power-to-weight ratio of a motorcycle far exceeds that of a car. Motorcycles are very light, and the motors of the high-performance bikes pump out 150, 160, even 170 horsepower. Think about your own car. How much horsepower does it have? Maybe 150 or 200 horsepower? And what does it weigh? Maybe 3,000 pounds, compared to maybe 400 or 500 pounds or less for a high-performance bike? You do the math.

Plus, the high-performance motorcycle market is extremely competitive. The manufacturers have to employ cutting-edge technology to make their motors powerful and to keep their suspensions up to snuff to handle the performance. Otherwise they'll drop out of the market.

Even motorcycles that aren't considered high-performance bikes can smoke cars on the quarter-mile. Maybe a few high-performance production cars that cost hundreds of thousands of dollars have higher top speeds than today's motorcycles. But high-performance motorcycles can go up to 186 mph (300 kph). The motorcycle manufacturers have a gentlemen's agreement to cap the top speed of their bikes at 186 mph because of rumblings in Europe a while back that motorcycles were being made to go too fast.

The bottom line is that even bikes that aren't high-performance machines generally can outperform a car. "So what?" the car guys may say with their feelings hurt. High performance isn't just for bragging rights; although that's fun, too. High performance gives motorcycle riders a safety edge to get out of the way quickly when a car changes lanes into the path of the motorcycle, or to stop quickly to avoid a collision.

The Glamour of Motorcycling

Okay, quick quiz. What do the following people have in common: Ben Affleck, Jessica Alba, Catherine Bell, James Belushi, Nicolas Cage, George Clooney, Tom Cruise, Billy Ray Cyrus, Leonardo DiCaprio, Fabio, Laurence Fishburne, Harrison Ford, Mel Gibson, Sammy Hagar, Hulk Hogan, Kate Hudson, and Lauren Hutton?

And what about Billy Joel, Angelina Jolie, Perry King, Queen Latifah, Hugh Laurie, Jay Leno, Lyle Lovett, Ricky Martin, Ewan McGregor, Juan Pablo Montoya, Kyle Petty, Richard Petty, Brad Pitt, Dennis Rodman, Arnold Schwarzenegger, Bruce Springsteen, Billy Bob Thornton, Bruce Willis, and Dwight Yoakam?

They're all celebrities — the "beautiful people" — and they all ride motorcycles. In fact, a lot of them are hard-core motorcyclists. Sure, Ewan McGregor is well known for portraying Obi-Wan Kenobi in the *Star Wars* movies. But many movie-lovers also followed his filmed exploits with buddy Charley Boorman when they traveled from London to New York by way of Europe, Mongolia, and Canada. The television series was called *Long Way Round.*

Or consider Catherine Bell, a star of the television series *JAG,* who also starred in the movie *Bruce Almighty.* At last count, she had a dozen motorcycles. And singer Lyle Lovett loves to ride motorcycles on the street *and* in the dirt.

Before he died in 1990, multimillionaire Malcolm Forbes was famed for taking bike trips with his motorcycle club, the Capitalist Tools — and with actress Elizabeth Taylor as a passenger!

Today riding motorcycles is chic. And it's fun to know that, as a motorcyclist, you have such good company. After all, we can't all be famous celebrities, but we can do something that they do. Or, if you look at it backward, famous celebrities and millionaires want to be like us! So you, too, can be part of the "in" crowd. All it takes is about a thousand bucks for a used motorcycle.

Riding makes you feel Marlon-Brando cool

A famous poster made from a photograph from the 1954 film *The Wild One* shows Marlon Brando sitting on a Triumph motorcycle. (I discuss this movie in Chapter 2 and in Chapter 21.) He looks soooo cool. In fact, he's cool throughout the movie. At one point in the movie, this motorcycling rebel is asked, "What are you rebelling against, Johnny?" To this he replies, "Whaddya got?"

All of us have a little Johnny in us. Maybe we have to wear a suit and tie when we go to work; or we need to punch the clock at the factory at a certain time, eat lunch at a certain time, and punch out at a certain time. We have bosses at work telling us what to do; we have responsibilities at home we have to take care of. Maybe we want to rebel against everything, but we can't. We can, however, feel like a rebel and feel cool when we ride our motorcycles.

After all, motorcycling isn't just about motorcycles. Motorcycles are a key component, of course, but motorcycling, really, is all about how it makes you feel. And when you put on your black leather jacket, black pants, and motorcycling boots and then pull on your gloves and hop on your bike, you can feel like Johnny in the movie. Go ahead, add a little sneer right after you fire up your machine and take off down the road. It's fun, and nobody gets hurt.

Maybe you're looking for a different kind of cool. Maybe you don't want to be a rebel. Maybe you want to be (and be seen as) an adventurer, ready to ride thousands of miles at a moment's notice — willing to ride 500 miles just to have lunch at a cool restaurant. You can do that, and you can have tales from your adventures to tell anyone who asks.

Admit it, you don't feel very cool when you hop into the family minivan. But when you hop on your motorcycle? It conjures up a whole different world in your head. You can live your fantasy. In fact, on a bike, your fantasy can become reality. You can feel very, very cool.

Being the envy of friends and strangers

When you take up motorcycling, people look at you in a different light — especially if you're the kind of person others wouldn't expect to ride a motorcycle. Based on our own life experiences, we all have our own perceptions of who a motorcyclist is and what type of person he or she is. Your friends and family may lecture you, telling you that motorcycles are dangerous and that you're too old to be riding a bike. However, the reality is that most of your friends will be envious and wish they could be motorcyclists, too.

And they have good reason to be envious. Motorcyclists are daring, adventurous types; otherwise they wouldn't ride motorcycles. They would be happy just riding around in cages, which is what motorcyclists call cars. Folks who don't ride motorcycles are envious for a number of reasons. One is the freedom that a motorcyclist has to just hop on his or her bike and ride, searching for adventure. A motorcyclist doesn't need a destination. He or she just needs a bike and some gas money.

Outsiders are also envious of the fun a motorcyclist has riding his or her machine. Most people have been driving cars for so long that they're on automatic pilot when they slide into the driver's seat. Not motorcyclists. On a motorcycle, they're hyperaware of what's going on around them, and they're in total control of the machine, making many quick-as-a-thought decisions during a ride: how to best take this turn, how to avoid that pothole, what gear to be in, how hard to brake, whether a car might pull out of that driveway.

People may think that just cruising down a country road on a motorcycle hearing the rumble of the engine, feeling the sun in your face, and smelling the flowers along the road must make the ride a pleasurable experience. And they're right. Or they may imagine the fun you have strafing tight corners on your high-performance bike; turning left, right, left; going up and down on a roller-coaster ride in the country. Again, they're right. And they're envious.

The bottom line is that friends, and strangers, want to be you. They probably won't admit it, but it's true.

Speaking the unique motorcyclist language

Attitude separates motorcyclists from car drivers. Motorcyclists are more adventurous. They're willing to step out of their comfort zones and try something new, and they're really part of a special group. As part of that special group, motorcyclists also have their own language, which is some of the fun of being a motorcyclist. You can talk biker talk with other motorcyclists that the car drivers don't understand. Being fellow motorcyclists is like knowing a foreign language or having a special handshake.

Biker language, of course, evolved out of the need to communicate with other motorcyclists about certain characteristics of motorcycling. And when talking about biker language, I'm not just talking about the special words that motorcyclists use — I'm also talking about what riders talk about. For example, motorcyclists talk an awful lot about tires. Do car drivers? Ask one of your car-driving buds what size tires are on his or her car, or whether they're high-performance tires. Your bud probably won't know.

A motorcyclist, however, will know all sorts of stuff:

✔ The size of his or her motorcycle tires

✔ The brand of tire they have

✔ Whether they're high-performance tires or tires designed to last a long time

✔ Whether they're radial or bias-ply tires

✔ How many miles he or she gets out of the tires before they need to be replaced

Imagine that you hop on your *Hog* (the trademarked nickname for a big Harley-Davidson motorcycle), and cruise down to a local restaurant that's a popular gathering place for motorcyclists. You park your bike next to a *bagger,* which is a big touring machine with saddlebags or luggage. Another motorcyclist greets you and asks whether you're a member of the *AMA.* That motorcyclist is talking not about the American Medical Association, but about the American Motorcyclist Association, the largest association of motorcyclists in the world.

In the restaurant, you sit down with other bikers and order a cup of coffee and a big slice of apple pie. Someone asks you what you're riding, and you say "a Hog." He replies that he's riding a *Duck* (Ducati). You then get into a discussion of your ride to the restaurant. He asks whether you had any problems on your big machine with the *sweepers,* which are long, gentle curves or turns in the road; or with the *twisties,* which are tight, sharp turns. He then asks whether you saw a bike on its side just off an *off-camber* turn (that is, a turn in which the asphalt tilts down in the opposite direction of the turn). He says he heard that some rider earlier got into the turn too *hot* (fast) "and *threw it in the weeds* (crashed)."

The discussion then turns to the size of the motor in your bike, the tires, how far you've ridden this riding season, your longest trip, what accessories you have on your bike, and other fun stuff all related to motorcycling. As a motorcyclist, if you aren't having fun riding your bike, you're having fun talking about motorcycling. I cover basic motorcyclist language in Appendix A.

Dressing the part of a motorcyclist

Besides riding and talking about motorcycles, what makes motorcycling fun is the wide variety of clothes you can wear that are related to the sport. Like motorcyclists, even nonmotorcyclists like to wear Harley-Davidson and West Coast Chopper T-shirts. Motorcyclists also like to wear and collect special shirts, like from the Harley-Davidson shops in areas where they've visited, or shirts that only other motorcyclists recognize.

For example, a motorcyclist may have a T-shirt from the Smiling Skull biker bar in Athens, Ohio; from Sturgis, South Dakota, which was bought while attending the mega-motorcycle rally there; and from Pacific Harley-Davidson in Honolulu. The collection may also include a foxhead shirt made by Fox Racing; a Gary Nixon Enterprises T-shirt sold by legendary motorcycle racer Gary Nixon; or a fancy Team Suzuki pit-crew shirt. Besides T-shirts and pit-crew shirts, you can buy motorcycle-themed Aloha shirts, dress shirts, tank tops, and more.

Motorcyclists always wear a motorcycle-themed T-shirt under their jacket when they ride. These shirts are part of the culture, and most motorcyclists have a large collection of motorcycle-related T-shirts. But for protection from the road when riding — and to look really cool — a motorcyclist needs a great jacket and other safety gear. Even nonmotorcyclists are dressing the part of motorcyclists nowadays. And why not? The jackets are so cool.

The great thing is that you can choose from an awful lot of great jackets. Dressing up for the ride in black or colorful riding gear is part of the fun of motorcycling. You can dress in a black jacket, black chaps, and black boots for a bad boy/girl look. You can wear a tight-fitting, colorful jacket and pants for a professional racer look. Or you can go with synthetic riding gear to have an adventure-across-Africa look. You can even change your looks, depending on what bike you ride. Though, you do need to wear the right gear for the bike you're riding. Why? To fit in with that subculture of motorcycling. Or, go ahead, be a rebel — wear whatever you want!

You want fringe on your jacket? You can get it. You want an orange and purple jacket? You can get that, too. The fun part of motorcycling clothes is the look, so have fun with it. But remember, motorcycling clothes serve an important safety function: They're made specifically to help protect you in a crash. I discuss riding gear in detail in Chapter 5.

Racing: Mikey (Michael Jordan) likes it!

Motorcycling is glamorous not only because of the people who ride motorcycles, but also because of the popularity of motorcycle sports even among non-motorcyclists. The top two motorcycle sports are *Supercross* and *roadracing*.

Supercross is racing that takes place in a stadium on a dirt course that features high jumps, tight turns, and rows of small hills that racers stutter over. These events are like rock concerts, with bright lights, giant megatron TV screens, fireworks, and professional riders who are as glamorous and popular, and almost as highly paid, as rock stars. If you go to any Supercross race around the country, you'll find thousands of fans screaming for their favorite riders, and probably only a small portion of the fans are motorcyclists. Supercross is great entertainment, something that motorcyclists are proud to be a part of.

Roadracing isn't actually racing on roads. This racing is exciting professional racing that occurs on asphalt tracks around the nation. In these races, riders hit 180 mph or more on their machines, and they ride elbow-to-elbow with other riders. The riders lean so far over in the tight turns that they scrape the knees of their leather racing suits, which have special protection. Some riders lean so far over that they scrape their elbows!

If you attend a professional roadrace, you may see former basketball legend Michael Jordan, who has his own racing team called Michael Jordan Motorsports. He has a two-rider team that races in Superbike and Superstock classes. Or you may bump into actress Catherine Bell or other celebrities who enjoy attending the races. With the colorful race team semitrucks, the carnival atmosphere at the track, and the big money that's put into professional motorcycle roadracing, these events have about all the glamour that you can stand.

Of course, you can find a lot of other motorcycle racing disciplines. But Supercross and roadracing are the two big glamour sports. I discuss some can't-miss races in Chapter 16.

Women in a Man's World

More women are getting into motorcycling. In fact, an estimated 10 percent of the motorcyclists on the road today are women. And that's great. After all, why should men have all the fun?

Motorcycle manufacturers and safety-gear makers recognize this growing market and are catering to women in various ways. Bike manufacturers have special programs to help women learn about motorcycling, and the safety gear producers are making products specifically for women. Women no longer have to buy ill-fitting men's jackets and pants that may not offer all the protection needed in a crash when the gear moves around upon impact with the asphalt.

Also gone are the days when a female rider had to buy a man's motorcycling boot in a small size to be able to stay safe while riding, or when she had very limited choices in jacket or pants styles. Women today have almost as many choices as men in jackets, pants, boots, gloves, and helmets. You can even find them with a feminine look. I discuss women's styles more in Chapter 6.

Some of the most beautiful women in the world ride motorcycles. For example, Catherine Bell, Lauren Hutton, and Angelina Jolie all ride bikes. A woman doesn't need to be big, look tough, and have a ton of tattoos to ride a motorcycle. And as more women ride motorcycles, more male motorcyclists are accepting them into the world of motorcycling not as women, but as fellow motorcyclists.

If guys are cool on bikes, then women are supercool

Male motorcyclists get a lot of respect when they have the skills to handle a motorcycle (which most men don't have) and when they're adventurous and look cool in their riding garb. Even so, they're men. As such, among motorcyclists men are no big deal. Women, on the other hand, *are* a big deal.

Women who ride are still a minority both among women in general and among motorcyclists. So for male motorcyclists, and even nonmotorcyclists, a woman who rides is a dream woman. Why? The perception may not match the reality, but women riders are seen as adventurous, outgoing, willing to take risks, and willing to step outside their comfort zones to enjoy life.

Female riders are supercool because they're strong women who decide to do something and then do it, who can stand up for themselves, and who can talk about motorcycling. Plus, they look great in today's motorcycling clothes cut specifically for women, with feminine designs. When a female motorcyclist walks into a restaurant, everyone knows she's special without her having to say a word.

And although guys have a great time giving women rides on their motorcycles and feeling the women hold them around the waist, true male motorcyclists prefer when women ride their own bikes. Why? The dynamics of a motorcycle change with a passenger, and a bike is a lot more fun to ride alone.

Dealing with special gender-related problems

Motorcycling is still very much a man's world, so women do face some problems. For example, on the whole, motorcycles are still made for men, so most are simply too big for women. However, motorcycles can be modified to make them safe for smaller women to ride, so don't think that you're forever locked out of motorcycling because of your size. (I talk about how to make these modifications in Chapter 6.)

And sometimes gaining acceptance as a motorcyclist by some men can be tough. But don't worry about those guys. Plenty of male motorcyclists will accept you and help you enjoy the joys of motorcycling.

Plus, along with the increase in female riders comes an increase in resources for them. You can join women's motorcycling clubs, where women socialize and ride together. And, today, more Web sites and magazines are geared specifically for female riders to share their stories and advice. Now truly is a good time to be a woman in the world of motorcycling.

Even Kids Can Ride

Motorcycling may seem difficult if you've never done it. But, really, how hard can it be? After all, 4-year-olds race motorcycles! Granted, they're very small motorcycles . . . and they don't go very fast . . . and they're riding in dirt. But, hey, those are 4-year-old kids riding them!

Talk to any motorcycling family in which the kids ride motorcycles in the dirt with dad (or even dad and mom) or race at a local track, and you discover a special bond. The kids are doing something they love, and the parents know exactly what their kids are up to every weekend because they're right there with them riding in the woods or at the racetrack.

How many other activities can you participate in with your kids? Plenty. But how many can you participate in that your kids actually think is cool? If you're a riding family, your kids are the envy of all the other kids on the block and at school. It's good, clean, wholesome recreation for the whole family. (I discuss children and motorcycling in further detail in Chapter 7.)

Getting kids started in motorcycling

It's great if your child wants to ride a motorcycle. In fact, it's something to encourage. After all, it's a lot better than having your kid hang out at the local mall. And it's a safer sport than you think, provided you ensure that your child has the proper training and safety gear and is well supervised.

Your child may not be old enough to drive a car or ride a streetbike, but he or she certainly can ride a dirt bike. And there are a lot of good pint-sized bikes available on the market for them. Safety gear and excellent training also are available for the youngsters. And while this hobby can be expensive, it also can be done cheaply if you pick your bike and safety gear wisely. (I discuss buying a used bike in Chapter 9.)

Riding a dirt bike will make you a better street rider, as I discuss in Chapter 3, so it will give your child valuable skills if he or she decides to get a streetbike later.

Kids + motorcycling = fun

Get your child a dirt bike, get one for yourself, get some dirt bike training, and then head out on the trails and have a ball. Riding with your kid is fun, and it's a great way to enjoy being with each other riding at a slow, leisurely pace. If you ride at your child's pace, you'll both stay out of trouble, no matter how much of a novice rider you are.

Take along some snacks and water or sports drinks to enjoy while stopped alongside the trail. Chat a little about riding and what's going on in your child's life, and I guarantee you'll make memories that will last forever.

Keys to Riding Safely

It's unavoidable. After you start talking about getting a motorcycle, your well-meaning family and friends will look at you like you've grown a second head. Then they'll start telling you tales of people they know who got motorcycles and then proceeded to seriously injure or even kill themselves. While some of the stories may be true, it's also true that people are killed driving a car, walking across an intersection, or even playing a sport like football or baseball.

Sure, motorcycling is dangerous, especially when compared to driving a car. After all, if a car hits another car, the drivers have a good chance of escaping serious injury because of the safety features of the car and because the driver is surrounded by heavy metal to absorb some of the impact. A motorcycle rider is much more vulnerable and likely to suffer injury if hit by another vehicle.

But motorcyclists have some big advantages over drivers of other vehicles when it comes to safety. For example, a motorcyclist on a nimble bike can accelerate out of the way of trouble or stop more quickly than a car or truck driver can to avoid a collision. And motorcyclists spend a lot of time practicing safe riding techniques to ensure their survival on the road.

Enrolling in basic training for motorcyclists

Although there's no boot camp for aspiring motorcyclists, there are great beginner motorcycle safety training classes run by friendly instructors. These classes are available to anyone with the desire to learn how to ride a bike and the tuition money to plunk down. This basic training is a great way for anyone interested in motorcycling to learn a couple things:

- ✔ Whether they would enjoy riding a motorcycle, since the class gives a taste of what the experience is like.
- ✔ Whether they even have the coordination needed to ride a motorcycle. Some people don't.

More importantly, though, basic rider training classes teach new riders how to be safe while riding their motorcycles. They do so not only by teaching basic riding techniques such as accelerating, stopping, turning, and swerving, but also by teaching what dangers to watch for while riding, such as a car making a left turn and pulling into a rider's path or a car merging into the rider's lane on the freeway. I discuss getting the best motorcycle safety training on the planet in Chapter 3.

Developing special riding skills

Besides basic training, motorcyclists have the opportunity to take advanced training and to attend classes held at racetracks to hone their accelerating, braking, and cornering skills. And all the skills they learn in basic classes, advanced classes, or even on the racetrack, they practice every day when they ride their motorcycles.

Motorcyclists know that practice is the key to using important skills, such as braking and swerving, without having to give the technique any thought. They see every curve as a challenge to determine whether it can be negotiated with perfect technique. Every stop sign is an opportunity to practice smooth stops and starts, and every empty parking lot presents an opportunity to practice slow, tight turns. (I discuss safe riding techniques in Chapters 14 and 15.)

Chapter 2

From the First Wooden Horse to Today's Iron Pony

....

In This Chapter

▶ Surveying the beginnings of American motorcycling

▶ Exploring the influx of British and Japanese machines

▶ Discovering how Americans' attitudes have changed toward motorcyclists

....

Motorcycling has a long, rich history that runs from the late 1800s to today. And that history has almost as many twists and turns as your favorite mountain road. From the first motorcycle — which was either simply a wooden testbed for a motor or a steam-powered bicycle, depending on which side of the debate you're on — to the hyperbikes of today that are so fast that some governments have even threatened to limit their speed, the world of motorcycling has gone through a lot of changes.

Some motorcyclists consider the very early days of the motorcycle as the glory years: You had to be a good rider and a good mechanic to navigate your machine over the rough dirt paths that were back then known as roads. Men raced motorcycles on giant, banked board tracks that could pierce a rider with foot-long slivers if he fell. And hundreds of separate motorcycle manufacturers built bikes in the United States.

Others argue that the late 1950s through the 1960s were the best days of motorcycling. The European manufacturers were selling their motorcycles in the United States, and motorcyclists spoke fondly of their Triumphs, Matchlesses, and BSAs. Then the Japanese manufacturers decided to take on the Europeans head-on in the U.S. market, bringing with them a notable advertising campaign that made motorcycling acceptable to Americans. Finally, the chopper craze hit, leading to some of the most stunning custom machines to ever explore the nation's highways and byways — at least, up until then.

You can easily romanticize the past, but the glory days of motorcycling are right now. Some 6 million motorcyclists share a passion for this timeless sport. Bikers today ride a wide variety of reliable, state-of-the-art machines; they watch the fastest racers ever to throw a leg over a motorcycle seat; and they buy the most innovative and protective motorcycling gear ever produced. If ever there was a great time to get into motorcycling, it is now.

In this chapter, you explore the beginnings of motorcycling, examine the motorcycle's explosion in popularity and fall from favor, discover how British and Japanese machines influenced American riders and the public, and consider how Americans' attitudes toward motorcyclists have changed over the years.

The Rise and Fall of American Motorcycling

Soon after the first motorcycles appeared in the late 1800s and early 1900s, people began to buy them. Early motorcycles were little more than bicycles with motors, but to many, it beat riding a horse or riding in a horse-pulled buggy to get around. Motorcycles were transportation, pure and simple.

Bicycle racing was a great form of entertainment back then, so it wasn't long before motorcycles were on the racetracks providing entertainment of their own. The factories put efforts into racing with hopes of boosting sales, and some of the hardy racers of the time became legends; their exploits were noted in the newspapers of the day.

But then motorcycles fell out of favor with the American public, primarily due to the cheap production of automobiles. Motorcycle racers were no longer the heroes they once had been. Almost all American motorcycle manufacturers went out of business; only war and the production of motorcycles for the military kept the biggest manufacturers alive.

The Europeans (particularly the British) and then the Japanese saw great market potential in the United States and took advantage of it, producing machines that Americans would buy. Ultimately, the Europeans couldn't compete with the Japanese in terms of quality and price, and today Japanese machines dominate the U.S. market. The Harley-Davidson Motor Company is the only surviving American motorcycle company from those early days, when as many as 300 American motorcycle manufacturers may have been producing bikes.

The golden age: 300 American motorcycle manufacturers

In the early 1900s, the internal combustion engine had been perfected and as many as 300 motorcycle manufacturers may have been operating in the

Gottlieb vs. Roper smackdown: Who built the first motorcycle?

When it comes to determining who created the first motorcycle, only two contenders emerge: Gottlieb Daimler and Sylvester Roper. It may be easy to say, "Well, which was built first? Then that, surely, is the first motorcycle." Well, things are a lot more complicated than that. The first motorcycle was built more than 100 years ago, yet debate over who built it still makes for lively conversation among motorcyclists who know a bit of the history.

Born in 1834 in Germany, Daimler was an engineer and industrial designer. In 1872, he worked for a company that made engines (primarily steam) that powered equipment. But he wanted a new motor and something that could propel a vehicle, like a stagecoach. Daimler teamed up with another inventor and industrial designer, Wilhelm Maybach, who worked at the same company, to try to realize this dream. They needed a good gas-powered motor for their experiments, and they found one created by Nikolaus Otto, one of the owners of the company that Daimler and Maybach worked for.

While perfecting the Otto motor, Daimler put one into a wooden, two-wheeled bicycle-like frame in 1885. The invention worked. Daimler went on to put an Otto motor in a stagecoach, and, in 1899, Daimler and Maybach built a car. Daimler, by the way, is the name in the modern company name Daimler-Chrysler.

So was the Daimler motorcycle really just a test platform for the Otto motor? Or was it, in fact, meant to be a motorcycle and it was a fanciful idea that became reality for Daimler and Maybach, who wanted to create propelled transportation? Also, were they just a step ahead of their time, which explains why their motorcycle-like invention never caught on with companies that would take a chance building it or the public that would take a chance buying it? These questions all figure into the debate over whether the Daimler machine can truly claim the title as the world's first motorcycle.

In the other corner, we have a man who set out to create a motorcycle: Roper. Born in 1823 in New Hampshire, Roper was a machinist and inventor. He attached a steam engine to a bicycle in 1869 to create a steam-powered motorcycle that he showed off at county fairs. He tried to get bicycle companies interested in his invention, but he didn't have much success. However, he didn't give up and kept improving on his invention, even when the internal combustion engine came on the scene. He built a total of ten machines.

In 1896, he took his latest machine to a bicycle racetrack to see if it could be used as a pacesetter for the bicycles. But while riding around the track, he crashed and died. Authorities determined later that he died of a heart attack, not from the crash. He was 72.

Since Roper's machine was steam powered, some argue that it wasn't the first motorcycle. Others argue that since the Daimler machine had two outrigger "training" wheels, it, in fact, had four wheels and couldn't be considered a motorcycle. What is certain is that the Daimler machine was the first internal combustion motorcycle, and the Roper was the first steam-powered motorcycle.

So then, what was the first production motorcycle? Many argue it is the Hildebrand and Wolfmuller. German brothers Heinrich and Wilhelm Hildebrand in the late 1800s had a dream to build a motorcycle, and teamed up with motor-builder Alois Wolfmuller. The result was the Hildebrand and Wolfmuller, a 1,498cc, gas-powered motorcycle built for sale to the public. Like all early motorcycles, it was basically a bicycle with a motor stuck on it. In three years they produced about 800 machines, but handling and starting problems with the bikes outraged customers, and the company went out of business.

United States alone (although others put the estimate at a little more than 50). How many of these actually produced motorcycles each year, or even survived a year, is unknown. But some famous American motorcycle manufacturers got their start during this time, including the Indian Motorcycle Company, the Harley-Davidson Motor Company, and Excelsior, later known as Excelsior-Henderson.

Why were motorcycles so popular in the early 1900s? The buying public wanted cheap transportation. In 1909, a standard Ford Model T car cost $850, or about a year's wages. The price for a 1909 Harley-Davidson? $325.

Indian Motorcycle Company

Indian actually began as the Hendee Manufacturing Company. George Hendee and Oscar Hendstrom teamed up to create Indian motorcycles. The first was built in 1901 and sold in 1902. Basically, they just stuck a motor on a bicycle frame, which is what everyone else was doing. However, the Indian proved to be relatively popular among the buying public. Hendee and Hendstrom sold 143 motorcycles that year; by 1913 they were producing a variety of models and selling 32,000.

Harley-Davidson Motor Company

The story of the Harley-Davidson Motor Company starting life in a 10-foot-by-15-foot shed in Milwaukee in 1903 is well known. What's not as well known is how few motorcycles were actually built in that shed: 1 prototype and 13 bikes. But those models were enough to convince the Harley brothers — William, Walter, and Arthur — and William Davidson, the company founders, to move to a 2,400-square-foot facility. In 1913, the company sold 13,000 motorcycles.

Excelsior

Excelsior built its first motorcycles in Chicago in 1905. In 1911, the Schwinn Company bought Excelsior to get into the motorcycle business. Meanwhile, the Henderson Company in Detroit began producing motorcycles in 1912. Excelsior bought out Henderson in 1917. At its high point, the company made only about 1,800 machines a year.

The demise of American motorcycling: Curse you, Mr. Ford!

With so many motorcycle manufacturers in the early days, the companies decided they needed to get into racing as a sales tool, primarily to prove the reliability of their machines. The racetrack battles between the Indian and Harley-Davidson factory riders in the 1910s and later were legendary. Harley-Davidson and Indian were later able to survive during the lean World War I years with military contracts. Indian sold the military about 50,000 machines, and Harley-Davidson sold about 20,000 from 1917 to 1919.

During those years, Indian sold no motorcycles to the public, and Harley-Davidson sold few. Many other American motorcycling companies that were struggling didn't survive the war years. Why were they all struggling and eventually going out of business? You can thank Mr. Henry Ford.

Although a lot of motorcyclists today buy a motorcycle for cheap transportation, most buy a motorcycle for recreation. They just want to have fun. That wasn't true back in the day. In the early 1900s, people wanted to get around and needed cheap transportation to do it. A motorcycle fit the bill, with a cost of $125 to $325 or so, depending on the model. That was at a time when cars cost as much as $2,000 or $3,000, and even Ford's cheap Model T was $850 in 1909.

But Ford was making a lot of cars. And he was learning a lot about how to produce cars cheaply. With his high volume and assembly-line innovations, he was able to cut the price of his cars over the years. The Model T went from $850 in 1909 to $440 in 1915. Suddenly, the Model T was within reach of the average American family. Ford built about 15 million Model Ts between 1909 and 1927. In 1927, a Ford Model T touring car cost $380. So a family could buy a motorcycle or, for a little more, buy a car. Most opted for a car. So by 1930, only two major American motorcycle manufacturers were left: Indian and Harley-Davidson.

And then there was one: Harley-Davidson

Indian and Harley continued their epic racetrack battles to boost sales and, during the years of World War II (1941–1945), sold bikes to the military. Harley-Davidson produced 90,000 military machines, while Indian sold 35,000 for war use.

After the war, Indian still sold its big Chief but also began producing smaller machines, hoping to compete with small, agile British imports. It couldn't. A combination of factors led to the demise of the Indian Motocycle Company in 1953, including bad management and stiff competition from Harley-Davidson.

Harley-Davidson was the lone American motorcycle manufacturer after 1953. But British imports were cutting into Harley-Davidson sales. By the late 1960s, Harley-Davidson was owned by American Machinery and Foundry (AMF), the bowling machine–making company, and suffered from a reputation of building very poor-quality machines. In 1981, a group of employees, including Willie G. Davidson, grandson of one of the company founders, bought the company, improved production, and made it a success.

Salute to the Sportster

The Sportster has remained incredibly popular over the years. You can still walk into a Harley-Davidson dealership today, more than 50 years after the first Sportster was built, and buy a new one. The initial XL didn't sell very well, but Harley-Davidson quickly redesigned the bike to give it a small peanut-shaped gas tank, staggered exhaust pipes, and a minimalist look that captured the attention of American buyers. This bike was designated the XLH. It received minor updates over the years and then a performance boost in 1966 and again in 1972, when the engine displacement was increased to 1,000cc.

Variations of the machine were built, including a touring model. Then in 1986, the Sportster got a new motor, called the Evolution. Even more changes have been made since then, and the bike is now available with engine displacements of 883cc and 1,200cc. But the Sportster has remained true to its original mission of being an affordable performance machine, particularly for those who want to get into motorcycling and who want a Harley-Davidson. On the other hand, the Sportster, particularly the 883, has the reputation of being "the girl's Harley" because this model is so popular among female riders.

Motorcycling's Popularity Rises Again

In motorcycling's early days, motorcycles were wildly popular because they were cheap transportation. They became popular again in the 1950s because they were fun to ride and people could afford them as recreational vehicles in the post–World War II boom years. Dominating the American market at the time were primarily British machines from companies with names like Triumph, BSA, and Norton.

The machines were smaller, lighter, and faster than Harley-Davidsons. By the late 1950s, British machines were everywhere, from the racetrack to Main Street. Harley-Davidson knew it had to improve its performance image to survive the British onslaught, so in 1957, it unveiled its secret weapon: the XL Sportster. Powered by a motor with 54 cubic inches of displacement (883cc), the Sportster was relatively quick and light, and shouted performance.

The British came into the market with lighter and faster machines than Harley-Davidson was selling and gained popularity among U.S. riders. The Japanese followed by offering bikes that were lighter, faster, and more reliable than the British machines.

Honda backed up its move into the United States with a genius advertising campaign meant to show that motorcycles were fun. The slogan is probably the most recognizable slogan in all of motorcycling: "You Meet the Nicest People on a Honda." And with that slogan, Honda captured the imagination of the American public and introduced them to their smaller-bore, unintimidating machines.

The campaign used a small Honda 50 step-through scooter as its centerpiece and showed moms and young couples smiling and riding the machine. The campaign was wildly successful and boosted Honda sales significantly. By 1963, Honda was selling about 200,000 machines a year in the United States.

The Japanese, led by Honda, continued to make inroads into the U.S. market through the 1960s. The British, unable to compete, eventually died out in the early 1970s (although Triumph has since been reborn). In contrast, by 1970, Honda alone was selling 500,000 motorcycles a year in the United States. Its flagship was the CB750, introduced in 1969. This bike was considered well built and sophisticated, and was relatively cheap, at $1,495. Motorcyclists from the 1970s fondly remember it as a high-performance streetbike.

The Japanese motorcycle manufacturers — Honda, Kawasaki, Suzuki, and Yamaha — dominate the American market today. Harley-Davidson is still going strong, particularly with good overseas sales. A variety of motorcycles from Europe — BMW, Ducati, Moto Guzzi, Triumph, and others — also are available in the United States, although their sales figures are dwarfed by those of the Japanese manufacturers and Harley-Davidson.

Changing Attitudes Toward Motorcyclists

Americans' attitudes toward motorcyclists have fluctuated from acceptance in the early years to disdain following World War II, to acceptance again in the 1960s, to the popularity and acceptance of today.

Why is the American public so fickle? What caused attitudes to fluctuate so dramatically over the years? Simply put, it was the media. Newspapers, magazines, and movies played a major role in shaping public opinion, and despite the best efforts of motorcycling organizations such as the then-small but feisty American Motorcyclist Association to counter negative press, motorcyclists have been portrayed at some points over the years as hoodlums or outlaws.

Although motorcyclists are generally accepted today, riders who have loud exhaust systems are causing a public backlash against all motorcyclists. Citizens are asking their lawmakers to do something about the noise. The problem has become so serious that major motorcycling organizations and even Harley-Davidson are asking riders to be responsible. In other words, they want them to pipe down.

How the media and Hollywood have shaped public opinion

From the first days of motorcycling in America through World War II, motorcycles were primarily viewed as transportation. The general public accepted motorcyclists. All that changed following the war.

Restless World War II vets formed motorcycle clubs and rode around together, sharing the camaraderie of motorcycling. Other clubs included nonvets as well, of course; the vet-dominated clubs were more free-wheeling and less likely to follow rules, though. For example, most motorcycle clubs associated themselves with the American Motorcyclist Association (AMA), took part in AMA-sanctioned rides, and competed for things such as AMA Safety Awards for safe riding. Many vet clubs had none of that.

Even long before World War II, the AMA sanctioned *gypsy tours,* which were (and still are) organized rides to a specific destination. Gypsy tours allowed riders to gather for a long ride and then to enjoy themselves at the destination for a day or two before heading home. Probably the most famous gypsy tour in American motorcycling history, and certainly the most significant for the reputation of motorcyclists, was the one that ended in Hollister, California, on the 4th of July weekend in 1947.

An estimated 4,000 motorcyclists descended on Hollister for the gypsy tour. Admittedly, some of the motorcyclists who ended up in Hollister as part of the Gypsy Tour got a little out of hand, drinking excessively, riding their bikes into bars, and, shall we say, putting on "exhibitions of speed" in the streets. What happened next, though, turned the American public against the American motorcyclist.

A picture is worth a thousand words

The *San Francisco Chronicle* reported on the Hollister Gypsy Tour, saying that motorcyclists had wreaked havoc in the town and forced police to impose an informal martial law. *Life* magazine, a popular news magazine of the day that was heavy on photographs, ran a staged photograph in 1947 of a motorcyclist in Hollister leaning back on his motorcycle seat and drinking a beer. About two dozen empty beer bottles littered the street beneath his bike. No story accompanied the photograph. The photograph carried a simple caption stating that this motorcyclist and his buddies had terrorized a town.

How do we know the famous photograph was staged? Simple. In the photograph is a bearded man in the background standing on the sidewalk. He later said the photo was staged. But it didn't matter. Because of the *Life* magazine photograph and caption, suddenly mainstream America feared motorcycle gangs and motorcyclists.

The dubious "1-percenter"

Members of outlaw motorcycle clubs that may be on the wrong side of the law at times like to refer to themselves as *1 percenters*. These clubs are called *outlaws* not because the members are criminals, but simply because they aren't associated, or chartered, with the American Motorcyclist Association (AMA). The club members have adopted the 1 percenter moniker, and even wear patches on their jackets or vests that say "1%." According to popular motorcycling lore, after the so-called Hollister riot, an AMA official, in an attempt at spin control, allegedly said that 99 percent of all motorcyclists are law-abiding citizens and only 1 percent are troublemakers. The AMA has been unable to confirm that an AMA official ever made such a statement, but the 1-percenter moniker has stuck.

The movies: Bigger than Life (magazine)

For Hollywood, the so-called Hollister riot had everything needed for a great movie. Well, not everything. It still needed a love interest. But, hey, Hollywood could just add that to the script, along with whatever else was needed to get people into the drive-ins and movie theaters. In 1954, Hollywood released a movie loosely based on the reported events in Hollister. This movie, called *The Wild One,* was directed by Laszlo Benedek, produced by Stanley Kramer, and distributed by Columbia Pictures Corp.

The movie portrayed motorcyclists as young punks ready to terrorize a town and rebelling against, well, everything. It also marked the beginning of a trend of motorcycle gang movies that lasted for about 15 years and did nothing to enhance the reputation of motorcyclists in the minds of the American public. Fortunately, in the early 1960s, Honda launched its now-famous "You Meet the Nicest People on a Honda" advertising campaign and helped offset some of the negativity toward motorcyclists that the movies spawned.

Then in 1969, the movie *Easy Rider* helped show that motorcyclists aren't just hoodlums. In that movie, Peter Fonda and Dennis Hopper set off to discover the United States on motorcycles. (You can read more about these movies in Chapter 21.)

When motorcycling became chic

In the 1970s and 1980s, motorcycling and motorcyclists became acceptable again, thanks in part to people like millionaire publisher Malcolm Forbes. Forbes became a motorcyclist in the late 1960s, and the news media followed his global motorcycling travels that he took with his club, the Capitalist Tools. He was often photographed with actress Elizabeth Taylor riding as his passenger. Americans saw that the rich and powerful rode motorcycles, so maybe motorcyclists weren't so bad after all.

In the 1990s and through to the present, riding a motorcycle has seemed cool. Famous actors and actresses, like Brad Pitt, Angelina Jolie, Tom Cruise, and George Clooney, ride motorcycles. So do doctors, lawyers, dentists, and politicians. Television shows related to motorcycling have even become popular among nonmotorcyclists, including *American Chopper,* featuring the battling Teutul family, and *Biker Build-off.*

What motorcycling is like today

With an estimated 6 million motorcyclists across the country today, you don't have to look far to see a motorcycle on the street. And despite the long and rich history of motorcycling, never has there been a better time to be a motorcyclist. Why? Consider the following:

- ✔ Choices in motorcycles are varied, and the bikes are extremely reliable
- ✔ The safety gear is the best it has ever been
- ✔ More women are getting into the sport
- ✔ Motorcycle safety training is better than ever
- ✔ The American public generally doesn't look at motorcyclists with distain

In fact, motorcyclists who make up the various subgroups of motorcycling are more accepting of the other subgroups than they have ever been. Now, more than ever, motorcyclists believe that it doesn't matter what type of motorcycle you ride — what matters is that you ride a motorcycle. That commonality is good enough to form a bond.

Nowadays, if they want to do so, getting your kids involved in motorcycling is easier, too. You can find organized kids' dirt rides, motorcycle safety training for the young set, and a lot of great safety gear made in pint sizes.

Plus, you can join international, national, and local clubs to help you get the most fun and excitement you can out of motorcycling. Enjoy the ride.

Chapter 3

You Wouldn't Fly a Jet Without Training, Would You?

In This Chapter

▶ Knowing why you shouldn't have a friend teach you to ride

▶ Getting motorcycle safety training from MSF

▶ Passing the test to get your motorcycle license

▶ Increasing your riding skills after you pass your licensing test

Motorcycles are complex machines compared to cars. In fact, they require a lot of skill to ride at all, let alone ride well. Consider a car, for example: you hop in, start it up, press on the accelerator to go, turn the steering wheel to steer, and press on the brake to stop. Simple. Not so with a motorcycle. With a bike, you've got a clutch lever on the left handlebar, a front brake lever on the right handlebar, a gear-shift lever that you manipulate with your left foot, and a rear-brake lever that you press with your right foot. And that's just the stuff on the bike. You also have to worry about turning the handlebars and leaning the motorcycle to steer, and you always have to stay balanced.

Sound complicated? It is. A lot goes on while you're riding a motorcycle, not only in your own actions to control the machine but also in the environment around you. Your environment can distract you and pose a real danger if you aren't paying close attention.

Pilots who ride motorcycles say that riding is the closest experience there is to flying. And as you know, pilots go through a lot of training to be able to fly their complex jet fighters. Similarly, motorcyclists need a lot of training to operate their complex machines.

In this chapter, you find out why it's a bad idea to let a friend teach you how to ride a motorcycle (no matter how long he or she has been riding). You also discover how the recognized experts teach newbies to ride, including the important lessons that students learn. I provide everything you need to know for when you visit your local department or bureau of motor vehicles to get your motorcycle license. Plus, I provide the facts that ensure that you have the skills needed to safely ride, and enjoy, your motorcycle.

If a Friend Offers to Teach You, Just Say No

Your motorcycling friend or friends will probably be excited when they find out that you want to learn how to ride. And, with the best intentions, they may even offer to teach you. Even if he or she is a certified instructor, it's not a good idea to learn from a friend.

Why? Well, it takes a special kind of person to be a good teacher. A good teacher is extremely patient, explains things in simple terms that anyone can grasp, understands the subject matter extremely well, and knows that each student must be taught at his or her own pace. A friend may not have that combination of knowledge and skills to be able to teach you.

Plus, a good motorcycling teacher is up on the latest research — not only on the best riding techniques, but also on how motorcycle crashes occur and how to avoid them. Unless I'm hanging out with the wrong crowd, there aren't very many motorcyclists who know the findings of the latest research. In fact, there aren't very many motorcyclists who know much about the findings of *any* motorcycle-related research.

For example, do you know that the most common car versus motorcycle crash is when a car makes a left turn in front of an approaching motorcycle? Or that you can just about cut your reaction time in half when you need to make a quick stop on your motorcycle simply by resting your right-hand fingers on your front brake lever and left-hand fingers on your clutch? You do now. And that means you know more than many of the motorcyclists on the road today.

That's the kind of stuff you learn in a safety class that you probably won't learn from your friend who tries to teach you how to ride a bike. And besides not giving you all the information you need to make you the best rider possible, your friend may even give you wrong information. For instance, your friend may tell you to ignore the front brake because it will flip you up over the handlebars if you use it. That advice is ludicrous. Most of your stopping power comes from the front brake, so you need that power when you make a quick stop. I cover quick stops in Chapter 14.

Even worse is the fact that you still see newspaper reports where motorcyclists say they had to "lay the bike down" to avoid a crash. But, wait a minute, laying a bike down while you're riding along *is* a crash! You certainly don't want a friend to teach you how to lay a bike down to avoid hitting something.

Another problem with having a friend teach you how to ride is that you may pick up his or her bad habits, such as:

- ✔ Not using enough fingers on the front brake
- ✔ Looking just ahead of your front tire instead of down the road
- ✔ Not turning your head far enough when you turn or ride through a curve or corner
- ✔ Putting your bike in neutral at a stoplight or stop sign
- ✔ Riding in the wrong part of the traffic lane

Your friend teaches you how to do things because that's the way he or she does it (even though it may not be the safest way to ride).

Another consideration is what happens if you get hurt while your friend is teaching you how to ride? Or what if you destroy the motorcycle that he or she is letting you learn on? Getting hurt or wrecking your friend's bike could put a real damper on your friendship. An organized class, on the other hand, is prepared to handle any medical emergencies and destroyed motorcycles.

Training with the Pros: MSF Courses

The *Motorcycle Safety Foundation,* known as the MSF, is the recognized leader in motorcycle safety training. It's a national, nonprofit organization sponsored by the major motorcycle manufacturers. The MSF has been providing training nationwide since the early 1970s, so its trainers know an awful lot about how to teach motorcycle safety. The foundation has also come to know how students learn best.

In fact, MSF training is so highly regarded that most states allow new riders to forego taking a riding skills test to get a motorcycle license if they have already passed an MSF course. So if you want the best motorcycle safety training in America (and probably on the planet), take an MSF class.

The MSF offers basic streetbike classes for people who have never been on a bike before and who want to see if they would enjoy motorcycling. It also offers classes for those who have already decided that they want to become motorcyclists. Plus, the MSF offers classes for experienced riders to brush up on their skills. The foundation offers a class for those who want to learn how to ride dirt bikes as well.

The MSF's mission with these training courses is to reduce motorcycling fatalities and injuries in the United States. Not only does the MSF provide rider training, but it also hosts international motorcycle safety conventions and helps fund motorcycling safety research.

In the motorcycling community, you gain respect from fellow riders if you've taken an MSF course. You gain even more respect if you take the basic course and then, later, the experienced rider course. And when you do take the experienced class, don't be surprised if lined up next to you on the riding range is a professional rider like a motojournalist. Some of these professionals take the experienced class every three years to brush up on their skills and stay sharp.

Another advantage to taking an MSF class is that many insurance companies give you a discount on your insurance if you prove that you have completed an MSF course within the past few years.

To find an MSF class near you, go to www.msf-usa.org. Sign up early because classes fill up fast, probably because people would rather pass the class than take the riding skills test in front of the police officers or government workers who give the tests. Plus, prospective, and even experienced, riders want the best training available.

If you can't get into an MSF class, you can still take the Rider's Edge safety course taught through Harley-Davidson dealerships or take other private lessons. However, it's unlikely that your state will accept those forms of training in lieu of passing an MSF course, which means that you're still required to take the riding skills test.

Motorcycle safety training classes aren't free, but they're well worth the price. Just think of them as part of the price of admission into the wonderful world of motorcycling. Prices can range from $60 to $100 or more.

Basic training: "This is a clutch, this is a brake . . ."

You should have absolutely no fear going into a beginner, or basic, motorcycle safety training class. After all, they are geared for, well, beginners. What does that mean? It means that the class begins with very basic terms and concepts and advances from there until you're out on the range actually riding one of the class motorcycles, which are small, easy-to-handle machines. You may be able to borrow a helmet from the class, but it's best to bring your own helmet, eye protection, and gloves.

To take a basic motorcycle riding class your state will probably require you to have a temporary instructional motorcycle permit. I explain how to get one later in this chapter.

What the basic course covers

It may seem silly, but a beginning class will start with basics such as discussing the difference between a car and a motorcycle. Almost every new rider has experience with cars (and not with motorcycles), so you have to begin thinking in different terms, such as how riding a motorcycle is different from driving a car.

A basic course also covers the following types of information:

- ✔ Protective gear, including helmets
- ✔ Managing risk on the road
- ✔ Avoiding crashes
- ✔ Inspecting your motorcycle before you go for a ride
- ✔ The different controls on a motorcycle, such as the clutch and brake levers

In addition, the class covers techniques for handling roadway obstructions and explains what to do if one of your tires skids, how alcohol affects your ability to ride, how to get a motorcycle license in your state, and more.

What happens on the riding range

The classroom instruction is interesting, but the real fun stuff happens out on the riding range, which is usually a parking lot where cones have been set up to run motorcycle riding drills. This is where students often get a little nervous, especially if they see someone drop a bike. But remember that the instructors are usually pretty kind and really do want you to learn how to ride. Don't think of them as drill instructors; think of them as a coach of your favorite sport.

On the riding range, the instructors first take time to go over the motorcycle and teach the controls and how to use them. You find out things such as how to find neutral, how to start and stop the bike, and how to use the throttle and shift. And that's all pretty much before even starting up the bike.

The basic class can be pretty slow going because you're learning from scratch. The first time on the riding range, your instructor will have you do straight-line drills that involve going very slowly so you get the feel for operating the throttle and clutch. In fact, you start out sitting on the bike and basically walking it under power. Really, this stuff shouldn't intimidate you.

Next you'll likely learn how to start, stop, and turn, which involves coordinating the throttle, clutch, and brake. Once you get the hang of those topics, you learn how to shift while moving. Then you learn other stuff like speeding up and slowing down, weaving around cones, stopping quickly, and making S- and U-turns.

But wait, there's more! You also learn how to properly lean a motorcycle, negotiate corners and curves, change lanes, and avoid hazards. You have a lot to learn, but every motorcyclist needs to master these basic skills.

Experienced rider training: Brushing up on key skills

The class for experienced riders forces students to think about riding and the dangers related to riding. It also allows them to brush up on their riding techniques. The class covers the basics, including what to inspect on your machine before you go for a ride and what protective gear to wear.

Students discuss risks involved in riding motorcycles and how to avoid those risks. A lot of time is spent on stopping distance and the affects of aging on a motorcyclist, such as slower reaction times.

The causes of crashes, both car versus motorcycle and motorcycle only, are analyzed. Students learn that most motorcyclists crash because they don't stop, swerve, or corner properly. The classroom talk also covers more esoteric subjects, such as how suspension works and how to maximize traction. Of course, the coach will also engage a discussion on drinking and riding.

After the classroom portion is over, it's out to the riding range where riders practice stopping, swerving, and cornering. When practicing on the range, these advanced riders are thinking about more than just technique, though. They're also analyzing things like how the suspension works or how much traction there is.

The coaches will try to spot bad habits and help riders correct them. For instance, they'll notice if you're looking down at the road when you corner rather than looking through the corner and to where you want to go.

It's good to brush up on your skills by taking the experienced class every three years.

Doin' it in the dirt to be a better street rider

If you want to improve your ability to ride your streetbike, take a dirt bike class. Even better, take a dirt bike class and then get a dirt bike and do a lot of trail riding. How can riding a dirt bike make you a better street rider? You'll encounter certain situations in the dirt that you also encounter on the street. In fact, the situation you encounter in the dirt will usually be more intense than the same one on the street. However, you're usually going slower in the dirt than you would be on the street, so there's less danger to you.

For example, if you ride in the dirt, especially after a rain, you'll often experience a front or rear wheel loss of traction and sliding. Or you may need to avoid an obstacle in the trail, such as a rock, but will have little room to do it because of trees on the side of the trail. You probably won't have to avoid a big rock on the street, but you'll likely have to avoid tire treads that have ripped off a truck tire or some other obstacle.

If you're used to the rear wheel sliding around on your dirt bike, then when you have to deal with that situation on your streetbike (if you hit gravel on the road, for example), you'll be better prepared. And if you're accustomed to getting around obstacles in tight spaces on the trail, doing the same on the street will be a snap.

Riding in the dirt also requires you to develop a good sense of throttle control and of tire traction. Otherwise you end up getting a ground-up view of the riding area. This ability to feel the traction of your tires obviously translates to the street as well. Other skills that relate to both streetbikes and dirt bikes include looking far down the trail (or down the street) and not fixating on targets, such as a rock on the trail or obstruction on the street. After all, if you look at something on the trail or in the street, you're going to hit it.

The MSF dirt bike class is for beginning dirt riders, and much of what a student learns is similar to what is taught in the basic streetbike class: They learn where the clutch and brake are, how to start the bike, what safety gear is necessary, and what to inspect on your bike before you go for a ride.

But the classroom portion of the dirt bike class also covers areas not covered in a street course, such as respect for the land and for other recreational users of the land, such as horseback riders and campers. After the classroom discussions are finished, it's time to hit the riding range.

This time, though, students aren't in a parking lot with cones. They're riding in the dirt. Like in the basic streetbike course, the dirt bike class begins with the basics, including how to start and stop the bike and walking the bike around under power to get a feel for how to use the clutch.

Next the students are riding around in circles, doing figure eights and riding over obstacles. Riding over obstacles is a skill that can translate to the street, because there may be times when you just can't avoid that tire tread in the road or that squirrel that darted out from nowhere.

In the dirt bike class, you ride up and down hills and tackle other challenges. It really is a lot of fun. The school provides everything from the bikes to the safety gear. Price? Around $75 or so.

Going Through the Process of Getting Licensed

The first step to getting on the road as a motorcyclist is obtaining a motorcycle license. And the first step in obtaining a motorcycle license is getting a temporary instructional motorcycle permit. It's easy to get and is usually good for six months to a year. (In fact, it's so easy to get that some motorcyclists get the permit and then, when it expires, get it renewed or get another one to avoid taking the required riding test! However, I don't recommend that route.)

In this section, I give you the lowdown on obtaining your learner's permit, knowing what to do once you have it, and eventually passing the test to get your full motorcycle license.

Obtaining your instructional permit

To get your instructional permit (or *learner's permit,* as it's often called), you must pass both a written test and an eye exam. To prepare, go online or call your state department or bureau of motor vehicles to find out how to get a motorcycle instructional permit. You can also visit a driver's license bureau and ask for the information.

No matter which way you do it, the license bureau will give you a packet of information that includes the requirements, instructional materials on how to ride a motorcycle, and a booklet explaining traffic laws. Some states charge a fee for this packet. If you're doing this in person, you'll probably need to take some form of identification, such as your car driver's license or a passport.

These materials are full of useful information, even for experienced motorcyclists. They cover, among other things, these topics:

✔ Proper riding gear

✔ The controls on a motorcycle

- ✔ Shifting and braking
- ✔ Turning, passing, and merging
- ✔ Handling curves
- ✔ Avoiding crashes
- ✔ Carrying passengers

After you get the materials home, study them. The information contained in the materials will be on the written test that you need to pass to get your instructional permit.

When you feel like you've studied enough to take the written exam, head on down to your license bureau. When you're there, examiners will test your vision and then give you the written exam. When you pass, you get your instructional permit.

These permits have restrictions. For example, you probably can only ride during daylight, must wear a helmet and eye protection, can't ride on the freeway, and can't carry passengers. That's because new riders are at serious risk for getting hurt, and you're supposed to be learning how to ride a motorcycle with the permit, not making cross-country trips. So, with your instructional permit in hand, get training. Don't venture onto the street on a motorcycle because that is very dangerous without training. But, just think, you're only months away from getting your full license.

You have your learner's permit, now learn!

After you have your learner's permit, you need to learn how to ride a bike so that you can pass the riding exam to get your full motorcycle license. The motorcycle license, by the way, is an endorsement on your car driver's license, if you have one.

Start by practicing in a parking lot, such as in a school parking lot on a weekend. Practice going in a straight line slowly, clicking up a gear, clicking back down a gear, and then stopping. Do this until you're comfortable with the maneuver.

Then practice riding in a straight line, turning around, and riding back. Get comfortable with these maneuvers, and then do some figure eights. Do big ones at first, and then get smaller and smaller.

Other maneuvers to practice in the parking lot are quick stops, swerving, riding as slowly as possible, and riding at various speeds. However, remember to always ride at a speed that's within your abilities.

Get comfortable with all these maneuvers in a parking lot before you even think about venturing into the street. You need to be able to perform these functions without thinking about them to survive on the road. Practice, practice, practice so that shifting, braking, and all the other basic skills needed to ride a motorcycle can be done without you having to think about them.

After you're comfortable, head out into the streets. Start out on country roads or roads with little or no traffic. Practice what you learned from your license branch informational materials about approaching intersections, passing, and so on. After a while you'll start to feel even more comfortable, and then you can venture onto more crowded streets. You may even decide to ride in the city at this point.

The big day: Receiving your official motorcycle license

After you feel comfortable riding, call the driver's licensing station at your local bureau or department of motor vehicles, and schedule a riding test. The riding test, normally called the *on-cycle skill test,* tests your ability to control your motorcycle and avoid crashes. Pass the test, and you get your license!

If your state accepts completion of a motorcycle safety training course in lieu of taking the state riding examination, it's better to take the course. You'll feel much less pressure, and you'll learn a lot. (See the earlier section, "Training with the Pros: MSF Courses," for more information.)

The on-cycle skill test involves maneuvers such as starting and stopping, turning, and swerving. The instructor runs you through drills between cones and marked off areas of a parking lot. The turns can be pretty tight, and some drills you need to complete within a specified amount of time. ***Remember:*** The test can be intimidating, so you need to be a master of basic skills to pass it.

You'll have to bring a properly licensed and insured motorcycle to take the test on (flip to Chapter 10 for more on insuring your bike). Also be sure to bring a helmet, eye protection, and gloves. It's a good idea to have good motorcycle boots and a motorcycle jacket as well.

What to Do After You Get Your License

Even after you earn your motorcycle license, you must remember that you're still a novice rider. The first six months after getting a motorcycle license or after getting a new or used bike are dangerous for a motorcyclist. For the newbie, it's dangerous because the rider lacks the skills needed to always ride safely. For the veteran with a new or used bike, it's dangerous because the rider is unfamiliar with how the bike handles.

After you get your license, keep practicing. Do more parking-lot drills, and ride in the country. Ride, ride, ride. Review the instructional materials that you received when you applied for your temporary permit again and again.

Also, if you have riding buddies, ride with them. But don't ride over your abilities. In other words, don't try to keep up with them if they speed it up or if they take curves faster than you want to. That's how motorcyclists (even experienced ones) get into trouble: by trying to keep up with their peers. Finally, if you haven't taken a basic motorcycle safety training class, take one.

Even though you have your license, don't carry passengers until you've been riding fairly regularly for at least six months. Why? Because the added weight changes the dynamic of the motorcycle. The bike will take longer to stop, take more effort to turn, and the suspension will feel different. These are all things that could complicate riding for a novice rider.

Street survival training and other continuing education

Besides taking the Motorcycle Safety Foundation's basic rider, experienced rider, and dirt bike classes (discussed earlier in this chapter), it's a good idea to take more safety classes. You can never learn too much about riding a motorcycle.

One good school in the eastern part of the United States that gives you real-world experience is the Stayin' Safe Motorcycle Training school, formed by the late Larry Grodsky. Grodsky was a motorcycle safety training expert who spent about 30 years developing his program. He was killed while riding in Texas in 2006 when he hit a deer, but his training team has kept the school alive. The school offers tightly controlled, on-street training for both novice and experienced riders. Plus, it offers tours that combine training with scenic rides. Visit www.stayinsafe.com for more information.

Effective Pacific Northwest classes are offered by the Evergreen Safety Council. Not only do they offer basic and experienced rider courses, but they also have a class called the Additional Riding Course for those who have completed the basic class but aren't ready for the experienced course. It gives the new rider the opportunity to practice riding skills. Check out www.esc.org for more details.

Streetmasters Motorcycle Workshops are held in Rosamond, California, where street riders learn cornering techniques. Go to `www.streetmasters.info` to learn more about these workshops.

You may be able to find other riding classes and safety training opportunities near you. Ask about them at local motorcycle dealerships.

Track schools: The need for speed

Track schools aren't just for racers anymore. A lot of schools that use asphalt racetracks to train racers also offer courses for street riders, so think of them as performance riding schools. These courses are great because they take place in a safe, controlled environment. For instance, there aren't any cars coming onto the track from side streets, you can go as fast as you want, and you can practice your skills without the fear of getting smashed by an 18-wheeler or another motorcycle.

Track school involves classroom and on-track instruction, with instructors showing you how to ride and then critiquing your technique. Even longtime riders with a lot of miles under their belts come away from track schools with new skills and a better understanding of how to ride safely. Plus, going to a track school can really boost your confidence and teach you how to focus while riding.

However, probably the main thing you learn in a track school is how to be smooth in everything you do on a motorcycle. You learn how to be smooth when accelerating, braking, turning, shifting your body weight, slowing, stopping, and more. It's more difficult than you think, but once you learn how to be smooth, you'll be a much better rider.

Some schools require that you use their bikes, and they'll rent you a helmet and safety gear if you don't have your own. Other schools require you to bring your own bike and safety gear. Classes range from one-day affairs to programs that last three days or more. The classes are priced accordingly.

Schools may require at least a year's experience on a streetbike before you can sign up for a class, and they may require special preparation of your motorcycle before it goes on the track. For instance, you may need to secure all critical nuts with safety wire. Check with the school about its requirements.

Here are some of the more popular track schools:

- **The Kevin Schwantz Suzuki School** (www.schwantzschool.com): This school, which is taught by former World MotoGP motorcycle racing champion Kevin Schwantz, takes place at the Road Atlanta racetrack in Braselton, Georgia. It's only for Suzuki riders, but if you don't own a Suzuki you can rent one from the school for the class.

- **Freddie Spencer's High Performance Riding School** (www.fast freddie.com): Taught by Freddie Spencer (another former World MotoGP racing champion), this school is held at the Las Vegas Motor Speedway in Las Vegas, Nevada. Students at this school use school-supplied Honda motorcycles.

- **STAR Motorcycle School** (www.starmotorcycle.com): Operated by former AMA racing champion Jason Pridmore, this school is actually named the Skills and Techniques Advanced Riding Motorcycle School. Classes are taught at racetracks around the country, from California to Illinois.

- **CLASS Motorcycle Schools** (www.classrides.com): Taught by former AMA racing champion Reg Pridmore, CLASS courses are conducted in California, and you use your own bike.

- **Team Hammer Advanced Riding School and Track Rides** (www.teamhammer.com/school): This school has been around since 1990 and it was formed by Team Hammer, a roadracing team. You use your own bike during these courses and rides.

- **The California Superbike School** (www.superbikeschool.com): Run by Keith Code (who has been the guru to many racers), this school offers training starting with the most common errors made by novice riders up to a unique program for each rider to work on problem areas. Code uses special training motorcycles to teach such things as braking and cornering.

- **The Ed Bargy Racing School** (www.edbargyracingschool.com): This school, which is run by former racer Ed Bargy, is offered at East Coast racetracks. The school is also known as Ed Bargy Racing Services.

You may be able to find a roadracing club in your area that offers rider training at a local racetrack. Check with your local motorcycle dealerships to find out. Plus, find out if your local roadracing club offers track days, where you're allowed on the track to hone your skills without instructors. The club usually divides the attendees into different groups based on the riders' skills and experience. These are much less expensive than track schools. A track day can cost around $150, while track school can cost $500 to $1,500 or more.

Part II
Welcome to the Club

The 5th Wave   By Rich Tennant

In this part . . .

The seemingly complicated world of motorcycling can be mind-numbing to the outsider or the person who wants to learn how to ride. So in this part, I unravel the mysteries of motorcycling, including describing the various subgroups of motorcyclists, what motorcycles they ride, and what safety gear they wear. After all, if you want to be a motorcyclist, you want to be sure you fall into a crowd you're happy with.

In this part, I also recognize the growing number of women getting involved in motorcycling. I explain the challenges they face being accepted in motorcycling circles, and I show how they can find properly-sized safety gear, make their bikes fit their bodies, and get in touch with other female motorcyclists to get as much fun and excitement out of the sport as possible. Also, we adults shouldn't have all the fun all the time. So I describe in detail how to get your kids safely involved in motorcycling so that you can share this family sport.

Chapter 4

Bikes and Biker Culture: You Are What You Ride

A lot of people have a vague idea that there are different types of motorcycles. And most folks believe that a motorcyclist is a motorcyclist. But the fact is that the colorful world of motorcycling has a dizzying array of motorcycles, from big, almost-lumbering touring machines to nimble sportbikes that are rocket ships on the road.

And motorcyclists are just as varied. They ride with their own clothing, attend specific gatherings, and have their own language — and it all depends on what they ride. Whether you ride a cruiser, tourer, sportbike, or streetfighter, you're sure to find unwritten rules for fitting in with a particular motorcycling subgroup.

In this chapter you discover the different types of motorcycles that are available. You get a peek at some of the trickest machines on the market, with some key specifications such as engine size, seat height, and dry weight. Finally, you also get a snapshot of different types of motorcyclists and what makes these subcultures of motorcycling special. Then you can decide where you think you'd fit in best.

Why are the specs important?

Throughout this chapter, I give the specs on various bikes. You may be wondering why. Here are just a few reasons:

✔ If you have a 30-inch inseam, you probably don't want a bike with a 32-inch seat height (unless you're a ballerina and are used to standing on your tippy-toes). Similarly, if you're a small person, you don't want an 800-pound motorcycle to push around in parking lots or garages. Finally, a longer wheelbase means a bigger bike and more straight-line stability, but the bike will turn more slowly.

✔ The key specs, such as engine size, seat height, claimed dry weight (which is claimed by the manufacturer and is usually optimistic, like the weight you give for your driver's license), wheelbase, and suggested retail, are the minimum specs that you need to know in order to compare machines before deciding what to test ride and buy.

✔ Motorcyclists love talking specs, even if it's just the basic specs such as engine size and seat height. Know a few key specs and you'll impress friends and strangers alike. Children, however, will remain unimpressed until you tell them that your bike goes a zillion miles an hour.

Cruiser Cool and Custom Chic

Cruisers, the most popular motorcycles in America today, are characterized by their high weights, low seat heights, comfortable, laid-back seating positions, and high-torque motors. These reliable, low-maintenance bikes are meant for cruising, whether it's down to the local hangout or across the country. No matter where you're headed, you're bound to look cool on a cruiser.

Discovering the flashy bikes

Cruisers look cool. So by default, riders look cool riding them. Plus, they're pretty comfortable to ride compared to some other styles of motorcycles. These are the reasons that motorcyclists buy cruisers. After all, other bikes stop better, accelerate better, turn better, and are cheaper. But a cruiser lets a doctor, a lawyer, or an accountant feel like a bad boy (or girl) on the weekends without getting into any real trouble.

In this section, I introduce you to the four basic divisions in the cruiser world, and I give you a look at some of the most popular cruiser styles on the market today.

Harley-Davidsons

The American-made Harley-Davidson is the quintessential cruiser (although Harley does make some other types of bikes). The 2008 Harley-Davidson

FXDL Dyna Low Rider (shown in Figure 4-1) is just one of the many Harleys you can choose from. Here are the key specs for this bike:

Engine: 96 cubic inches (1,584cc)

Seat height: 26.8 inches

Wheelbase: 64.6 inches

Claimed dry weight: 641 pounds

Suggested retail: $14,995

Figure 4-1:
The 2008 Harley-Davidson FXDL Dyna Low Rider.

Photograph courtesy of Harley-Davidson Photography & Imaging. Copyright Harley-Davison.

Japanese (or metric) cruisers

The Japanese Big Four manufacturers — Honda, Kawasaki, Suzuki, and Yamaha — began making cruisers in the 1970s, taking their styling cues from Harley-Davidson. They're called *metric cruisers* because their nuts and bolts are metric, not American SAE fasteners. Also, their engine sizes are normally given in cubic centimeters, 1,670cc for example, rather than in cubic inches, like 110ci, which is Harley-Davidson's tradition. The 2008 Kawasaki Vulcan 1500 Classic (see Figure 4-2) is an example of this type of cruiser. Here are the key specs on this machine:

Engine: 90 cubic inches (1,470cc)

Seat height: 27.6 inches

Wheelbase: 65.6 inches

Claimed dry weight: 659 pounds

Suggested retail: $9,699

Photo courtesy of Kawasaki Motor Corporation USA.

Customs, choppers, and show customs

Following World War II, motorcyclists removed parts and cut parts up to make their bikes faster. Doing this also gave their motorcycles a unique look. These machines became known as *bobbers*. Motorcyclists continued this trend through the years. Riders in the 1960s chopped things off, added extended front forks, and made other changes with styling in mind to create bikes of their own, which came to be known as *choppers*.

Individual bike builders in the 1960s saw what motorcyclists were doing to their machines and began building similar bikes for cash-paying customers. These bikes, still popular today, are called *customs* because they're custom made and include few parts from the big motorcycle manufacturers.

The *show custom* world is a whole different animal, with bike prices ranging from $40,000 to $350,000. They usually have outrageous styling and wild paint jobs, and some have more pointy additions than a porcupine. These custom bikes usually don't see much road time; instead they appear in bike shows. Show bike motorcyclists aren't interested in the usual specs for their machines. Sure, size matters for the engine, but riders are more interested in the parts on the bike, and who made them, rather than things like seat height or claimed dry weight. Figure 4-3 shows an example of a custom American show bike. Here are the specs for that bike:

Engine: 106 cubic inches (1,737cc)

S & S Tanks: Skunkworx three-gallon gas tank on right, three-quart oil tank, battery box and electrical on left

Exhaust: Custom stainless by Skunkworx and Tubular Techniques

Suggested retail: $85,000

Figure 4-3:
The Skunkworx Custom Cycle "The Panhandler."

Photo courtesy of Skunkworx Custom Cycle.

Power cruisers

Modern cruisers have always been known for their relative comfort, reliability and ease of maintenance, but these days some riders want more. They want performance. And this desire has spawned machines called *power cruisers,* which feature high-performance motors, brakes, and suspension straight from the factory. The 1,670cc Star Warrior, made by Yamaha, is a popular power cruiser (see Figure 4-4). Here are the specs on this power cruiser:

Engine: 102 cubic inches (1,670cc)

Seat height: 28.7 inches

Wheelbase: 65.6 inches

Claimed dry weight: 613 pounds

Suggested retail: $12,449

Photo courtesy of Yamaha Motor Corp USA.

Figure 4-4:
The 2008
Star
Warrior.

Sporting the cruiser rider's uniform

Cruiser riders typically sport traditional biker's garb, which consists of these:

✔ Black leather jacket

✔ Black leather pants

✔ Heavy black boots

✔ Black leather gloves

However, as a cruiser rider, you can thumb your nose at tradition if you want. Black leather became the garb of choice back in the day when bikes were unreliable and a lot of time was spent on the roadside repairing them. Bikers would throw down their black leather jackets to kneel on and the jackets wouldn't show as much dirt or oil stains. Those days are over thanks to the super-reliability of motorcycles today, but many riders stick with the black garb because they like the bad-boy or bad-gal look. So what if it gets really hot? It looks really cool.

Looking like a Harley-Davidson rider

In Harley-Davidson culture, if you want to fit in, you pretty much have to wear — at a minimum — a black leather jacket and black boots. Sometimes, however, you will see rebels wearing (gasp!) brown leather. Leather chaps are favored over black leather pants, although you'll see the pants some-times. A sleeveless denim jacket with patches of skulls or playing cards is also popular attire.

In states where the law doesn't require riders to wear helmets, it's popular for Harley-Davidson riders to wear bandannas tied around the head to keep their hair from being blown around and getting tangled in the wind. Other riders wear a special *do-rag* that looks like a bandanna but is easier to wrap around the head —because it has a hook-and-loop fastener. Similarly, women with long hair like to keep their hair neat by wearing special ponytail sleeves that are usually made of leather.

In states where helmets are required, most Harley-Davidson riders like to wear the smallest helmet possible — a *beanie* helmet that covers just the top of the head. (I describe helmets in more detail in Chapter 5.)

And when riding a Harley-Davidson, you've got to wear a Harley-Davidson T-shirt. Those shirts are popular even among non–Harley-Davidson riders. For added coolness, you need shirts from the neat places you've visited, such as the Honolulu Harley-Davidson shop or one in Daytona Beach, Florida. T-shirts from biker bars, such as the Smiling Skull in Athens, Ohio, are also popular.

Heavy, black engineering boots are a favorite of the Harley-Davidson bunch. Any of the several styles of boots made by Harley-Davidson are fair game as well. All in all, Harley-Davidson riders like to wear stuff that says "Harley-Davidson" on it. Some of the riders even get Harley-Davidson tattoos because they're so loyal to the American brand.

Custom bike riders tend to mimic the Harley-Davidson crowd in their appearance.

Dressing like a metric cruiser biker

When riding metric or power cruisers you can pretty much wear what you want, but you'll definitely still see a lot of black or brown leather. Jackets made of synthetics, which aren't as hot as leather, aren't frowned on either. The bottom line is this: Wear whatever makes you feel good. If you like bad-boy black, go for it. Or, if you want to be more comfortable, go the synthetic route. Either way you'll fit in. (Check out Chapter 5, where I provide all the information you need to gear up — regardless of the style you choose.)

Bandannas and do-rags are popular when riders aren't wearing helmets. When wearing a helmet, cruiser riders don't really have a favorite style. Each rider picks what he or she likes. As far as footwear goes, most cruiser riders favor heavy engineer boots or other motorcycle styles, such as lace-up boots, that are made for cruising.

Brand loyalty and the Harley rider

Most motorcyclists are fiercely loyal to the brand of motorcycle they ride, particularly Harley-Davidson riders. (Harley riders truly are different!) This brand loyalty has sparked the creation of brand-specific clubs like H.O.G. — the Harley Owners Group — or the STAR Touring & Riding Association. (Check out Chapter 19 for more on these and other brand-specific clubs.)

Although attitudes are changing, a lot of Harley-Davidson riders are still trying to portray an outlaw image, and they tend to look down on other makes and models. Japanese sportbikes (see the later section "Sportbikes: 0 to 60 mph in 2.8 Seconds"), which Harley riders call "rice-burners," are particularly held in contempt. Old-school Harley riders despise Japanese machines, and sometimes they even have a sacrificial Japanese bike at their rallies for rally-goers to take turns whacking with a sledgehammer. As if it isn't already obvious: Tread cautiously around Harley riders if you own a Japanese machine.

You don't have to go to the Japanese bike-bashing extreme to fit in with most Harley crowds, but you do have to know the different Harley models by their alphabet soup designations: XL (Sportster), FXD family (Dyna), FXST (Softail Standard), FXSTSSE (Screamin' Eagle Softail Springer), and so on. Go to the Harley-Davidson Web site (www.harley-davidson.com) for more details. In fact, I suggest you make that site your new best friend.

Where to go and how to be cool

Cruiser riders are known for their short hops, which usually mean cruising on a Saturday from bar to bar. Go on the ride, share the camaraderie, just don't drink! In fact, staying sober and watching your buds' alcohol-induced antics may prove to be quite entertaining! (But as always, if you notice someone who's entirely too buzzed to be riding, be sure to find him or her a ride home.)

Bike nights are another ritual for cruiser riders. They're simply gatherings of motorcyclists at a local bar, restaurant, or motorcycle shop to eat, maybe drink, talk bikes, and look at the machinery in the parking lot. Some bike nights attract 1,000 or more bikers. It's a great place to feel like you belong. And luckily these gatherings have a built-in excuse for not drinking: They usually happen on work nights.

Motorcycle clubs also have organized rides, whether to raise money for charity or just to enjoy the countryside. They're usually advertised at local motorcycle shops or at biker bars. Cruiser riders also get together with a couple buds to take trips every now and then. They may travel to a rally or even just visit a different part of the country. (I cover rallies and trips in Chapter 16.)

And, finally, remember that you're a cruiser rider, so you can be a lone wolf. When you feel the need to ride, just head out to the beach, the mountains, or wherever. And if you run into another cruiser rider stopped somewhere, take the time to chat.

Talking cruiser speak

Like all motorcyclists, cruiser, power cruiser, and custom riders like to talk about bikes. So if you want to fit in, you have get in on the lingo. For instance, if you ride a metric cruiser, get to know the various models available and their basic specs. If you ride a Harley, you *must* at least know the different families sold: Sportster, Dyna, Softail, VRSC, and Touring, for example, and the variations of the families, such as Softail Springer. It may seem complicated. And, well, it is.

All you Harley riders out there should absolutely know that Willie G. Davidson (who's also known as "Willie G.") is the Harley-Davidson Motor Company's styling guru. He's a descendant of the company founders and a god among Harley riders.

All cruiser riders have a unique language when it comes to their bikes. Why? Because all their machines have things that others don't. So you'll hear talk about all sorts of different terms, including some of the following:

- ✔ **Floorboards:** These are platforms for your feet.
- ✔ **Heel-toe shifters:** These are shifters that you can manipulate with your heel or toe.
- ✔ **Shotgun, slash-cut, or other styles of mufflers:** *Shotgun mufflers* are basically round tube designs; pipes with a slash-cut are just that, pipes with a slash-cut at the end.
- ✔ **Straight pipes:** These are mufflers with their baffles taken out. Straight pipes make the bike loud and very annoying to nonriders (and many other motorcyclists as well). I talk about straight pipes more in Chapter 12.
- ✔ **Knucklehead, Panhead, and Shovelhead motors:** These are some of the different Harley-Davidson motors made over the years. They get their names because the Knucklehead looks like it has hand knuckles on the head, the head of a Panhead looks like a pan, and, of course, the head of a Shovelhead looks like the business end of a shovel.

The quickest way to learn the language is to read lots and lots of cruiser magazines. You can find magazines for metric cruisers and Harleys. Some examples of these magazines include *American Iron Magazine, American Rider, Cruising Rider, Easyriders, Motorcycle Cruiser, RoadBike,* and *V-Twin.* Also helpful when learning cruiser lingo is hanging around cruiser riders and listening to what they talk about.

Touring with the Long-Distance Bikes

Touring machines are long-distance motorcycles built for comfort. They're big, heavy, and able to click off thousands of miles on the road without a whimper. And they're expensive.

But, on the upside, they hold their value relatively well and most buyers won't balk at high mileage on the machine, since that's what they're made for. These aren't bare-bones bikes either — they have a lot of the luxuries that you'd want for a long-distance ride, like a plush seat and stereo.

If you plan to do any long-distance traveling with a passenger, a touring machine is the way to go. Your passenger will thank you. After all, you as the rider are pretty busy handling the machine while your passenger is just sitting back enjoying the sights. A touring bike allows the passenger to be very comfortable during the ride.

Checking out bikes built for the long haul

You can choose from three basic types of touring machines: luxury tourers, sport tourers, and adventure tourers. Luxury touring riders are modern-day cowboys discovering America on long treks at their own pace. Sport-touring riders enjoy spirited riding on twisty back roads during their cross-country jaunts. Adventure touring riders tool around on machines that look like big dirt bikes, but they spend most of their time on the road. The following sections provide details about these three types of machines and show popular examples of each.

Luxury tourers

Luxury tourers, also known as *full dressers,* or to old-timers, *baggers,* are the granddaddy of touring machines. Why? Pure comfort. Luxury touring machines are big, heavy, and relatively slow handling. They also feature an upright seating position. In fact, these bikes have almost as many luxuries as a car. You can get a luxury tourer decked out with a high windscreen, big front *fairing* (the bodywork on the front of the bike to help protect you from the wind and weather), plush seat, luggage, cruise control, heated seat and handgrips, radio and CD player, global positioning system, an intercom so you can talk with your passenger, and much more. You want an airbag like in your car? Honda's Gold Wing (see Figure 4-5) has one. Here are the specs on the Gold Wing:

Engine: 1,832cc

Seat height: 29.1 inches

Wheelbase: 66.5 inches

Claimed dry weight: To be determined

Suggested retail: $22,099

Figure 4-5:
The 2008
Honda Gold
Wing.

Sport tourers

The *sport tourers* are machines that combine the adrenaline-pumping acceleration, braking power, and handling of a high-performance bike with the luggage of a touring machine. Of course, they weigh more than a high-performance sport machine because of added luggage, bigger bodywork, and other touring necessities, but they're a lot more fun to ride on twisty roads than luxury tourers. See Figure 4-6 for an example of a sport tourer. Here are the specs on this bike:

Engine: 1,298cc

Seat height: 31.5 inches

Wheelbase: 60.6 inches

Claimed dry weight: 582 pounds

Suggested retail: $13,799

Figure 4-6:
The 2008
Yamaha
FJR1300A.

Photo courtesy of Yamaha Motor Corp USA.

Adventure tourers

Adventure tourers are street-legal off-road machines on steroids. Outfitted with luggage, these bikes are designed to cross hundreds or even thousands of miles of rugged country and ask for more. They have high ground clearance, big gas tanks, and motors with lots of stump-pulling torque. Even though they look like they should be crossing the African desert, most adventure-touring riders spend their time on freeways and paved roads, with occasional jaunts down gravel or dirt roads. But hey, the bikes look really cool and the riders feel like adventurers. Figure 4-7 shows an example of an adventure tourer. Here are the specs of the machine:

Engine: 1,170cc

Seat height: 35.2 inches

Wheelbase: 59.5 inches

Claimed dry weight: 492 pounds

Suggested retail: $16,350

Figure 4-7:
The 2007
BMW
R1200GS
Adventure.

Stylin': The right looks for touring riders

For a luxury tourer rider, dressing in the proper gear is easy: Almost anything goes. Leather jackets and pants offer the best protection, and they come in many styles and colors. But many in the touring crowd prefer synthetic riding gear, which offers more comfort in hot weather. And synthetic gear offers plenty of protection for the touring rider with its built-in armor protection. A three-quarter, flip-up or full-face helmet is the way to go for head gear. (I discuss various types of helmets in Chapter 5.) For boots, luxury touring riders generally go with the same types of boots that cruiser riders wear (you can read about cruiser gear earlier in the chapter).

Sport-touring riders, however, like to wear clothes that lean more toward the "sport" than the "touring" side because of the chance of a crash while riding twisty roads at a spirited pace. A leather jacket with a tighter fit than the luxury touring riders wear is the way to go. Equally popular, though, are synthetic jackets and pants. Sport-touring riders wear full-face helmets, and generally wear sport boots, which I discuss in Chapter 5.

For the adventure tourer, the right look is all function. Don't even think about leather: It's adventure-touring gear, Baybee! You need a synthetic three-quarter length jacket that reaches below the waist and is chock-full of big pockets to provide wind protection, storage pockets, and the signature look. Your pants will be synthetic as well. These riders generally wear full-face helmets, but their boots are either sport or tall lace-up boots.

If there's a uniform among the touring crowd, especially BMW riders, it's the Aerostich Roadcrafter one-piece suit or the Roadcrafter jacket and pants. These synthetic suits slip on easily over your clothes and have a lot of special touches, like big pockets, protective padding, and reflective panels so you're easy to spot in the dark. Check out www.aerostich.com for more details.

Fitting in with the touring crowd

Touring riders are often lone wolves (though sometimes they run in small packs), so you probably won't see them gathering together on weekends for group rides. However, you'll likely bump into them alone or in small groups during their long-distance travels. Or you may find them at major rallies for touring riders where they gather to swap stories and go on short rides. It's easy to fit in. All you have to do is talk about motorcycles, riding, trips, gear, or anything else motorcycling related. They're very accepting of all riders.

Touring riders especially like to talk about their machines and the special gadgets on them, like global positioning systems or extra lights. Touring riders also like to talk about great trips, great roads, and getting caught riding in bad weather!

To get a feel for the touring crowd and pick up some of the lingo, check out some of the touring magazines, including *Rider* and *Road Runner.* You can also take a look at the publications of touring clubs, such as the BMW Motorcycle Owners of America or the Honda Sport Touring Association. In fact, if you join a touring club you'll make new friends and pick up the lingo pretty quick. I discuss some touring clubs in Chapter 19. Last but not least, you can flip through the *American Motorcyclist,* the magazine of the American Motorcyclist Association.

Sportbikes: 0 to 60 in 2.8 seconds

Sportbikes, also called *crotch rockets* by non–sportbike riders, are the thoroughbreds of the street motorcycling world — race bikes with turn signals and license plates. The acceleration takes your breath away, and the G-forces you feel when braking make your heart stop. You don't sit on a sportbike, you crouch down in it. Sportbikes are characterized by their lightweight, powerful motors, short wheelbases, exceptional stopping power, and razor-sharp handling.

You'll hear nonriders call a sportbike a *Ninja*, but that's wrong. Kawasaki produces a Ninja line of sportbikes, so don't call a sportbike a Ninja unless it is, in fact, one of the Kawasaki machines.

The Suzuki GSX-R sportbikes are considered among the best. Check out Figure 4-8 to see a photo of this bike. Here are the specs:

Engine: 999cc

Seat height: 31.9 inches

Wheelbase: 55.7 inches

Claimed dry weight: 379 pounds

Suggested retail: $11,399

Figure 4-8: The 2008 Suzuki GSX-R1000.

Photo courtesy of American Suzuki Motor Corp.

Dressing like Ricky Roadracer

For the hard-core sportbike rider, one-piece or two-piece, zip-together roadrace leathers are the way to go. Most sportbikers, however, wear a tight roadrace-cut leather jacket and bluejeans or other pants.

Synthetic jackets, even some made of mesh, are becoming more and more popular because they're cooler than leather. However, these jackets don't offer the same high level of protection. For this crowd, colorful garb that matches the colors on your bike is the only way to go.

A full-face helmet is the helmet of choice for sportbike riders who wear helmets — and most do. Also, roadrace-style boots are the footwear of choice. These days you may see a lot of young people on sportbikes who aren't wearing helmets or other proper safety gear. In fact, they may be riding with tennis shoes or flip-flops. While they may think they look cool, when they crash they are going to get very hurt. *Remember:* True sportbikers wear all the safety gear they can.

Fitting in with the sportbike crowd

Sportbikers are a lot like cruiser riders in that they're very social, but they tend to hang with friends rather than sportbikers they don't know. They gather in groups in which everyone knows each other for spirited weekend rides, and they spend time together before and after the ride talking about riding and bikes. You can't just show up for one of these rides, however. You have to be invited by a friend who's already part of the group. Sportbikers also like to gather at *bike nights,* which are gatherings of motorcyclists hosted by a restaurant or other business, usually on weekday evenings. Make a friend there, and you'll probably be invited on a ride. Note to women: Drop a hint that you're looking for someone to ride with and you'll get more invitations than you can handle.

To talk the talk, remember that this crowd is all about performance. Know the following details inside and out:

- The hottest sportbikes on the market, the key specifications, the different performance tires available, and the popular upgrades, such as a rear fender eliminator kit that makes a sportbike look even more like a race bike
- The top stars of AMA Superbike and international MotoGP racing (and don't forget to follow their careers)
- Roadracer language, such as "throw it in the weeds," which means go off the road and crash, usually because a rider went too fast into a turn

Simply hang out with sportbikers, listen, and nod when they talk. You'll pick up the lingo quickly. Read sportbike-related magazines to stay up on the latest racing news, lingo, and performance products. Some popular magazines include *Cycle World, Motorcyclist, Sport Rider, 2 Wheel Tuner,* and *Road Racer X.*

Naked Machines

Naked bikes are bikes with minimal bodywork. The minimal bodywork allows you to show off the motor. These machines are generally considered *standard* motorcycles. They have an upright seating position and motors with smooth power delivery (which make them relatively easy to ride), and they're also comfortable. They're all-around machines that can go across town or across the country.

Naked riders, that is, riders of naked bikes, are probably the only motorcyclists who woke up one day and said, "I want to ride a motorcycle" (rather than saying "I want to tour the country on a bike" or "I want to look bad" or "I want to go fast"). As such, they don't have their own crowd or events. You'll find some of them hooking up with cruiser riders and others falling in with the sportbike crowd, depending on the type of riding they like.

Another naked bike you may hear about is called a *streetfighter,* but it doesn't fall into the conventional naked bike category. Streetfighters are generally stripped-down sportbikes ridden by young riders with a reputation for hooliganism — popping wheelies, doing wheelstands on the front wheel, burning donuts, and performing other stunts. Streetfighters are more popular in Europe than they are in America. Streetfighter riders tend to run with the sportbike crowd.

Kawasaki's Z1000, shown in Figure 4-9, is a perfect example of a naked machine. Here are the specs:

Engine: 953cc

Seat height: 32.3 inches

Wheelbase: 56.9 inches

Claimed dry weight: Not available

Suggested retail: $8,899

As for attire, naked bike or standard riders generally wear sedate leather or synthetic jackets and bluejeans or synthetic pants. But almost anything goes. So if you want flashier garb, go for it. A black leather jacket is okay, but don't go for a full-on Harley-rider look. That would be considered bad form. Full-face helmets are the helmet of choice, while footwear can be cruiser chic or sportbike cool. The great thing about this crowd is that you'll likely be accepted no matter what way you dress.

Because standard riders tend to gravitate toward the cruiser or sportbike crowd, they need to know the lingo of the people they ride with. Check out the cruiser and sportbike sections earlier in the chapter for more tips on getting in with the crowd you're hanging with.

Figure 4-9:
The 2008
Kawasaki
Z1000.

Dual-Purpose Bikes and Dirt Machines

You don't have to ride on the street to be a motorcyclist. Go ahead, have some fun in the dirt. This section shows you a couple of options.

Getting to know bikes made for the dirt

Many motorcyclists got their start as kids riding in the dirt, and their love of motorcycling included street riding as they got older. Most dirt riders also have streetbikes. However, most street riders don't also have dirt bikes. Either way, riding in the dirt is a lot of fun, and it's a great family sport too. As I explain in Chapter 3, dirt riding even makes you a better street rider. If you pick up a 25-year-old dirt bike for $500, you can have a million dollars worth of fun. (And learn a lot about fixing and maintaining a motorcycle!)

Riding the street and the trails

Dual-purpose or *dual-sport* bikes are at home on the road or in the trails. They're tall, street-legal machines with an upright seating position and tires that are made for both street and dirt use.

A dual-purpose bike is a compromise between a street and dirt machine, so you have to be mindful of that fact. For instance, you may not want to lean the bike over as far on the road as you would on a pure streetbike, and you may not want to do much freeway riding. And, because of their weight, these bikes can be a handful when on the trails. But owners of these bikes nonetheless love them because they're all-around machines that are easy to ride in traffic and they're cheap.

Kawasaki's KLR650 (see Figure 4-10) is one of the more popular dual-purpose machines. Here are the specs:

Engine: 651cc

Seat height: 35 inches

Wheelbase: 58.3 inches

Claimed dry weight: 386 pounds

Suggested retail: $5,349

Figure 4-10: The 2008 Kawasaki KLR650.

Photo courtesy of Kawasaki Motor Corporation USA.

Going for dirt only

If you don't want to compromise with a dual-purpose bike, get a strictly off-road machine, like an *enduro* or a *motocrosser*. Simply put, an enduro is a dirt bike with lighting and a spark arrester on the muffler. Motocross bikes are like enduros but are lighter racing machines with a little more power. However, motocrossers don't have the lights and other enduro-related equipment.

If you decide to get a motocrosser to play with, start small. Otherwise you may find yourself getting a worm's eye view of the trail a lot more often than you'd like because of the big bike's power.

Yamaha builds a well-liked off-road machine, shown in Figure 4-11. Here are its specs:

Engine: 449cc

Seat height: 38.6 inches

Wheelbase: 58.5 inches

Claimed dry weight: 248 pounds

Suggested retail: $7,199

Figure 4-11: The 2008 Yamaha WR450F.

Photo courtesy of Yamaha Motor Corp USA.

Dressing the part and fitting in

Dual-purpose riders wear three-quarter length jackets with lots of pockets and synthetic pants for protection. They may also sport a motocross jersey and pants if they plan to spend the day on the trails. Generally speaking it's strictly motocross gear for enduro and motocross riders in the dirt. What I mean by motocross gear is light, padded jerseys (like football jerseys) and pants made specifically for riding off the road. Motocross jerseys are even popular among kids for everyday wear, even if they don't ride motorcycles.

Dual-purpose riders generally wear a sport-style boot when riding on the street. In the dirt, dual-sporters and motocrossers prefer boots made for motocross, which are heavily padded and armored tall boots made to withstand a pounding against tree limbs and other off-road obstacles.

For helmets, dual-sporters wear full-face street helmets on the street. They, along with the motocrossers, wear specially designed motocross helmets in the dirt. These full-face helmets have large eyeports so riders can also wear goggles. These helmets also have a visor to help block the sun and deflect small branches and rocks tossed by your buddy's bike ahead of you.

Dirt riders love dirt riding and they enjoy the company of other dirt riders. To fit in, simply show up for a ride or join a club. (I tell you how to find an organized trail ride in your area in Chapter 16.) Be sure to learn the lingo, including terms like *auger in* (fall off your bike landing head first) and *face plant* (fall off your bike and land face first). Sprinkle stories of your latest trail ride with these two terms and you'll get a smile from your fellow riders. They've all been there with sheepish grins under their helmets. Read dirt- and trail-riding magazines to catch on to the lingo and to get riding tips. Some magazines you might check out include *Dirt Rider, Racer X,* and *Transworld Motocross.*

Chapter 5

Dress for Success

*M*any folks say that the clothes make the man (or woman), and nowhere is that more true than in the diverse world of motorcycling. Riding gear says a lot about a motorcyclist. One quick look, and you know that he or she is a cruiser rider, sportbiker, tourer, or whatever. For the rider, wearing the right gear means fitting in with the crowd you're hanging with on that particular day. Or it can mean feeling like you wore your tux or classic little black dress to a square dance.

The most important thing to consider, though, is that your motorcycle gear must protect you in a crash. How good your jacket looks just won't matter, for example, if its seams explode and shred when you hit the pavement. And boots are no good to you if the soles are slick leather that slide around every time you put your feet down at a stoplight or stop sign.

The uninitiated may think they can just look at a garment and know it's safe for motorcycling. But certain aspects make safety gear true motorcycling jackets, pants, helmets, and gloves. Other "features" make them fashions that have no business being worn while riding a motorcycle. To be blunt, the wrong gear can result in serious injury in a crash.

In this chapter, you discover the array of helmets, jackets, gloves, boots, and pants available to motorcyclists that are designed to protect in a crash. They're all important parts of your package of safety gear. Here you survey the different types and styles available, get a feel for the prices, and find out what to avoid. When you start wearing your protective gear consistently, you'll feel like something is wrong every time you leave the house on your bike without wearing your helmet, jacket, gloves, boots, or riding pants.

A Helmet: The Best Protection Next to Your Brain

A motorcycle helmet says you're a true motorcyclist. After all, anyone can walk around wearing a motorcycle jacket or even a jacket and chaps. But when you see someone carrying a helmet, you know that person is a rider, not someone just dressed up like a motorcyclist. In fact, a nonrider probably would feel pretty goofy carrying around a helmet.

But riders don't have helmets because they want to show the world they ride. They want to protect their noggins, and a helmet does that well. Imagine just sitting on your bike in a parking lot and tipping over, hitting your head on the asphalt. That fall alone could seriously injure you. Now imagine riding down a nice, scenic country road at about 35 mph. You bank your bike into a corner and hit some gravel. At that point, your rear tire loses traction, you get spit on the ground, and then you hit your head on the road. In this type of situation, a helmet will save you.

Even if you don't want to wear a helmet, you need one. Your state may require motorcyclists to wear a helmet, or this may be the law in a state you plan to ride to or through. (You can find out the requirements by checking the state-by-state motorcycling laws summarized in Appendix B.) So you may as well get a comfortable helmet that you're willing to wear.

The following sections discuss the different types of helmets available, how to get a great fit, and more.

Deciding which type of helmet fits you

The helmet market is very competitive, so companies are always coming up with new designs and new features — which is great for motorcyclists. You can find all sorts of different helmets, including the following:

- **Full-face helmets,** which cover your entire head, including your face
- **Flip-up helmets,** which are full-face helmets that allow you to flip up the entire front
- **Three-quarter helmets,** which cover the top and sides of your head
- **Half helmets,** also called a *shorties* or *beanies,* which just basically cover the top of your head

The following sections discuss each of these types in detail so you can choose the one that suits your needs.

Protecting your eyes

All states require that you wear eye protection when you ride. However, some states let you ride without if you have a windscreen on your motorcycle that's above eye level. With a full-face or flip-up helmet, the faceshield serves as your eye protection. But if you ride with the front of your flip-up helmet flipped up, you need to wear eye protection, such as glasses or goggles. That eye protection must be able to withstand an impact (from a rock, for example). Your best bet for getting eye protection that truly protects your eyes is to visit a motorcycle shop. Forget about going to the local drugstore and picking up a pair of $5 sunglasses; they won't save your sight.

Full-face and flip-up helmets

For maximum protection, a full-face (see Figure 5-1a) or flip-up helmet (see Figure 5-1b) is the way to go. Full-face and flip-up helmets all have a polycarbonate *faceshield,* also called a *visor,* over the eyeport that you can flip up and down. Helmets come standard with a clear shield, although most riders also like to purchase a smokeshield to use on sunny days. Other colors are also available.

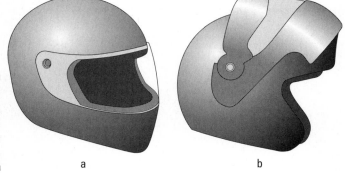

Figure 5-1:
A full-face helmet and a flip-up helmet.

a   b

Not only does a full-face or flip-up helmet protect all sides of your head and your face from a nasty pounding or scraping if you get in a crash, but this type of helmet also protects your eyes, nose, and face from serious injury from rocks, bugs, and even birds. Imagine cruising down the highway only to have a stone kicked up by a truck tire hit you in the face; or what if a bird flies right into your nose? It happens. And it hurts.

Three-quarter helmets

Some riders prefer three-quarter helmets (see Figure 5-2), because they want to feel the wind in their faces when they ride, or maybe because they feel claustrophobic in a full-face helmet.

Figure 5-2:
A three-quarter helmet.

You'll find some very good, comfortable three-quarter helmets on the market. The downside, of course, is that your face is unprotected not only in a crash, but also from stones, bugs, and even rain that can really, really sting when you're riding 55 mph.

Half helmets

The half helmet, sometimes called a *beanie* (see Figure 5-3), offers little protection because motorcyclists rarely fall directly on the top of their heads. But a half helmet is better than no helmet — at least it offers a little bit of protection. Half-helmets are favored by hard-core cruiser types who are forced to wear helmets by state law.

Figure 5-3:
A half helmet.

Protecting your head in style

Helmet styles and colors abound in the marketplace, so you're sure to find something that you like in prices ranging from less than $100 to $700 or more. If you want to be really unique, you can buy a white helmet in a style you like and then have it custom-painted. This is a pricey option, ranging from $500 to $1,500 for the paint job alone, but you'll really like your helmet, and nobody else in the world will have one like it. Ask a custom bike builder in your area to steer you to a helmet painter. Or use your favorite search engine to browse the Internet for a custom painter.

Ensuring that a helmet meets federal safety requirements

Nonmotorcyclists may have an image of bikers cruising down the road on their big motorcycles wearing jean jackets with the arms cut off and donning World War II–style German helmets. That may be a popular image from the movies, but when is the last time you saw a motorcyclist wearing that type of helmet? Probably never. If you did, you can be sure it was illegal.

That's because all helmets sold in the United States must meet strict federal Department of Transportation (DOT) impact standards. And to show that a helmet meets that standard, it must have a DOT sticker attached to the back of it. If you're considering buying a helmet and find one that doesn't have a DOT sticker, don't buy it. It's illegal and it won't protect your head. These are called *novelty* helmets for a reason.

When looking at helmets, you'll sometimes find that they also have a sticker from the Snell Memorial Foundation. This certification differs somewhat from the federal DOT certification. The Snell certification offers more protection from impacts sustained at higher speeds. Do you need a helmet with Snell certification? Not legally, but it's good for peace of mind.

A helmet is made up of a shell (usually a fiberglass or polycarbonate composite), expanded polystyrene foam designed to crush upon impact so that the force of the impact isn't transmitted to your brain, and a chin strap. Helmets are designed to survive only one solid impact, so even dropping your helmet on the sidewalk can seriously reduce its ability to protect your head. Handle your helmet carefully — and don't set it on your motorcycle mirror because doing so can crush the expanded polystyrene foam. Also, it's recommended that you get a new helmet every five years. Why? Gas fumes from riding, or even from your garage (if you store your helmet there), can break down the foam. Besides, with advances in helmet technology and designs, you'll want a new helmet within five years anyway.

Getting the proper fit

A helmet is the most important piece of safety equipment you can wear. And to get the most protection, you need a helmet that fits well. After all, you don't want a helmet that's too big and will twist on your head if you get in a crash. And you don't want a helmet that's so tight and uncomfortable that you won't wear it as often as you should.

No matter what size head you have, you'll find a helmet that will fit you well. To get a proper fit, you should do the following:

1. **Get a cloth tape measure and measure the circumference of your head at just about the level of your eyebrows.**

   Use a tape measure that measures in centimeters because that knowledge is crucial for a good fit.

2. **After you know your size, look for a label inside the helmet that tells the size, such as XS, S, M, L, XL, or XXL.**

   Remember that a medium helmet made by one manufacturer could be the same size as a large one that's made by another manufacturer. This is where you use the notes you jotted down about the circumference of your head in centimeters (see Step 1). Besides using the S/M/L designations, most helmet manufacturers give the size in centimeters. For example, an L may also say 59–60 cm.

3. **Try on a lot of different helmets, even different helmets made by the same manufacturer.**

   Different helmet brands and even different models within the same brand can have different shapes and can fit differently.

4. **Feel for pressure points.**

   Some riders complain that certain helmets put too much pressure on their foreheads, so be on the lookout for this feel in a helmet. Other riders may believe the padding in the cheek area is way too tight. You want a snug fit, but not a painful one.

   Some manufacturers offer different-sized padding for the inside of their helmets so you can customize your fit if the ear or cheek paddings are too tight for you.

5. **Put on the helmet, strap it up, and shake your head left and right and up and down.**

   When you perform these movements, the helmet should stay put. Push up on the chinbar of a full-face helmet to make sure it won't slide up a whole lot under pressure. Make sure you can't roll the helmet forward off your head. Try to get a helmet that centers your eyes in the eyeport.

Is a $700 helmet worth it?

You want the best protection you can get for your head, but that doesn't mean you have to shell out big bucks for a helmet. For a helmet to be legally sold in the United States for street or off-road use, it must meet federal Department of Transportation (DOT) standards. And if a helmet meets those standards, it will have a DOT sticker on it. So whether you spend $100 or $700 on a helmet, it really doesn't matter when it comes to protection. All the helmets pass the same tests. When you spend more money on a helmet, you're paying for things such as a lighter weight, better ventilation, maybe more comfort, better graphics, and usually a better ability to cut wind noise. Some riders are perfectly happy with their $100 helmets, while others have moved up to $500 helmets and now will never go back. Unfortunately, there's no easy (meaning, inexpensive) way to try out various helmets on the road. Ask your riding pals what they wear and why, to get an idea about the differences in helmets.

Every time you buy a helmet, which should be at least every five years, go through this process, as if you're buying a helmet for the first time. After all, helmet makers may have changed the sizing of their helmets in the years that have passed.

Keeping your helmet new, and your scalp from itching

A helmet is a big investment, especially if you spend big money for a high-end one. You'll want to keep it looking shiny and new. But you don't want to use any harsh cleaning fluids on it. Chemicals can damage the outer shell and even speed up the deterioration of the foam liner inside that absorbs impacts.

One problem you'll face as a rider, especially if you ride at night, is bugs. Very small bugs can pose a very big problem. Why? The carcasses dry up and get hard while you ride, and if you don't take care in how you get them off, you could end up scratching your helmet or faceshield.

The best way to get bugs off your helmet is to first place a wet cotton cloth or towel on the front of your helmet for 15 minutes or so. This softens the hard bodies of the bugs and makes them easy to get off. In a pinch, a wet paper towel will work.

To clean the outer shell of the helmet, it's best to use a mild detergent, like dishwashing soap. To clean the faceshield, pick up a cleaning product at your bike shop made specifically for that purpose. When the shell and faceshield are clean, you can use a bit of automotive wax to give the shell a protective coat.

A mild soap is also best for cleaning the inside liner of the helmet, which can get a little, umm, ripe, if you don't clean it occasionally. The liners of some helmets come out, which makes cleaning easy. If your liner doesn't come out, first dab it with a mild detergent and then with a wet towel. Then let it dry. Make sure your helmet liner is absolutely clean.

If you find that your helmet makes your scalp itch, you can take some steps to try to correct that. First, make sure that your ventilation system is open so that air is circulating through the helmet. Also try using a different shampoo. Your shampoo could be drying out your scalp so much that if your head sweats, it starts itching. Finally, check with a dermatologist to be sure you don't have some kind of skin problem. You also can consult an allergist to see whether you're allergic to something in the helmet.

No, it won't break your neck: This and other helmet myths busted

Faced with arguments about the safety of helmets, some motorcyclists who don't wear them argue that a helmet actually poses more dangers to a motorcyclist than riding without one. These bikers have four main arguments, which I debunk in the following sections.

The bottom line is that there are compelling safety reasons for wearing a helmet. But it's your choice, unless your state has a law requiring you to wear one.

Argument 1: "A helmet will break my neck"

One popular argument is that if you get in a crash wearing a full-face helmet and hit the road with the chinbar, it will snap your head back, breaking your neck. Then, they say, the motorcyclist is left bedridden for the rest of his or her life. On the other hand, they say, such an impact would kill you if you weren't wearing a helmet, and they would rather be dead than unable to move. Hmmm. It's an interesting argument, but no facts can back it up.

In fact, research shows that a motorcycle rider is less likely to suffer a severe, crippling neck injury — I'm talking about the spinal cord here — than a rider without a helmet. Or, looking at it backward: If you ride without a helmet, you're more likely to suffer a crippling injury than if you wear a helmet.

Argument 2: "I can't hear anything with a helmet on"

Helmet opponents argue that riders who wear helmets can't hear anything with the helmet on, such as the blaring of the siren on an approaching police car or ambulance, or even the sounds of nearby vehicles. Again, this is untrue. Yes, helmets reduce sounds — the blasting wind noise rushing by your ears while you ride when you don't wear a helmet is muffled significantly, for example — but you can still hear sirens, cars and trucks, and even people yelling at you. Helmets protect you from the possibly damaging whistling wind noise as well as other loud noises you may encounter on your rides.

Argument 3: "A helmet reduces my peripheral vision"

Helmet haters often say that a helmet reduces peripheral vision. They say that they need every advantage they can get to see car drivers and other dangers approaching from the side while they're riding. Well, guess what? Research again shows that a helmet doesn't reduce peripheral vision. In fact, remember those DOT safety standards discussed earlier in this chapter? Those standards require that a helmet allow for 210 degrees of peripheral vision, which is about the peripheral vision that the average person has.

Argument 4: "Helmet laws don't save lives"

A common argument is that more motorcyclists die in states that require helmets than in states that don't require helmets. You can't compare one state with another to argue that more motorcyclists wearing helmets die on the road; the comparison needs to be made in the same state because you need to compare the number of riders on the road. And the fact is, normally when a state that required riders to wear helmets repeals the mandatory helmet law, motorcyclist deaths go up. Plus, motorcyclists don't just die from head injuries; they can also die from internal injuries.

Motorcycle Jackets: Looking Cool While Staying Protected

The way the story goes, motorcyclists used to always wear black leather jackets because, besides gaining wearable protection, motorcyclists could take off their jackets and throw them on the ground when they were working on their broken-down bikes alongside the road. The bikers wouldn't get dirty, and the black wouldn't show the dirt so much. Plus, grease and road grime don't show up as well on a black jacket.

This theory may be true, since motorcycles of yesteryear weren't as reliable as they are today, or it may not be true. It doesn't really matter, though, because today's motorcyclist isn't stuck with just one choice in a jacket. Besides black leather, today's rider can pick from leather jackets in all different colors, including pink. They can even choose jackets made from synthetic materials with built-in armor offering loads of protection.

So you can make a fashion statement with the jacket you wear or project your desired image. If you want to look like a bad boy or girl, go with the black leather. If you want to look like you just rode off the racetrack, you can get a colorful racing-style jacket. If you want to look like you just came from a long-distance riding trip through the desert, you can do that, too. You just need the right jacket. Expect to pay about $130 for a basic synthetic jacket and up to $900 or more for a custom-made leather jacket with a lot of built-in protection and other features. Have some fun with your jacket. After all, motorcycling *is* about having fun.

Old Faithful: Nothing beats a leather jacket

For uncompromising protection and a great feel, you can't beat a motorcycle jacket made of thick, competition-weight leather that's 1.1 mm to 1.3 mm thick. When you hold the jacket in one hand, it feels heavy, but when you wear it, it doesn't.

Motorcycle roadracers who circle racetracks at 180 mph or more wear one-piece leather suits with built-in armor because they offer the most abrasion protection. These racers fall off their bikes and go sliding off the track at high speeds; they walk away from these crashes because sliding on the asphalt didn't grind away the leather.

When buying a leather jacket, it's vital that it's a *motorcycling jacket.* A fashion jacket isn't thick enough to protect against abrasion if you fall off your bike at any speed.

What's great about leather jackets besides the protection is that leather can be dyed, so you'll find a lot of great-looking jackets out there besides classic black. You can spot-clean your leather jacket when it gets dirty, but eventually, to have it thoroughly cleaned, you should take it to a professional cleaner who's skilled in cleaning leather. You also should treat your jacket with leather conditioner every now and then to keep it supple. Expect to pay $250 and up for a leather jacket.

Opting for synthetics when leather is too hot or too expensive

A lot of motorcyclists have a leather jacket to wear when the weather is cool or cold, and opt for a synthetic mesh jacket when the weather is hot. Or they have a synthetic jacket that isn't mesh but has a lot of big pockets because they want to be able to carry a lot of stuff.

Synthetic jackets are a lot cheaper than leather ones. So if you're on a tight budget, you can opt for a synthetic jacket. Synthetic jackets don't quite offer the abrasion protection of leather, but, hey, it's pretty unlikely that you'll be sliding down the asphalt at 100 mph like a roadracer might.

Synthetics still offer good abrasion protection and have armor protection in key areas like the elbows and shoulders. Like leather jackets, they come in a variety of colors and styles. Just make sure you get one that's made specifically for motorcycling. Cleaning synthetic jackets is easy: Take out the padding and throw it in the washing machine. Expect to pay $120 and up for a synthetic jacket.

Finding a good fit and protection

Motorcycling jackets are made for, well, motorcycling, so they have a different fit and feel compared to jackets you normally wear. Motorcycle jackets for street riding need to be snug so they aren't flapping around in the wind and so that the armor protection in them stays put over critical areas of the body in a crash.

Don't get a jacket that's too tight. You want to avoid a too tight jacket for two reasons:

✔ You'll rarely wear it because it's uncomfortable (and a jacket can't protect you unless you're wearing it).

✔ Much as we all hate to admit it, most of us gain a little weight as we get older, so it may not fit after a few months or years.

Besides being snug, a motorcycle jacket has longer arms than a regular jacket. Why? When you're on your bike and are reaching out in front of you to hold the handlebars, you need that extra sleeve length to keep your wrists protected. A motorcycle jacket is also designed so that it won't get tight around your shoulders as you reach for the handlebars.

Most motorcycle jackets have zippers at the wrists so you can snug up the lower part of the sleeve after you put on your jacket. The pockets also have zippers so that the stuff you have in there doesn't fall out while you ride. And there's usually an inside breast pocket and a breathable liner. Some leather jackets also have zippered vents so you can let air in while you ride. Many synthetic jackets are made of a mesh to keep you cool.

Motorcycle jackets vary in the level of extra protection they offer, and your riding style dictates how much protection you need. For example, if you're a cruiser rider, you can wear a leather jacket that just has an extra layer of padding in key areas: the shoulders and elbows. Or, as a rider of any machine, you may want to opt for a leather or synthetic jacket that also has padding in the shoulders and elbows. If you ride a sportbike, you'll want to consider a jacket that has *hard armor* in those key areas, which is padding with a hard shell.

The more protection you get, the better off you are, but adding protection also adds cost, especially if you have your jacket custom made. But it's a worthwhile investment, especially considering that your jacket will last you many, many years — unless, of course, you gain weight and can't fit into it anymore.

Boots Aren't Just for Cowboys

Often riders don't give enough thought to their riding boots. Different boots are made for different riding styles — cruiser, touring, sportbike — so it's important to pick the right boot.

Some riders just pick up a cheap pair of work boots or even combat boots to ride in. Well, that foot wear is better than flip-flops, but it really isn't the best choice for motorcycle riding. Motorcycle boots are specifically made to provide protection in the event of a crash. They also help to keep you from slipping when you put your feet down at stoplights and to make it easier to move your feet around on the bike's footpegs.

Good motorcycle boots aren't cheap. You can expect to pay from $100 to $350 or more. But these boots are well worth it and will last for many years. Plus, if you really like the boots, you sometimes can have them repaired when the soles wear out or you scrape up the protection mounted on the sides or back of the boots.

If you have a great idea for boot graphics or you just want boots that fit perfectly, consider buying custom boots. Expect to pay $450 or more.

Determining the important fits and features

Your riding style determines the features you need in a boot. Cruiser riders, for example, need fewer safety features than a sportbike rider. You'll find a lot of different boots out there, and if they're made for motorcycling, you'll know that they'll at least meet your basic needs.

Many cruiser riders opt for a black or brown engineer-type boot or a lace-up work-type boot. You can get these boots "off the rack" or custom made. A basic boot has a hard toe and nonslip sole. Boots with more features may have an extra layer of leather where the boot manipulates the shifter as well as padding or other protection around the ankles and heels.

For a sportbike rider, a sport/roadracing boot is the way to go. These boots are lightweight and are designed for easy movement on the footpegs as well as for feel of the shift and brake levers. The heels are low, the soles are relatively flat, and you get hard protection in the toes, ankles, heels, and elsewhere.

A motorcycle boot should be snug, but it shouldn't be so tight that it's uncomfortable. It should be comfortable for walking as well as riding. Some new riders need a little time to get used to the tightness around the ankle caused by built-in ankle protection. If you're uncomfortable in a really snug boot, get one that's a little looser. Just make sure the boot isn't so big that your foot can move in it, giving you blisters on your heel.

A lot of motorcycling boots are made in Europe, so they come in European sizes. For example, a European 45 is an American men's 10.5, and a European 45.5 is an American 11. But sizing differs among various manufacturers, so one boot maker's 45 may, in fact, be equivalent to an American 11 instead of 10.5. In fact, sizes vary among manufacturers even in American sizes. You may find that you wear a 10.5 boot from one maker and an 11 from another. Before you buy, actually go to a store and try on the boots, or make sure you can return them if you mail-order them and they don't fit.

Protection: Not all boots are created equal

A lot of boots out there offer various levels of protection. Your best bet is to get the most protection you can afford. For example, at a minimum, the boots should be water resistant so that your feet won't get wet in the rain. For more money, you can opt for a waterproof boot, which will let you ride through a deluge or walk through 6 inches of water without getting your feet wet. Keeping your dogs dry is important for your own comfort and for the sheer enjoyment of motorcycling. And, of course, it's important so you can safely operate your machine.

Also, at a minimum, a motorcycle boot should have a nonslip sole and a hard toe. The boot may offer other levels of protection, such as padding or hard armor around the ankle and heels and on the shin; it's up to you to decide what you need.

Sport/roadrace boots also feature *toe sliders* on the outer edge of the toes so that if the rider touches that part of the boot to the asphalt while taking a corner, the asphalt won't grind away the boot. Good boots also feature protection, usually hard armor, for the Achilles heel.

Caring for your boots

Take care of your boots, and they'll last you a long time. To clean them, just wipe off the dirt with a damp cloth or sponge. Then dry them with a soft cloth. If your boots have any plastic parts on the outside that are articulated, you can use a silicone lubricant on them to make them stop squeaking. Don't use any harsh cleaners; otherwise you may wreck those protective parts.

Store your boots in a well-ventilated area, and stuff them with newspaper over the winter so they maintain their shape. If your boots get wet — and there will be days they will — dry them with a cloth as best you can and then leave them in a well-ventilated area away from direct sunlight to dry.

Covering Your Legs: The Right Pants Are Important

Most riders ignore picking up a pair of motorcycle riding pants and, instead, opt to ride in blue jeans. Big mistake. Riding pants are important because of the abrasion protection they offer in a crash. Imagine sliding down the road on your butt in blue jeans: Your flesh would look like hamburger in seconds.

If you want the right image, you need to match your riding pants with your riding jacket. If you wear a black leather jacket, then black leather pants or chaps are the way to go. If you wear a synthetic jacket, then synthetic pants would look best. In either case, you can get blue or black jeans made specifically for motorcycling that would work well.

It may seem like a hassle to have to put on special pants for motorcycling, but, hey, nobody said motorcycling is easy. And riders aren't dressing for the ride as much as they're dressing for the possibility of a crash.

Leather pants: Great protection made sexy

For the same reason that leather makes for great riding jackets, it makes for great riding pants. Leather offers great abrasion protection. Plus, leather pants look great on both men and women because, for motorcycling, you need a snug fit.

You don't need competition-weight leather for pants because the impact areas in a crash are the knees, hips, and less likely, the butt, which should have padding or other protection. But you do need something thicker than the leather pants you'll find at a fashion shop. With motorcycling-specific leather pants, you get more than a good fit for riding. The seams also should have a very strong nylon or other material thread and, even better, be double-stitched so the seams don't explode when the pants hit the pavement in a crash.

Leather riding pants basically come in two different styles: a blue jean-type style for cruising and touring riders, and a roadrace style for sportbike riders. The blue jean-style pants usually don't have any extra protection, but roadrace-style pants have tons. They have extra leather and padding, and maybe even hard armor, in the hips and knees. They may have *knee sliders,* which are hard plastic pucks that hook to the sides of the knees with hook-and-loop fasteners so you can touch a knee to the asphalt in a turn without grinding away leather. The pants also may have zippers at the end of the leg for a snug fit.

Roadrace-style pants may even have elastic panels in the crotch and back to allow for easy movement on the motorcycle. They come in a variety of colors, and you can even find jackets with matching pants.

If you can't find pants you want off the rack, or if you're hard to fit, consider getting custom leather pants in either style. It's pricey, but you'll know your pants will fit perfectly and have all the pockets, protection, and other features you want.

Leather overpants, which are pricey but convenient, are also available. They are leather pants with zippers all the way up the sides of the legs so that you can wear these pants over your regular pants. Overpants are great for commuting to work on a motorcycle: When you get to work, you just take them off and, voilà! No unsightly bug stains on your pants! Price? About $300 to $400.

Chaps: The cool alternative to leather pants

Black or brown leather motorcycling chaps are extremely popular with the cruiser crowd. Chaps are cheaper than leather pants, aren't as hot, are easy to put on, and still look way cool on men and women.

Chaps are so popular that you can usually find vendors at motorcycling rallies selling them at relatively cheap prices.

Examine chaps carefully before buying, or they may protect you only slightly better than blue jeans would. Check the buckle construction to make sure it's well attached and won't fall apart. Make sure the leather is of a decent thickness, and check the stitching to make sure it's stitched with a strong nylon and, even better, double-stitched.

Good chaps will cost around $200 or more, but will offer good abrasion protection in all key areas except your bottom.

Synthetic pants and blue jeans

Some riders find leather to be too hot to ride in. Fortunately, some alternatives offer good protection, including synthetic pants, and blue and black jeans made specifically for motorcycling.

Synthetic motorcycling pants are abrasion resistant, although not as much as leather, and come in a regular pants style or a sportrider style. You also can get synthetic overpants. Generally, synthetic pants offer padding or armor in the knees and hips, which are impact areas in a crash, and may have stretch panels for ease of movement on a bike. They cost about $200 or more.

Some companies also make blue and black jeans specifically for motorcycling. These pants have extra protection in impact areas and are made to be abrasion resistant. Plus, they offer a little extra room in the crotch, for ease of movement on a bike. They cost about $60 and up.

Gloves: Style and Protection in One Neat Package

Good gloves are very important for a motorcyclist's safety, not only because they protect the rider's hands in the event of a fall, but also because they offer protection against bugs and stones kicked up by truck tires on the freeway. They also provide some protection in bad weather. Expect to pay $60 to $350 for gloves, depending on the style and features.

Surveying the different styles

Motorcycle gloves have precurved fingers to fit comfortably around the motorcycle's handgrips. Most times they also have padding on the back of the hand and along the little finger to provide protection in a crash.

You'll find many gloves on the market. Consider the following:

- The motorcycling glove that offers almost no protection and that, fortunately, isn't very popular, is the *fingerless glove.* This glove would protect the palm of your hand in a get-off, but that's about it.

- The next level up in protection is a *full leather glove,* like a workman's glove. This style will help protect against stones and rocks while riding and abrasions during a crash (as long as the leather is thick enough and the stitching is strong enough that the glove doesn't explode on impact).

Ridin' in the rain

Every motorcyclist should have a good set of rain gear, which is a rain suit that goes over your riding clothes. You never know when you may need to ride through heavy rain to get somewhere. A rain suit will keep you comfortable, warm, and dry, making your ride safer. You can get either a one-piece or a two-piece rain suit starting at around $60. Rain suits are usually made of nylon. Try to stay away from plastic or PVC suits because they don't breathe well, meaning you can overheat in them. Try the rain suit on in the store over the gear you'll be wearing when you ride to make sure it fits and doesn't become too tight in a riding position.

✔ Another style of glove is a *regular leather motorcycling glove.* This type of glove is made to be snug and offers various levels of protection, ranging from extra leather on the palm to extra leather and padding on the palm, the knuckles, the outside of the little fingers, along the edge of the hand, and maybe even along the tops of the fingers — all possible impact areas in a crash.

✔ *High-zoot sport-riding* or *roadracing gloves* fit tight and have padding and even hard armor just about everywhere. These gloves also have a long gauntlet so they fit easily over the sleeve of a motorcycle jacket, a strap to make the glove snug around the wrist, and even a ventilation system, if you want it. These gloves come in many different colors.

You can also find special gloves for warm-weather riding, cool-weather riding, and even cold-weather riding. (Yes, some motorcyclists do ride even when there's snow on the ground.) Whatever you put on, just remember that any motorcycle glove is better than no glove at all.

Tips for trying out gloves

A large glove made by one manufacturer may be an extra large made by another manufacturer, so be sure to try on the gloves before you buy them. They should fit snugly so they don't come off in a crash, but they should still be comfortable enough that you'll wear them when you ride. When trying on gloves, make sure that none of the stitching cuts into your hand anywhere and that any hard armor doesn't press painfully on any pressure points.

Whether you're buying a synthetic glove or a leather glove, make sure that it's well constructed, with strong stitching, and that it has the protective features you want. Consider buying different gloves for different seasons. After all, you can't control your motorcycle well if your hands are numb; likewise, hot and sweaty hands can pose a danger for control.

Chapter 6

Leather and Lace: Women in Motorcycling

Motorcycling has traditionally been a man's sport, but more women are deciding they don't want to take a back seat to any man and are learning to ride their own bikes.

Granted, riding on the back of a bike through the countryside with a significant other can be a lot of fun, but being in control of the machine yourself is even more fun. Just ask any of the 10 percent of the approximately 6 million female motorcyclists on the road today or any of the female roadracers, motocrossers, and other motorcycle racing competitors.

The face of motorcycling is definitely changing. Today when a couple walks into a motorcycle dealership, smart salespeople don't automatically assume that the guy, not the gal, wants to buy a bike. The motorcycle manufacturers acknowledge the growth in female riders and are now designing more gear and holding more events specifically for women. And you'll be surprised by how many famous women ride motorcycles, including actresses Angelina Jolie, Catherine Bell, Kate Hudson, and Jessica Alba; TV personality Mary Hart also rides.

In this chapter, you get tips on how to gain acceptance by your motorcycling brethren, find the right jacket and other gear to fit your body, adjust your machine for a comfortable and safe fit, and get in touch with other female motorcyclists to share secrets of the women's motorcycling world.

Getting the Respect You Deserve

Motorcycle safety instructors will tell you that women are the best students and learners. Why? Women usually don't come into the courses with anything to prove. They have no macho image to try to uphold, and they admit, at least to themselves, that they don't know how to ride a motorcycle. Because of that, women are typically attentive and eager to learn — they aren't just in class to get the certificate.

Now, not all men go into a motorcycle safety training class thinking they know everything and trying to uphold a macho image. But many do. And those men are the Neanderthals who give women a hard time when they become riders. Why do they do that? They're probably afraid women are better riders than they are!

In some motorcycling circles, guys still call women by derogatory names (you'll even see them on T-shirts) and treat women like property. That attitude is all part of the macho, bad-boy image those guys are trying to portray. You obviously don't have to stand for it. Let people in your riding group know you won't tolerate it. Or, if you want to, find yourself a group that's more open-minded about female riders. It's really easy to do.

Fortunately, jerks aren't any more common in the motorcycling world than they are in the regular world, which means that most fellow motorcyclists will treat you great. In fact, just being a woman who rides gains you more respect from guys than a new male rider gets initially. A man has to prove himself among the other riders before he can gain respect. (I know, it's that stupid macho thing again.) But women get instant respect just by climbing on and grabbing the controls of a bike.

You'll lose that respect immediately, though, if you don't know the difference between a cruiser and a sportbike, or if you hop on your bike and then make a beeline right into the side of a parked car. Each motorcycling subgroup has its own way of thinking (which I explain in Chapter 4), but all motorcyclists talk about some common things, so you need to learn those basics first. When you understand the basics, just hanging around motorcyclists will help you pick up more motorcycling knowledge and gain you even more respect.

Do what bikers do, and know the lingo

You don't need a tattoo to fit in with a biker crowd, but you do need to do what your crowd does and know the lingo. Otherwise you may be labeled as a "wannabe" motorcyclist. But don't worry; the following sections give you some ideas of how to fit in with the crowd.

Walking the walk (or riding the ride)

Does your crowd like to take part in organized rides to raise money for charity? Go on some of those rides. Do group members hang out at Bike Nights? If so, check them out. Maybe they like to plan daylong rides on Saturdays or Sundays. Go along. Obviously you don't have to go on every single ride your group puts together (though it's perfectly fine if you want to). But you do need to show up now and then to show that you are a rider, not a poser or wannabe.

The more you go to these group events, the more you'll be hanging around motorcyclists. And the more you hang around motorcyclists, the more you'll learn about motorcycling.

Talking the talk

Initially, you'll likely do a lot of listening when other riders talk about tires, bike modifications, new machines, and tough riding situations that they were able to get out of. But, eventually, you'll learn enough to be able to join the discussions and offer insights of your own.

Here's just one example of what motorcyclists like to talk about: tires. They *love* delving into this topic. For instance, they'll look at someone's tires and note that they are sport or "sticky" tires, meaning that the rubber is soft and provides a better grip on the road. But they'll also note that the life of a sticky tire isn't very long.

Or they may peg a tire as a touring tire, meaning that the rubber is hard and doesn't have the extreme grip of a sport tire. And, of course, they'll comment on the long life of the touring tire. You may also hear riders talk of sport-touring tires, which are a compromise between sport and touring tires. Motorcyclists also look at the wear on a biker's tire to see how leaned over the motorcyclist has had the bike on the road, meaning how fast the motorcyclist has taken corners. They may even comment on whether it's time to change the tire.

"How do you like those tires?" is a pretty common question among bikers because you'll find differences in tires among different manufacturers. This is when the talk may get a little more detailed: Riders may say the front tire "steers heavy," meaning it takes some effort to turn the bike, or they may say the tread pattern makes the bike really wobble when riding over rain grooves in the road.

All this is the type of knowledge that you need to tuck away in the back of your brain — not only so you can talk about tires, but also so you have a wealth of knowledge about different tires and how they work in the real world when it comes time to buy your next set.

In fact, if you want to learn anything, just ask a rider, "Do you like . . . ." A thoughtful motorcyclist will give you an answer chock-full of information. After hearing the answer, you'll be able to talk about that subject and also file away that knowledge for later. Consider this example of the question you may ask and some answers you may get. "Do you like that . . ."

- **Helmet:** "I like it a lot. It fits great, although it was a little tight at first. It feels light, the venting works great so it keeps me cool in the summer, and you can get a lot of different tinted faceshields for it. It's expensive, though — maybe around $500."

- **Seat:** "This seat isn't the stock seat. That one was too hard. I bought this one at (company name), and it has a lot more padding. Plus, it's a little wider than stock, so it's a lot better for the long haul."

- **Style of gloves:** "They're a little hot, but they fit well and offer some extra protection, with another layer of leather on the fingers and palms. They were cheap. I need to buy some vented ones for summer riding, though."

- **Tire:** "This type of tire is pretty good, but it's a little slippery in the rain. And I didn't get as many miles out of it as I thought I would. I'll probably get a more expensive tire when I replace it."

Besides talking about equipment and gear, motorcyclists talk about roads and riding. They talk about nice roads with *long sweepers,* which are long, flowing turns; *tight hairpins,* which are turns that turn back on themselves; and *tight corners,* which are, well, tight corners. Sportbike riders talk about "taking a line through a turn" and "hitting the apex." The *apex* is the tightest point in a curve. Check out Appendix A for more of the basic biker lingo.

You'll pick up more knowledge as you hang around motorcyclists. Just remember, to be a motorcyclist, you really do need to know the lingo. Plus, it's fun to speak a language that most people on the road find foreign.

Ride, ride, ride

The best way to get respect from fellow motorcyclists, even if you don't know much of the lingo, is to ride. Motorcyclists respect riders. Put a lot of miles on your bike. Not only will you gain respect when fellow riders sneak a peek at your odometer, but the more you ride, the better a rider you'll become. You'll always be using your skills and improving. It doesn't matter where you ride or whether it's with a group or alone — what matters is that you do ride. By the way, in case you didn't know, being called a "wannabe" or a "poser" is an insult.

Long-distance rides also gain you a lot of respect. If you can tell tales of riding from Missouri to Daytona Beach, Florida, or from Minnesota to Colorado, you'll be right up there with the experienced riders in your crowd.

One more thing: Don't let worry over dropping your bike in front of others stop you from riding. Motorcyclists get off balance and drop motorcycles. Let's face it, bikes have two wheels, not four, so they can be heavy and unstable when they aren't moving. Sure, it's embarrassing to drop a motorcycle in a parking lot, but it happens. If you drop your bike, you may take some good-natured ribbing over it, but other riders won't have any less respect for you. Chances are extremely good that they've done the same themselves.

Curves Ahead: Finding Gear That Fits

Not too long ago, women had to settle for guys' motorcycling clothes in small sizes if they wanted to be safe on a bike. But the jackets never fit quite right, for obvious reasons, and even the gloves many times were too long in the fingers. And leather pants? You could pretty much forget about finding a pair that fit in the hips. Chaps were pretty easy to find — just don't fall on your butt!

Thankfully, women now have choices in their own riding gear. Granted, it's not the wide variety that men enjoy when shopping for protective gear. But nowadays manufacturers make jackets, pants, and boots especially for women, and in different styles.

If you want to go for the tough biker-chick look, you can do it. If you want a very feminine look, you can get that, too. And, of course, you can achieve some middle ground: good-looking, cut-for-a-woman protective gear with just a hint that it was made for a girl, like a single rose on the side of a boot. Some companies even make dirt bike riding jerseys and pants specifically for women.

Don't expect to be able to march down to your local motorcycle dealer and pick a jacket off the rack. You may be able to do that at a mega-motorcycle accessories store, but you may have to travel a ways to get to a store like that. (But just think, this gives you another excuse to ride your bike!) With a little perseverance, though, you'll find riding gear that offers protection in a style you like. Best of all, it will fit. Motorcycle rallies where thousands of motorcyclists gather to have a good time also have vendors selling everything from helmets to jackets to pants. Women's sizes and styles are always available there. (I describe various rallies in Chapter 16.)

If you're a woman with a body shape that is difficult to fit with gear off the rack, you can still get great jackets, pants, and boots. Do what hard-to-fit men do: Have them custom made. In fact, if you can afford it, I recommend that you get a custom-made jacket anyway. (I recommend that for men also.) A custom-made jacket gives you a perfect fit, the style and colors you want, and all the features you're looking for — well, all that you can afford, anyway.

My favorite jacket is a custom one with lots of built-in armor that I had made more than ten years ago. (I had the foresight to ask the maker to add a couple extra inches in the tummy to allow for growth.) The cost at the time? $950. But, hey, I'm still wearing it. So that figure works out to be less than $95 a year for a jacket with protection that equals that of professional motorcycle roadracers' jackets.

Jackets, pants, and helmets just for women

The motorcycling industry sees a great opportunity with the influx of women into the sport. Fortunately this means that women now can find a wide variety of safety gear that not only offers protection but fits well and looks great. In fact, some jackets look so good that you may want to wear them casually, even when you aren't on a motorcycle.

Okay, you may look great in a designer leather jacket and figure you'll just buy that for when you ride. Or you may really like your tall leather boots that you wear for a night on the town, so you figure that you don't need to buy a new pair for riding your bike. Forget it. The leather on a designer jacket is too thin, the stitching is too weak, and it will probably shred and the seams will burst if you fall off your bike. Ouch! And the boots won't offer the foot and ankle support and protection you need for riding a bike. Plus you won't have a good sole for gripping the road when you stop at slippery intersections for stoplights.

When you're looking for motorcycling gear, think safety first and style second. Good motorcycling gear is made to protect you in case of a crash. You should be able to find gear that offers protection, comfort, and style all in one package. And some inexpensive gear will do the job of protecting you, but don't skimp. If you aren't happy with your gear, you won't wear it. And if you won't wear it, you won't have the protection you need. Go ahead, splurge — get the gear you want. You'll feel good riding in it, and you'll be happy you got it if you do get in a crash.

Jacket

If you shop around, you'll find jackets in those sizes that perplex men, such as 0, 2, 4–6, 16–18, and 24–26. The manufacturer may give those sizes or may list the sizes as women's XS, S, M, L, XL, and so on, with a sizing chart that gives the equivalent in the numeric sizes such as 0, 2, 4, 6, and so on.

The manufacturer may even give more information, like bust size, hip size, arm length, and more, in inches. This helps you compare measurements; one manufacturer's L may be another's M. So shop around to make sure you get a good fit.

It's best that you go to stores and try jackets on. But if you don't find one you like, consider ordering by mail. (I discuss this later in this chapter.) If you go that route, however, consider calling the manufacturer and giving the operator your measurements. He or she can then tell you what size to buy.

Your jacket, in particular, should fit well. Why? Because your jacket should have extra padding or even armor in critical areas, like the elbows. You want a good fit so that the protection doesn't twist around your arm in a crash, leaving your elbow unprotected. You also want a good fit around the waist or hips so that the jacket doesn't ride up in a crash, exposing your lower back to the road. The wrists of your jacket should be snug — and they usually are with the help of a zipper on each wrist — so that the sleeve doesn't ride up in a crash and expose your lower arm to abrasion. (I give more tips on what to look for in good riding gear in Chapter 5.)

You aren't stuck with buying a black, police-style motorcycle jacket. Women's jackets come in black, white, and even pink. You can even find a variety of styles, including jackets with collars, jackets with fringe, or even a real tight-fitting roadracer style jacket. Plus, you can find synthetic jackets that offer a lot of protection. The key is to get a jacket that fits well and offers as much protection, such as built-in armor, as you can afford.

Pants

Good riding pants for women are harder to find, but they're out there. If you're a Harley-Davidson rider or you run with a cruiser crowd, consider getting leather chaps. They look way cool and fit in with the cruiser crowd. In fact, Harley-Davidson embraces women riders and offers a wide variety of gear for women.

If chaps aren't your thing, you want leather or synthetic pants, or even reinforced blue or black jeans made specifically for riding. Those jeans have Kevlar, the stuff they use to make bulletproof vests, in critical areas to offer protection against punctures and abrasion.

Again, you don't have to settle for men's sizes when it comes to riding pants. Women's pants come in sizes just like you'd find in a department store: 0, 2, 4, and so on. You may also find them in women's XS, S, M, and so on down the line.

Boots

Manufacturers are crafting some great motorcycling boots for women these days. Not only do these boots offer a lot of foot and ankle protection, but if you're short, you can even get boots that have a taller sole. This sole can help you reach the ground when sitting still on your bike. You can get regular-looking boots like the guys wear, or you can get something with a feminine touch, like fringe or a rose.

Helmet

Women's helmets are like guys' helmets, only prettier. (I discuss the ins and outs of helmets, and what to look for, in Chapter 5.) You can find helmets with graphics designed specifically to appeal to women. For example, you can find some with pink graphics. Motorcycling is fun, so have some fun with your helmet design. Get one with cartoon characters, if you like. Or, if you're willing to spend the cash, work with a custom helmet painter to design your own one-of-a-kind helmet. Who needs a tattoo when you can design your own helmet?

Where to find the stuff you need

So where can you find all this cool women's riding gear, anyway? The first place to start is at the dealer of the manufacturer of your motorcycle. For example, say you ride a Harley-Davidson. In that case, trot down to your local Harley-Davidson dealer and see what the shop is selling. Harley-Davidson knows that it doesn't just sell motorcycles — it sells a lifestyle. So the dealers usually have a lot of men's and women's riding gear for sale. Yamaha and its Star brand of motorcycles also offer women's gear. If the dealer doesn't have what you're looking for, a salesperson probably can show you a catalog of riding gear that you can order from.

Suppose you want a piece of gear that isn't branded with the manufacturer's name on it. Expand your search. Try to find a large motorcycle accessory store near you that offers a wide variety of women's riding gear from different manufacturers. Try on what you like, and then buy it.

If you can't find what you want at a dealer and don't have a motorcycling megastore near you, it's time for you to turn to the Internet. Just type something like "women's motorcycling clothes" into your search engine. You'll find links to cool stuff to buy (although do know that some of it you can purchase only through your local motorcycle accessories shop). Some of the companies that sell women's riding clothes include Firstgear, Tourmaster, Arlen Ness, and Icon.

You want a custom paint job for your helmet? Go to the Internet and search for custom helmet painters. You'll find a lot of good ones out there, and you can find examples of their work online, along with prices and other details.

What about clothing for playin' in the dirt?

If you've decided that you aren't a street rider, but you instead like to play in the dirt, you're in good shape when it comes to riding gear. Fox Racing and THOR, two famous names in motocross gear, are among the companies that make pants, jerseys, and even boots for women as well as for men. New companies, like the Girlyz Clothing Company, also make motocross gear specifically for women. Shop around and you'll find what you like.

If you buy gear online, make sure you know the return policy before you buy. You must be able to return your gear if it doesn't fit. As I said earlier, one manufacturer's large size may equal another manufacturer's medium size.

Finally, ask your girlfriends who ride where they got their riding gear. You may be surprised to learn that your friend got her cool Harley-Davidson boots at a local store.

How Low Can You Go? Making a Bike Fit You

After you have riding gear that fits, you need to make sure that your bike fits you, too. Guys have to make adjustments to their bikes to make them fit also, but usually not to the extreme that some women do. Because women are generally shorter than men, they need to either buy smaller bikes or lower their bikes so they can plant their feet as firmly on the ground as possible. (I discuss small bikes that may not need to be adjusted for smaller people in Chapter 8.)

Safety, after all, comes first in motorcycling. And you're not safe if you're on a machine that doesn't fit you. As a rider, you have enough to worry about (cars, deer, and other hazards). So you shouldn't have to worry about whether you can comfortably touch the ground with your boots at a stoplight or reach the gearshift lever with your feet. Taking the time to set up your machine properly will make riding a lot more fun.

Tricks to lower your machine

If you absolutely adore a machine that's a bit too big for you, don't worry. You can lower the machine (referred to as lowering the *ride height*) three-quarters of an inch or an inch — or even more. Lowering the bike just an inch can make a big difference for getting on and off the machine and keeping the bike comfortably in control at stoplights. Nothing else is much more embarrassing than pulling up to a stoplight and having the bike tip over because your legs aren't long enough to reach the ground.

Starting with the seat

A simple place to start when tackling the task of lowering your machine to make it fit you is with the seat. If you have a well-padded seat, you can take off the seat cover and trim some of the foam. The electric carving knife that you use to carve a turkey works great for this. You may be able to shave an inch or two off the seat height this way. The tradeoff, of course, is a harder seat when you're riding.

Another option is to get a custom seat that gives your bike a lower seat height. Custom seat companies like Corbin (www.corbin.com; 800-538-7035) Mustang (www.mustangseats.com; 800-243-1392), or Sargent (www.sargentcycle.com; 800-749-7328) can offer you some options. Check out seat manufacturers' Web sites, or give them a call and ask about their selection. However, do know that custom seating isn't cheap.

For example, a Corbin Gunfighter seat for a 2008 Harley-Davidson FXSTC Softail Custom costs $369. The seat height on a stock Softail Custom is 28.3 inches, or 26.4 inches *laden,* which means with a 180-pound rider sitting on the bike. Harley-Davidson is the only company that gives two seat heights for its bikes, laden and *unladen,* which means with no rider on the bike. The Gunfighter seat gives the Softail Custom a seat height of 26 inches unladen.

Moving on to the suspension, if necessary

If you don't want to carve up your seat foam or spend the bucks for a custom seat, or if you opted for one of those options but need to lower the bike even further, it's time to tackle the suspension — the front forks and the rear shock or shocks.

You have to do this carefully, for a few reasons:

- Motorcycles are tight little packages, and everything is designed to work together. So if you start messing around with the front or rear suspension, you may upset the geometry of the bike so much that it's unsafe to ride.

- Changing the suspension *will* change the handling of the bike. You may not notice it, which is fine. But when you do make changes, be sure to take it easy when you ride for the first time; be sure and think about how the suspension feels.

- If you need to loosen bolts to make adjustments, it's critical that you tighten them back up to factory specifications. You can find these specs in a service manual for your motorcycle. The last thing you need is for critical bolts to fall off while you're riding.

One trick to lower your ride height is to raise the front fork tubes in the *triple tree* (which is the part that the fork tubes are clamped into) a half-inch to an inch. This lowers the front of your bike. It also makes your bike steer more quickly, which means it takes less effort to turn it into a corner. You can also adjust the *preload,* which, simply put, is the amount of tension on your spring in each fork tube. If you reduce the preload — that is, lessen the tension on the spring — your bike will lower a bit when you sit on it. Your owner's manual shows you how to adjust the preload.

To complete the ride-height adjustment, you need to lower the rear as much as the front, if possible. Your rear shock (or shocks, depending on what kind of bike you have) probably has a preload adjustment. If you reduce the pre-load or tension — your owner's manual shows you how — you lower the bike's rear when you sit on it. If your rear shock doesn't have preload adjustment, or if you want to lower the rear end more, consider new shocks built for your bike that aren't as long as the stock shock.

This work isn't as complicated as it seems, but if you're uncomfortable doing the work yourself, take the bike to a mechanic who can do the job. If you really want it done right, take your bike to a shop that specializes in motorcycle suspension. They'll not only lower your bike, but they'll tune your suspension to your riding style and you'll have one sweet ride. This isn't cheap, though. Call around.

If you try these adjustments and motorcycling-specific boots with higher-than-normal heels, and the bike is still too tall for you, you need a different bike.

Adjusting or modifying your controls

After you've adjusted your machine so that you can sit on it with both feet firmly planted on the ground (or close to it), you can tackle the controls: the *shift lever, brake levers,* and *clutch lever.*

Shift lever

The shift lever is the lever on your motorcycle that you tap with your left foot to put the bike into gear or to change gears. You may find that your foot is too small to reach the end of the shift lever to operate it correctly, or you may need to move your foot a long way to move the lever to change gears.

If you have a small foot, you can shorten the lever by having an inch or so cut out of it and then welded back together. It may not be pretty, but it will work. Or maybe your local dealer can recommend a shorter lever from another bike that will bolt onto yours.

If, while you're riding, you find yourself accidentally kicking your shift lever and putting your bike in neutral as a result, or you find that you have to lift your foot a long way to change gears, consider adjusting your lever down. This fix is simple. The lever is held on with a bolt. Take out the bolt, pull the lever off the splined rod that it is attached to, and then put the lever back on at an angle that you think will work for you. Then just retighten the bolt.

The bike also may have an adjustable rod that connects the lever to the transmission, so you may need to make an adjustment to that rod. Ride the bike around and see if that works. If not, repeat the process. You may need to repeat this process several times to get an angle to the lever you're comfortable with. Eventually, you'll find a shift-lever angle you're comfortable with.

Brake and clutch levers

If the brake and clutch levers on the handlebars are too far out for you — that is, if your fingers won't reach around them comfortably — you need to pull the levers closer. To do so, you can spin the wheels on the levers and pull the levers closer to the handlebars. If that fix doesn't work, or if your levers aren't adjustable, you may need to see if you can find other lever assemblies that will fit on your bike that have shorter distances between the levers and the handlebars.

While you're sitting there on your bike, you may as well adjust the levers up or down so that they're comfortable for you to manipulate. On most bikes two bolts on the perch hold the lever. You can loosen these bolts so you can twist the entire assembly on the handlebar. *Note:* Some bikes are constructed so that you can't twist the levers on the handlebars. But don't worry; the adjustment isn't critical. It just makes the bike more comfortable to manipulate.

When your hands are on the handgrips, your fingers should lie flat on the levers. In other words, your arm should form a straight line from the crook in your arm at the elbow to your fingertips. Make this adjustment to fit the riding position you'll be in most of the time that you're riding (such as sitting up rather than crouched down out of the wind). You should be able to comfortably put your hands on the handgrips and your fingers on the levers with your eyes closed. Taller riders will find they need to turn the levers down or lower the levers to get the proper fit. When you do it once, you shouldn't have to adjust it again. Be sure to tighten up those bolts.

Your rear brake lever that you press with your right foot should offer some adjustment much like your shift lever.

Solidarity, Baby: Resources for Women Riders

Female motorcyclists, like male motorcyclists, have a lot to learn about motorcycling and a lot of stories and information to share. The quickest and easiest way to learn important stuff for female riders is to ride and talk with other female riders.

Although female motorcyclists are still a minority in the male-dominated sport, their numbers are growing daily. As a result, you'll find more women to talk to and pal around with, and you'll also find more information out there about motorcycling for female riders.

The motorcycle manufacturers also recognize the growing importance of women in motorcycling and are trying to make it easier for women to get involved in — and stay involved in — motorcycling. For example, Harley-Davidson holds women-only events. At these events, women gather at a dealership and learn about bikes, riding gear, and other stuff. They also get to chat with other female motorcyclists. Kawasaki and Ducati let women ride their bikes and hone their riding skills on racetracks in women-only events.

Similarly, the American Motorcyclist Association holds a popular Women & Motorcycling conference every few years that features activities, seminars, and rides for women.

If you take the time to get to know other female riders, join motorcycling clubs specifically for women, take part in manufacturer-sponsored motorcycling activities for women, and seek out other resources, you'll have even more fun as a motorcyclist. Plus, the more you support women's motorcycling groups and for-women-only activities, the stronger they will become. It's a win-win situation for everyone. The following sections offer some options for ways to get involved.

Joining a club like the Motor Maids

Joining a women's motorcycling club is a great way to share the joy — and sometimes frustration — of being a female motorcyclist. Not a lot of women's clubs are out there, but there are some, ranging from international and national organizations to small local groups. If you hunt around, you're sure to find a group or two you can join.

Do your homework before you join a local club. Some clubs are squeaky clean, promote a positive and wholesome image of motorcycling, and do charity work and a lot of riding. Others pride themselves on being bad girls' clubs. Hey, wait a minute — this is just like the men's clubs! (Well, except for the "bad girl" part.) A common denominator for all clubs, men's and women's alike, is that they promote camaraderie and focus on having fun on motorcycles.

National and international organizations include the following:

- **Motor Maids:** This group is one of the greatest organizations on the planet. Founded in 1940, this national organization is the oldest women's club in the United States. It's a riding club that's proud of its long history and tradition, and it's passionate about motorcycling. Some of the most influential woman in motorcycling are Motor Maids. This is a riding/social club that accepts riders of all types of bikes. See www.motormaids.org for more details.

- **Women in the Wind:** Although this organization isn't as old as Motor Maids, Women in the Wind has built up a strong, wholesome reputation since its founding in 1979. The organization has more than 60 chapters nationwide, and, like the Motor Maids, these gals ride. But they also do charity work and socialize. The group accepts all types of bikes. For more information, visit www.womeninthewind.org.

- **Women on Wheels:** The Women on Wheels Motorcycle Organization is the third of the best-known women's motorcycling groups in the United States. Founded in 1982, Women on Wheels promotes a positive image of motorcycling, socializes, and supports charities. The group accepts all types of bikes. Check out www.womenonwheels.org for more information.

- **The Women's International Motorcycle Association:** This organization isn't as well known, but the Women's International Motorcycle Association has a long history, stretching back to its founding in England in 1950 by an American woman. The association is very active in England and has divisions around the world, including in the United States (although the U.S. operations are in a rebuilding mode). This wholesome association organizes a lot of activities in Great Britain and elsewhere, and is sure to become a force in the United States with the proper support. The group accepts all types of bikes. See www.wimagb.co.uk.

- **Women's Motorcyclist Foundation:** This group is made up of great riders and has a strong charitable focus, raising money for breast cancer research. The group sponsors a lot of events for women motorcyclists to get together, to learn about motorcycling, and to enjoy the sport. See www.womensmotorcyclistfoundation.org to find out more.

After these big national and international organizations are the state and local clubs. It pays to do your homework with these groups. Some of these clubs have names that can't be published in a family book. Ask your motorcycling friends and motorcycle shops about women's clubs, and search the Internet — you'll find them.

Visiting the Internet

The Internet is a great tool for motorcyclists to find out everything from how to change your oil to how to build a full-blown racing machine. But the Internet also has problems. For example, anyone can post anything, so not all the information is correct. In fact, some of the information is flat-out wrong and can be dangerous.

Also important to remember is that Web sites come and go quickly. It takes true dedication to create and maintain a Web site. The Web sites of the motorcycle manufacturers, big motorcycling organizations, and big motorcycle accessories stores have been up a long time and probably will stay up as long as those companies and organizations exist. Other sites that seemed like a great idea at the time may disappear quickly.

With that said, the following great women's motorcycling news and information Web sites will probably continue to operate for a long time:

- *Women Riders Now* (www.womenridersnow.com) is an online magazine chock-full of motorcycling information and features for women. Some of the Web site's departments include "Way to Go Girl!," which provides a snapshot of recent accomplishments of women riders, like setting a land speed record; "Riding Right," which features stories on proper riding technique; and "Lifestyle" articles about women and their riding adventures.

  The Web site is professionally done and is updated frequently. Genevieve Schmidt, a well-respected motojournalist, runs the site. She previously worked in television, and besides being an avid motorcycle rider, she knows how to ride ATVs. Her site is current and informative; all motorcyclists, not just women, should read it.

- *Helmet Hair* (www.helmethair.com) is a quarterly online magazine that is professionally done and has great stories about women riders as well as interviews with women who make a difference in motorcycling. Whereas *Women Riders Now* may be considered more of a hard-news type of site that tells you what's going on in the motorcycling world, *Helmet Hair* is more geared toward features and pop culture.

  This site is a lot of fun to read, with features like "Favorite Female Motorcycle Movie Scenes," "Carole Bennett: Digital Art Revolutionary," and "The Mamalogues: Riding with Children." I highly recommend it.

- A newcomer in the online female motojournalism world is *Women Motorcyclists Monthly* (`www.womenmotorcyclistsmonthly.com`). It's too early to tell whether this magazine will survive, but it's off to a good start, with an attractive layout and a good mix of stories. Its features include articles about a female stunt rider, news about women custom bike builders, and event coverage. The editor promises more stories from and about regular women riders. This site also has a discussion forum that may prove to be a great resource.

- *Real Divas Ride* (`www.realdivas.ride.com`) is a Web site run for motorcycling women. It has some interesting stories about female motorcyclists and clubs.

If you like your magazines printed on paper, *Biker Ally* magazine is a motorcycle magazine written by women for women. This family-friendly magazine offers news, features, and product reviews. It even sponsors a Biker Ally Rally. See `www.bikerallymag.com`.

Enrolling in racetrack organizations for women

I mentioned earlier that Harley-Davidson, Kawasaki, and others hold special events for women only. Consider taking part in other women-only events to share the camaraderie of other female riders and to hone your skills. These events include the following:

- **Femmoto:** Femmoto organizes women-only rides on racetracks in which women ride loaner bikes from Kawasaki, Triumph, or other manufacturers and sharpen their skills. Femmoto also organizes track days when women can ride their own bikes. See `www.femmoto.com` for more details.

- **Women's Motocross Association:** If you want to ride motocross, the Women's Motocross Association can steer you in the right direction. The best female motocross racers in the world run in Women's Motocross Association events. In fact, female motocrossers from around the world come to compete in Women's Motocross Association races to test themselves against the best. Visit `www.womensmotocross association.com`.

Chapter 7

What to Do if Your Kid Wants to Ride Too

*I*f you have a child who wants to ride, consider yourself lucky! Motorcycling is a great family sport. It allows families to spend quality time together; plus, when the family is out riding together, parents know exactly where their kids are and what they're doing. Would you rather have your kid hanging out at the mall or motorcycle riding with you?

I'm not talking about streetbikes here; I'm talking about off-road motorcycling for kids ages 4 to 15. These tips also apply to 16- and 17-year-olds, although kids in this age group may want to get streetbikes. Older teens who want streetbikes should have off-road bikes as well, to improve their riding skills.

In this chapter, you find out how to select the right bike for your child, in terms of both the bike's size and power characteristics. I show you how to ensure that your youngster gets the best safety training possible and is properly attired in safety gear (without making you go broke). I also prepare you for your child's first day at the racetrack (if your child decides to go that route).

Finding a Bike That Fits Your Child's Needs

Thinking about putting your child on a motorcycle for the first time can be a little scary. As the adult, you get to make the decisions, and one of the most important decisions you can make is picking the right machine. Kids' bikes come in a lot of different flavors, from mild trail-riding machines to high-strung racers meant only for experienced riders. You also find different features on different machines that can help put your mind at ease, such as *restrictors* to restrict the power and *limiters* to limit how far open the child can turn the throttle, which determines how fast the child can go. True beginner bikes have automatic transmissions, but with other bikes the child needs to learn how to shift gears. You can even get aftermarket training wheels for small machines (by *aftermarket,* I mean from a non-motorcycle manufacturer).

When looking for your child's first bike, do your homework, get to know the machines available and what they feature, and shop around. Sometimes you can get a good deal on a child's bike that has been sitting on a dealer's showroom floor for a year or two, or even three. Plus, as you know, kids grow fast. They grow out of just about everything you buy them, and a motorcycle is no different. So look for a used machine that another child has outgrown, and you may find a deal. The parent really has no use for the bike, so don't be afraid to haggle. (I cover what to look for in a used bike and how to negotiate a fair price in Chapter 9.)

Considering trail bikes and racers

A kid's *trail bike* is an off-road motorcycle that offers more mild power delivery; these bikes are easier to ride than an off-road race bike. A trail bike is the best choice for a new, young rider because it's easy to ride and doesn't require a lot of maintenance like a race bike does. In fact, you can even get beginner trail bikes with a *shaft drive,* whereby power is delivered to the rear wheel through a shaft, rather than a *chain drive,* which delivers power with a chain. A chain drive requires more maintenance than a shaft drive.

For younger kids

For a young child, the best way to go is a trail bike with an automatic transmission, a restrictor to limit power, and a limiter to limit how far a child can twist the throttle. The Yamaha PW50 (shown in Figure 7-1) is an example of a trail bike for a young child. The KTM 50SX (shown in Figure 7-2) is more of a racing machine with long suspension travel, disc brakes (as opposed to drum brakes), and high-quality — which also means higher-cost — components.

Here are the key specs for the Yamaha PW50:

Engine: 49cc

Seat height: 19.1 inches

Wheelbase: 33.7 inches

Claimed dry weight: 82 pounds

Transmission: Automatic

Final drive: Shaft

MSRP: $1,149

Figure 7-1:
The 2008 Yamaha PW50.

Photo courtesy of Yamaha Motor Corp. USA

Here are the specs for the KTM 50SX:

Engine: 49cc

Seat height: 25.59 to 26.57 inches (adjustable)

Wheelbase: 40.55 inches

Claimed weight: 85.55 pounds (without gas)

Transmission: Automatic

Final drive: Chain

MSRP: $3,598

Figure 7-2:
The 2008
KTM 50SX.

KTM North America, Inc.

An important consideration when choosing a bike is where your child will be riding. If he or she will only be riding in your backyard, just about any bike will do. However, you should avoid getting a race bike if you live close to neighbors. Non-motorcyclists can find the sound of race bikes annoying because they can be loud. And when annoyed, neighbors may complain to government officials about the noise. This can lead to an ugly fight, not only with your neighbors but also with City Hall. It's not fun. Also, if you plan to ride in national forests or in other public riding areas, your child's bike will probably need a *spark arrester* that keeps any sparks from coming out of the exhaust system. After all, you don't want to catch the forest on fire! The bike also needs to meet sound limits. The exhaust pipe will be stamped with words saying that it meets federal sound limits (if it in fact does). That info also may be spelled out on a sticker on the frame of the motorcycle.

For older kids

An older child won't fit on a small machine like Yamaha's PW50, so you need to look at a trail bike that's a little bigger, like an 85cc or even a 125cc machine. Even on these bigger machines, you can find features such as throttle limiters, so shop around for the ones you want. Kawasaki's KLX 110 (shown in Figure 7-3) is a good machine for young riders (or even small adult women) to develop riding skills on.

Here are the specs for the KLX 110:

Engine: 111cc

Seat height: 25.6 inches

Wheelbase: 41.9 inches

Claimed dry weight: 141.1 pounds

Transmission: Three-speed

Final drive: Chain

MSRP: $1,749

Figure 7-3:
The 2008
Kawasaki
KLX 110.

Photo courtesy of Kawasaki Motor Corporation USA.

If your child has outgrown small bikes like Yamaha's PW50 and is ready to go the race bike route (meaning he or she has the skills to handle a more powerful machine with stiffer suspension), many good bikes are available with 85cc motors. The Suzuki RM85 (shown in Figure 7-4) is a good example. This bike also comes in an "L" designation, the RM85L, which has bigger wheels and a longer wheelbase so that the bike fits bigger kids better.

If your child gets into 125cc race bikes, remember that they're a handful to ride. Make sure your child has the proper skills before jumping on one of these thoroughbreds. The 125s are what the young professional racers race.

Here are the key specs for the Suzuki RM85:

Engine: 84.7cc

Seat height: 33.5 inches

Wheelbase: 48.8 inches

Claimed dry weight: 143 pounds

Transmission: Six-speed

Final drive: Chain

MSRP: $3,099

Figure 7-4:
The 2008
Suzuki
RM85.

Photo courtesy of American Suzuki Motor Corp.

Making sure your child fits the machine

No matter whether you decide to get a trail bike or a racer for your child, making sure that the bike you choose is the right size is critical. To be sure your child fits a machine, at a minimum the child should

- Be able to place both feet flat on the ground
- Be able to reach the handlebars comfortably with a slight bend at the elbows
- Have long-enough fingers to operate the clutch and brake levers on the handlebars

You may be tempted to buy a bigger bike for your child with the thought that he or she will grow into it and get more years of use out of it. However, thinking that way is a mistake. Here's why:

✔ **Buying a bike that's too big can be dangerous.** Remember, your child knows absolutely nothing about motorcycles. It's up to you to ensure that your child is as safe as possible. Your youngster has enough going through his or her mind while learning how to ride. Don't endanger your child by putting him or her on a machine that's difficult to control because it's too big.

✔ **A bike that's too big may frustrate your child.** Your child is excited about learning to ride. Don't dampen his or her enthusiasm, and maybe even sour the entire motorcycling experience, by putting him or her on a machine that is too big, too heavy, and too frustrating to control.

✔ **A bigger machine costs more.** Instead of spending the big bucks on a big machine, plan on getting a right-sized machine and selling it later. Or, better yet, use it as a hand-me-down for your next youngest child, and the next, and the next. That way the whole family can be involved in motorcycling.

Presenting Dirt Bike Safety Training Your Kid Can Understand

Safety training is vital for a young, new rider, just as it is for an adult. But training young riders can be a challenge because those riders can't even guess at basics like what a clutch is, what a brake is, what a throttle is, how fast they're going, and so on.

Your job, as a responsible parent, is to ensure that your child gets the best, safest training possible. Before the training even begins, you need to know the child's bike thoroughly. You need to know the basics like how to start the bike, where to find the *kill switch* (the button you push to stop the engine), and how to adjust the throttle limiter. If you bought the bike new, read the owner's manual thoroughly. If you bought it used, ask the previous owner to explain the basics to you, including whether you need to mix oil with the gas (as is customary with some bikes).

You can't help your child learn if you don't know the machine yourself.

Leaving the teaching to the pros

The best way to get safety training for your child is to enroll him or her in an organized dirt bike school for beginners. The Motorcycle Safety Foundation, a national organization best known for its street motorcycle safety training classes for adults, offers a dirt bike school that trains adults and children as young as age 6. For more information on a class near you, go to www. dirtbikeschool.com. Other options are also available, so ask your local dealer if he or she knows of a local school.

Letting the pros do the teaching is a good idea for several reasons. Among them are the following:

- ✔ The instructors know how children learn and the best way to teach them.
- ✔ Your child may feel less intimidated and feel less pressure to succeed learning from a stranger rather than from you.
- ✔ The instructors won't get frustrated, mad, or flustered if your child isn't catching on to something quickly. They're used to it.
- ✔ The school provides the motorcycle and safety gear for the class. So if your child takes the class and then decides he or she doesn't want to ride motorcycles after all, you aren't out the cost of a bike and safety gear.
- ✔ The class is composed of a small group of kids, which may make learning even more fun for your child.

Kids' classes, like adult classes, start with the very basics — the controls, how to start the machine, and so on — and involve just pushing the bike around a bit before learning how to ride the machine under power. Your child learns steering, turning, dealing with obstacles like rocks, climbing hills, judging different terrain for traction, and a bunch of other stuff that you may forget to cover if you do the teaching yourself.

Taking a do-it-yourself approach

If there isn't a dirt bike school near you, and you don't know how to ride, find an experienced dirt-riding friend with kids to teach your child. That parent will have experience working with dirt-riding kids, and probably will know some of the pitfalls in training kids since he or she has provided guidance and instruction for his or her own. If you're an experienced rider and there's no dirt bike class near you, you can do the training yourself.

Following are some key points to keep in mind if you're doing the training:

- ✔ Stay calm.
- ✔ Accept that your child may not learn as quickly as you think he or she should.
- ✔ Take your time.
- ✔ Keep everything very simple.

You need to adjust your vocabulary to fit the child's experience. For example, you can't say, "Give it some gas" or "Hit the brakes" because your child won't have a clue what you mean. You have to first explain that twisting the throttle ("this thing on the right handlebar") makes the bike go, and twisting it further makes the bike go faster. You also need to point out the brake levers, and then explain that to make the bike stop, the throttle has to be twisted closed and the front brake lever has to be squeezed with the right hand while the rear brake lever has to be pushed with the right foot. Keep everything simple and take one step at a time. Your child has a lot to learn, so don't rush things. Also, offer a lot of encouragement during the training.

Always stress safety. Stay close to your child to keep him or her safe, and keep the speed slow. Don't let your child try anything that may be dangerous, such as climbing a small hill, until you know he or she is ready to tackle that challenge. Ask often how your child feels about doing or trying something — riding a bike over a log, for instance — and if your child doesn't feel comfortable with it, don't make him or her do it.

Similarly, stress the importance of using proper safety gear. Don't allow your child to even sit on a motorcycle without wearing a helmet. Wearing safety gear should be something that feels natural to your child. For more on purchasing this gear, check out the following section.

Considering Cool and Safe Kid's Gear

A lot of gear is available for kids: helmets, goggles, boots, jerseys, pants, chest protectors, neck rolls, special riding socks, knee guards, elbow guards, wrist guards, and kidney belts.

Safety gear not only helps protect your child from injury, but it also looks cool and is fun to wear. The makers of kids' gear offer styles that appeal to the younger set, like helmets with cartoonish skull graphics. Go shopping with your youngster and you'll find the helmet, boots, gloves, jersey, pants, and so on that your kid not only should wear, but *wants* to wear.

Like adult gear, the best way to buy kids' gear is to go to a dealer so that the child can try stuff on to make sure it fits comfortably. You may get cheaper prices by mail order, but you can't be sure that what you order will fit.

If you're worried about the cost, remember that you can sell the gear after your child outgrows it. Safety gear is critical.

Ensuring a proper fit

You want your little one to be safe while riding, and that means outfitting the young rider with safety gear. But no matter how good the gear is, it won't protect your child if it doesn't fit right. For instance, consider these situations:

- Helmets that are too big can twist around and even come off.

- Boots that are too big can twist and injure a foot and make it difficult to shift and use the foot brake.

- Ill-fitting gloves can make it more difficult to manipulate the hand controls, and they also can cause blisters.

Do your own peace of mind, and your child, a favor, and make sure the gear you buy your little one fits correctly. I give you pointers on how to do this in the following sections.

Helmet

The first thing you should buy is a helmet. (I explain how a helmet protects a rider's head in Chapter 5.) Expect to buy a helmet probably every year as your child grows. Make sure the helmet has federal Department of Transportation (DOT), Snell Memorial Foundation, or American National Standards Institute (ANSI) certification to show that it has been tested and operates properly. If the child will ever wear the helmet on a streetbike, such as while riding as your passenger, the helmet must be DOT approved and have a DOT sticker on it.

You don't want to buy a child a helmet that's too big or too small. Here's what you need to do to check for a proper fit:

1. **Have your child put on the helmet.**

   First pull the helmet opening apart slightly using the chinstrap, and then fasten the chinstrap. (Be careful not to fasten it too tightly.)

2. **The helmet should fit snugly, but it shouldn't be so tight that it's uncomfortable.**

   Ideally, the child's eyes should be centered in the helmet's eyeport.

3. **Push the helmet forward, backward, and from side to side.**

   The helmet should remain snug. It shouldn't be loose enough to be pushed over the eyes.

4. **If you have the time, have your child wear the helmet around the store for a half hour or so to be sure it doesn't begin to hurt.**

   Remember that a snug helmet will loosen a little bit as it conforms to the head, but it should never be so tight that it's uncomfortable or painful to wear.

Never buy a used helmet. A helmet is designed to be destroyed with one hard whack, so that a rider's head isn't injured. A helmet can lose its ability to protect the rider just by being dropped on the floor, even though it may show no signs of damage.

Boots

Boots are another critical safety item that your child needs to wear when riding. Good, sturdy boots help protect the feet and ankles from injury due to twisting or hard knocks against branches or rocks. They also help the rider maintain a grip on the motorcycle's footpegs.

Like helmets, boots must be tried on to ensure they fit, especially since one boot maker's child Size 6 may be a lot smaller than another maker's child Size 6. Be sure that your child is wearing thick, off-road socks when trying on boots. The boots should be snug, with no movement of the foot in the boot, but they shouldn't be so tight that they cut off blood circulation or are painful to wear.

Pants and jersey

Off-road jerseys look like football jerseys and offer a little bit of padding in the elbows for protection. They come in various materials for hot-or-moderate-weather riding. The jersey should be loose, especially if you plan to fit elbow and wrist guards plus a chest protector under it.

Off-road pants should fit well and offer room for knee and shin guards. They usually have minimal padding in the hips. Have your child try them on with the boots, since the motocross-style pants are meant to fit inside the boots.

Outfitting your kid in safety gear without breaking your budget

You want the best protection possible for your child, but you're a little short on cash. What to do, what to do. Start with the critical safety gear, and then add items as your budget allows. Keep in mind that if your child will just be riding in the backyard or trail riding, and not hitting the racetrack, he or she doesn't need the most expensive, most extensive list of safety items available today.

At a minimum, your child should have a good helmet and goggles. For boots, your child can wear sturdy, over-the-ankle, work-type boots. And any sturdy gloves should do. Next, add a sweatshirt and bluejeans, and your child is ready to ride for a minimal outlay of cash. The coolness factor may not be as high as your child would like, but you can feel good knowing that your child's basic safety needs are met.

When you're financially ready to step up a little, you can swap out some items in your kid's basic protection package. Your child still needs the helmet, but now it's time to spring for

- ✔ Some motocross-style boots that offer plenty of protection for the feet and ankles
- ✔ An over-the-jersey chest protector to protect against rocks kicked up by other bikes or tree limbs hanging over trails
- ✔ Motocross gloves designed specifically for dirt riding
- ✔ Motocross-style pants that offer a better fit and more protection than jeans
- ✔ Knee guards that go under the pants and protect the knees and shins from whacks

That's all most kids need for riding. But if your child wants to get into racing, you'll want to add more safety gear, such as

- ✔ An under-the-jersey chest protector
- ✔ Elbow guards, wrist guards, and a neck guard
- ✔ A kidney belt

Plus, you may want to opt for top-of-the-line stuff: helmet, jersey, pants, and boots. Hey, nobody said racing was cheap. But it *is* dangerous, so you really should go with the best gear possible.

Making Trail Rides Fun

Your child will probably spend most of his or her time trail riding rather than racing and, being the responsible parent that you are, you'll be along for the ride. Remember that it's your responsibility to keep your child safe, so it's best for you to ride behind him or her to keep a close watch. The ride should be fun, not a grueling day on the trail.

Even though you're both riding, your child's abilities and mental and physical condition should dictate whether you take easy, moderate, or difficult trails, how fast and how far you go, when to take a break, and when to call it a day.

Preparing for the ride

If you've ever taken your kids to the beach, you know that it can take some time to round up everything and everybody to head out the door and hit the road. Heading off for a trail ride doesn't have to be that way. In fact, you can do the following things the day before you head out to make sure your departure from home and your experience on the trail are as pleasant as possible:

- ✔ **The night before you go riding, let your kid practice getting geared up.** That way you can determine how long the process takes, plus your child, with your help, can learn how to put on the knee and shin guards and properly snap the buckles on the belt. This preparation shouldn't be a problem because kids love wearing their riding gear. They'd probably wear it to school if you'd let them.

- ✔ **Go over the motorcycles you'll be taking on the ride and make sure everything is working properly.** Check the clutch and throttle cables, make sure the tires have the proper air pressure, and find out if the machines have enough oil and are gassed up.

- ✔ **Have your child practice starting his or her machine, because you know it's going to stall during the trail ride.** Also have your child practice laying down and picking up the machine because chances are good that, at least at some point, the machine is going to end up on its side in the dirt.

- ✔ **Pack gear and other essentials, like gas, in your truck or trailer the night before.** Taking care of this ahead of time will ensure that you're ready to roll as quickly as possible in the morning.

Packing snacks, games, and other essentials

More than likely the ride from your house to your favorite riding area will be long. Plan accordingly, or you may end up with a cranky kid by the time you arrive. Take along games to play in the car or truck, and pack snacks for the trip to the trail as well as for breaks while riding. Apples, bananas, grapes, lots of juice, and water are good ideas.

Kids spill stuff, rip stuff, and even lose stuff. That's just what kids do. With this in mind, it doesn't hurt to bring along extra gear, like goggles, a jersey, and gloves, just in case. Plus, don't forget a first-aid kit in case you or your child get snagged by a tree branch, or worse.

For the ride home, have regular clothes your child can change into to be more comfortable. Your child may want to continue to wear his other gear, which is okay too. Bring towels to put on the car or truck seat so the dirty riding clothes don't get the vehicle dirty. And consider bringing towels and water to wash your child off and make him or her more comfortable. In fact, you may want to take a swipe at your own dusty face with a wet towel as well.

Facing Racing: When Your Youngster Wants to Race

While trail riding can be a lot of fun, sometimes a child may want to compete. Thousands of kids nationwide take part in organized competition, and *motocross* racing is by far the most popular form of racing for kids. Motocross involves racing on a natural-terrain track that features jumps, tight turns, and hills. A motocross race is usually divided into two *motos*, or races. The riders' finishes in both motos are tallied to give him or her an overall score. A moto usually lasts a specified number of laps and usually doesn't take more than a half-hour to complete. The racing is intense.

Other forms of organized racing also offer competitive riding opportunities for kids on dirt bikes. They include the following:

- **Hare scrambles:** *Hare scrambles* are off-road races run on looped courses over natural terrain. These races generally last a couple hours. The looped course is usually a mile or more long.

- **Hare and hound races:** *Hare and hound races* are much like hare scrambles except that they're usually held in the desert over a looped course 40 or 50 miles long. The rider must hit a series of checkpoints along the course. These races are normally held in the western United States.

- **Enduros:** *Enduros* are much like hare scrambles except that riders must try to stay at a designated speed throughout a race. For example, the race organizers may decide that the riders must maintain an average speed of 24 mph. There are various checkpoints along the course, and, depending on how the race organizers have set up the competition, riders who arrive at a checkpoint either too early or too late may be penalized.

- **Dirt track:** Your child is unlikely to want to get into dirt-track racing but, hey, you never know. Dirt-track racing involves racing on a dirt oval. While adults may run on a mile-long oval dirt track, kids generally race on half-mile or smaller tracks. Have you ever seen the Kentucky Derby on TV? That's the kind of track that dirt-track racers compete on.

Your local motorcycle dealership should be able to tell you about local tracks and clubs that organize racing. Or you can contact the American Motorcyclist Association (AMA), which sanctions thousands of motorcycling-related events nationwide every year. You can contact the AMA by calling 800-262-5646 or going to www.amadirectlink.com. The AMA can fill you in on events, dates, times, and who to call to get involved in races in your area.

Determining whether your child is ready

Just because your child wants to race doesn't mean he or she is ready to. As a responsible parent, it's up to you to decide for your child. How do you know? After all, racing can be pretty dangerous.

First, be sure your child has mastered the basic skills of riding, is a pretty good rider, and truly has an interest in racing. Then consider the following means of gathering information to help you decide:

- ✔ **Go to some local races with your child and watch the class your child would race in to get an idea of what the racing is like.** Note whether the racing is tight with a lot of bumping or whether the riders spread out pretty quickly.

- ✔ **Find out whether your local track has a practice day.** If so, take advantage of it. This lets your child ride on the track without experiencing the pressure of competition, and it gives you the chance to evaluate how well your child navigates the track, and whether he or she is, in fact, ready to race.

- ✔ **Talk to other parents to learn what their experiences have been related to having a little racer in the family.** Talk about everything, including how far they have to travel to race, how often, and how much racing costs.

- ✔ **Determine the rules so your child races legally.** Ask the organizer of a race you're considering where to get a copy of the rules that cover machinery and safety requirements, class eligibility, and other things you need to know to race legally.

- ✔ **Consider your child's temperament.** Does he or she easily get flustered? Will your little racer be horribly upset if he or she doesn't win, or will your child be able to accept the fact that just competing is a major accomplishment?

Knowing what to expect the first day at the track

Okay, so you've done your homework and decided that your child is ready to race. You're even ready to shell out the cash it takes to buy the best safety equipment and bike possible, maintain the machine, and take the trips to the tracks. In that case, you're ready to go racing!

Here are some things to keep in mind when your child is racing at a track:

- When you get to the track, you pay a fee at the gate to get in and another fee for every class your child enters to race. You also fill out an entry form and sign a liability release. The friendly people at the registration desk usually give you a sheet that tells the times for the practices and races for the classes.

  Ask if there are any printed rules for conduct at the track. For example, some race organizers don't allow parents on the track to help a fallen rider unless the rider is in a class for very young racers, say, 4 to 6 years old.

- If the race is AMA-sanctioned, and it probably is, your racer must be a member of the AMA. You can avoid a lot of hassle by contacting and joining the AMA before you even go to the track. But if you're not a member before you arrive at the track, you can sign up there.

- After you get set up in the pits, chat with other racing families, have a good time, and keep your eye on your watch so your child doesn't miss practice or the race. Have plenty of water, snacks, and other necessities to maintain the well-being of your child, just as you would on a trail ride. (Check out the earlier section, "Making Trail Rides Fun," for more information on going out for trail rides.)

- Encourage your child no matter how well or how poorly he or she does, and make sure your youngster is having fun. Too many parents let their own competitive juices overshadow the fact that the child should be having a good time. A parent's screaming, anger, and frustration are not only bad for the child, but they also ruin the fun environment for the rest of the parents and racers.

Part III
You and Your Machine

The 5th Wave   By Rich Tennant

"A new high performance air intake system should make it faster. If that doesn't work, I'll paint a few more flames on the gas tank and see if that does anything."

In this part . . .

You're ready to ride, but you don't have a bike. What to do? This part guides you by introducing good beginner bikes in terms of price and performance. I also explain the ins and outs of buying a new or used bike. Even experienced motorcyclists sometimes don't know what to look for when inspecting a used bike, so I tell you exactly what to look for. You also need insurance if you're going to ride, and it's a little different from car insurance, so I explain that in this part, too.

As a motorcyclist, you want to put a little bit of your own personality into your motorcycle with some custom parts or even some major custom work. I explain the best way to go about making your machine your own. Even if you don't customize your bike, you definitely want to take care of it. This way you're sure that it provides you with reliable service for years and that it's in good shape when you decide to sell. I explain how to maintain your machine in easy-to-understand terms.

Chapter 8

First Bikes

As an aspiring motorcyclist, you may have a vision in your mind of what you want your bike to look like. You may see yourself on the biggest, baddest bike on the block — one that has lots of chrome and flames in the paint and that makes a *potato-potato* sound when you start it up and it idles. Or maybe you envision riding the fastest sportbike in the city so you can get from stoplight to stoplight in less than three seconds.

Well, one day you can have that big cruiser with a lot of chrome or that hyperquick sportbike. But those bikes really aren't the best machines to consider when you're just starting your motorcycling career. You must consider a lot of things when you're contemplating your first motorcycle.

In this chapter, you discover what you need to consider in terms of size, performance, and even styling when you decide on your first bike. You also get a look at some of the best first bikes on the market today, and you look into some of the bigger machines as well — one of them may be the right first bike for you.

Determining Your Perfect First Bike

If you ask motorcyclists why they bought a particular motorcycle, they may talk about the great handling, the powerful motor, the comfortable seating position, or the great looks. But the bottom line is that motorcyclists buy a bike because they like it. Some people buy cars that they'll just live with because they're cheap (both the people and the cars). But motorcyclists aren't like that. A bike is an extension of the rider, with emotional ties. The bike has to be cool.

Of course, first-time bike buyers need to keep their emotions in check, or they may be riding home on the first motorcycle they sit on — and probably paying too much for it. (I cover emotions and the nuts and bolts of buying a motorcycle, including pricing, in Chapter 9.) The first-time motorcycle buyer needs to be practical. For example, is a dealer who can work on the bike located nearby? You don't want to buy an exotic foreign machine only to find out that the closest dealer is 200 miles away.

In this section, I clue you in on some important points and questions to consider when figuring out what kinds of bikes appeal most to you. I also point out what to look for when you begin checking out bikes to actually buy.

Picking a bike is picking a lifestyle

The first consideration in buying a new bike is what style to get. After all, the style you buy determines what motorcycling crowd you get to hang out with. Most crowds are forgiving of new riders and accept them no matter what bike they're on, but others, like the Harley-Davidson crowd, generally aren't so tolerant.

If you aren't quite sure about what style or crowd fits you, start by asking yourself what you'll use the bike for. If you plan to mainly ride around town and take only a few rides out in the country, a big touring bike isn't a good idea. (A big touring rig isn't a good idea for a first bike anyway because it's a handful.) You're likely in the market for a cruiser.

I discuss various biker lifestyles and the bikes associated with them in detail in Chapter 4. Simply put, though, motorcycling culture breaks down into these lifestyles:

- ✔ **Touring:** *Touring machines* are big, with a lot of cargo space for long-distance riding. Touring riders tend to ride alone or in small groups.

- ✔ **Cruiser:** *Cruisers* are long, low machines with an upright or laid-back seating position built for cruising. Cruiser riders usually take short rides, with an occasional long ride thrown in. They like to wear a lot of black and look tough.

- ✔ **Sportbike:** *Sportbikes* are racing-style machines that are favored by younger riders who like the low weight and high performance. They look like competition machines right off the racetrack, and some of the riders dress like professional racers.

- ✔ **Adventure-touring:** *Adventure-touring* riders have large, street-legal, off-road machines with luggage so they can venture onto gravel roads and even rougher terrain. They tend to ride alone or in small groups.

✔ **Dual-sport:** A *dual-sport bike* is a street-legal, off-road machine that isn't as big as an adventurer-tourer and doesn't have the luggage. These riders tend to ride alone. They like their bikes for their versatility and because they're easy to ride, especially in traffic.

If a friend got you into motorcycling, pick a bike like he or she has so you can ride with your friend's crowd. That group also knows a lot about the kind of bike you'll be riding, so you can get advice on maintenance and tires.

You need to choose a size, power, and performance you can handle

Although lifestyle is one of the first things to consider, it doesn't have to be the main factor when you're just starting out as a motorcyclist. The important thing right now is to get a bike that's easy to ride and comfortable to learn on. After all, you won't fit into any motorcycling group if you don't know how to ride a motorcycle.

If you're a beginning motorcyclist, other motorcyclists will forgive you if you don't have a big, powerful, flashy machine. After all, every motorcyclist had to start on something, and most start on something small. Besides, when you get comfortable navigating city streets, cruising country roads, and riding the twisty roads in the mountains, you'll probably want to get a bigger, more powerful motorcycle.

To start, get something small. Don't get something so small that you look like a clown riding one of those tiny motorcycles, but do get something that you fit on well, that has a smaller motor, and that's relatively lightweight.

When you're sitting on the motorcycle, you should be able to put both feet comfortably flat on the ground. You also should be able to easily reach the handlebar controls. In other words, you shouldn't be straining to reach the handlebars and the controls on the handlebars, and you should be able to comfortably manipulate the rear brake and shift lever with your feet.

All motorcycles perform well, whether you're talking about the motor, suspension, or brakes. So unless you buy a 20-year-old bike, you don't have to worry about buying one that won't work well for you in terms of performance. I recommend against buying an old bike, and I explain why in Chapter 9. Steer clear of the big machines as well — the weight alone can be too much for a novice rider to handle. Finally, be sure to avoid the high-performance motorcycles that are scary fast.

When you're considering the power of the motor, you want something that's a middleweight or smaller. You don't want a bike with a powerful motor that will spin the rear tire if you twist the throttle too fast and too far. What's a middleweight or smaller motor? That depends on the bike. For example, a 600cc cruiser is considered a small bike, whereas a 600cc sportbike is way too much for a beginner to handle. I describe small and middleweight motorcycles with tame, novice-friendly motors later in this chapter.

Keep it simple, cheap, and easy to sell later

You're a new rider, so you're bound to drop the bike in your garage or in a parking lot — maybe several times. So do you really want to be riding a big, expensive machine for your first bike? Get a small machine that you can pick up after you drop it; and get an inexpensive one with parts that you can cheaply replace, so you don't cry whenever it tips over.

Plus, it's best to start out with a small, inexpensive machine because you may find later that it isn't the bike — or bike style — that you really want. For example, you may buy a cheap sportbike for your first bike but then decide after six months that you don't like the crouched-down seating position; you may want a sit-up or even a laid-back cruiser instead. A cheap machine is easy to sell.

Styling is another consideration. Sure, you should get a motorcycle that you like to look at. In fact, when you become a motorcyclist, you'll find yourself in the garage just staring at your bike for half an hour, an hour, or even longer. Strange, but true. But for your first bike, you need to be realistic. You don't want a lot of extra chrome parts or plastic bodywork that can get smashed up when you tip over.

Also, suppose that you decide after a month or two of riding that you really don't like motorcycling after all. Maybe motorcycling was fun to dream about, but the reality isn't as romantic as in your dreams. (I know, this scenario will never happen, right?) Again, an inexpensive machine is a lot easier to sell than an expensive one.

Purely New-Rider Machines

With some motorcycles, an experienced motorcyclist can look at them and immediately know that the owner is either a new rider or a small person. But that's okay. Everyone has to learn somehow, and the smallest bikes are the easiest to learn on.

You can peruse a good mix of small machines, from cruisers and sportbikes to standards. They're light, inexpensive, and easy to ride. Long term, women generally buy these bikes (most guys are simply too big for them), but they're great for anyone to learn on. Here I show some of the popular small bikes on the market.

Cruisers

The Harley-Davidson Sportster 883 (see Figure 8-1) is the brand's smallest machine. However, this one isn't as small as the small bikes other manufacturers offer. The Sportster 883 is relatively cheap and, as such, allows for relatively inexpensive entry into the world of Harley-Davidson motorcycling. Here are the specs for the machine:

Engine: 53.9-cubic-inch (883cc) air-cooled V-twin

Seat height: Laden 27.3 inches; unladen 29.3 inches (*laden* means with a 180-pound rider sitting on it)

Wheelbase: 60 inches

Claimed dry weight: 563 pounds

Suggested retail: $6,695

Figure 8-1: The 2008 Harley-Davidson Sportster XL883.

Photograph courtesy of Harley-Davidson Photography & Imaging. Copyright Harley-Davidson.

The Star V Star 250 (shown in Figure 8-2) offers a lot of fun in a small, cruiser-style package. This pint-size cruiser is light, low, inexpensive, and looks great. Check out the specs on the bike:

Engine: 249cc air-cooled V-twin

Seat height: 27 inches

Wheelbase: 58.7 inches

Claimed dry weight: 302 pounds

Suggested retail: $3,599

Figure 8-2:
The 2008
Star V Star
250.

Photo courtesy of Yamaha Motor Corp. USA.

Sportbikes

It's hard to find a small sportbike. Fortunately, if you've decided you want a small, nimble machine that looks great and will let you perfect your quick cornering and other sportbike-related skills, Kawasaki has exactly what you need: the Ninja 250R (see Figure 8-3).

Engine: 249cc liquid-cooled parallel twin

Seat height: 30.7 inches

Wheelbase: 54.7 inches

Claimed dry weight: 333 pounds

Suggested retail: $3,499

Photo courtesy of Kawasaki Motor Corporation USA.

Figure 8-3:
The 2008
Kawasaki
Ninja 250R.

Naked, or standard, machines

A *naked bike,* also known as a *standard,* is another great first bike that's easy to ride and looks great. The 2008 Honda Nighthawk (see Figure 8-4) is a perfect example of a small naked bike. Here are the specs for the Nighthawk:

Engine: 234cc air-cooled V-twin

Seat height: 29.3 inches

Wheelbase: 56.3 inches

Claimed curb weight (ready to ride and full of fluids, including gas): 315 pounds

Suggested retail: $3,699

For something bigger, with double the motor size, the 2008 Buell Blast is worth a look (see Figure 8-5). This great entry-level machine features a relatively light weight, great power, and two seat-height options. So if you're height-challenged you can go with the seat that will bring you 2 inches closer to Mother Earth (25.5 inches compared to the standard seat's 27.5 inches). The specs of this bike include the following:

Engine: 30-cubic-inch (492cc) air-cooled single

Seat height: 25.7 inches (or low profile 25.5 inches)

Wheelbase: 55 inches

Dry weight: 360 pounds

Suggested retail: $4,695

Figure 8-4:
The 2008
Honda
Nighthawk.

Photo: American Honda Motor Co. Inc.

Figure 8-5:
The 2008
Buell Blast.

Photograph courtesy of Harley-Davidson Photography & Imaging. Copyright Harley-Davidson.

Bikes That Don't Scream "Rookie!"

You'll find an awful lot of motorcycles to choose from when looking for your first streetbike. Some machines are great for new riders but still work for experienced motorcyclists as well. After all, the manufacturers wouldn't keep making them if people weren't buying them. And there can't be *that* many new motorcyclists coming into the fold each year.

These bikes have tame motors, lighter weight, and a relatively cheap price, which make them fairly easy to acquire, ride, and maintain. And, who knows? Maybe you'll find that you really like your first bike a lot, and you'll keep it for five years or more.

These bikes are cruisers, sportbikes, and standards, so you do have to make a lifestyle choice when you decide which type of bike feels the most comfortable. One caveat is that women can choose smaller machines without facing the ribbing from fellow motorcyclists that men may get.

Cruisers you can't go wrong with

If you want to get into the cruiser lifestyle, you have a lot of choices. You can get a cruiser with a smaller motor that looks just as big and bad as its older siblings. You'll look cool cruising and can spend less money for that machine than you would getting a more powerful bike. The downside, though, is that even the middleweight cruisers can be heavy. Make sure it's light enough and balanced well enough that you can push it around a little bit in a parking lot.

An 800cc or 900cc machine may be as big as you want to go for a first bike. Cruisers can go up to 2,000cc. Depending on your size, you may want to start with a 600cc bike. These machines give you enough oomph in the motor department yet are relatively easy to handle. Honda, Star, Suzuki, and Kawasaki all make great bikes in this size.

When you're looking at and sitting on bikes, be sure to compare the specifications. For example, some bikes have seats that are 2 inches higher than others, which can make the difference between comfortably planting both feet on the ground and having to go around on tippy-toes. Plus, a liquid-cooled motor stays cooler than an air-cooled motor, especially if you plan to do a lot of stop-and-go city riding.

Because you do have a lot of choices in cruisers, you need to shop around. Find a look you like, a size that fits, and a cost you can afford. (I discuss buying a bike more in Chapter 9.) Also consider whether accessories are readily available so you can customize your machine to your liking. That's part of the fun of motorcycling — m   g your machine your own. (Check out Chapter 12 for more on customizing.)

The 2008 Honda Shadow Spirit 750, shown in Figure 8-6, has a long and low look. It features shortened fenders and a low seat height. Check out the specs for this machine:

Engine: 45-cubic-inch (745cc) liquid-cooled V-twin

Seat height: 25.7 inches

Wheelbase: 65 inches

Curb weight: To be announced (2007 claimed dry weight is 503.5 pounds)

Suggested retail: $6,799

Figure 8-6: The 2008 Honda Shadow Spirit 750 (VT750C2).

The 2008 Star V Star Classic (shown in Figure 8-7) has a retro look because it appears that it has no rear shock, but it does. It also has floorboards, steel fenders, and a lot of chrome. Here are the specs:

Engine: 40-cubic-inch (649cc) air-cooled V-twin

Seat height: 27.9 inches

Wheelbase: 64 inches

Claimed dry weight: 505 pounds

Suggested retail: $6,199

The 2008 Suzuki Boulevard C50T (see Figure 8-8) is a cruiser with some touring-bike touches, including a big windscreen and saddlebags. Check out the specs for this machine:

Engine: 50-cubic-inch (819.35cc) liquid-cooled V-twin

Seat height: 27.6 inches

Wheelbase: 65.2 inches

Claimed dry weight: 567 pounds

Suggested retail: $7,999

Figure 8-7:
The 2008
Star V Star
Classic.

Photo courtesy of Yamaha Motor Corp. USA

Figure 8-8:
The 2008
Suzuki
Boulevard
C50T.

Photo courtesy of American Suzuki Motor Corp.

The 2008 Kawasaki Vulcan 900 Custom, shown in Figure 8-9, is a mid-size cruiser with a lot of chrome, a big rear tire, and a light-looking front end. Here are the specs:

Engine: 55-cubic-inch (903cc) liquid-cooled V-twin

Seat height: 27 inches

Wheelbase: 64.8 inches

Claimed dry weight: 549 pounds

Suggested retail: $7,399

Figure 8-9:
The 2008
Kawasaki
Vulcan 900
Custom.

Photo courtesy of Kawasaki Motor Corporation USA.

Friendly standards

Standard machines, or naked bikes, also make good beginner machines if you pick wisely. Like sportbikes, some are novice-friendly machines and some are bigger, more powerful bikes that can be a handful for a new rider.

A standard machine offers a more upright position than a sportbike and includes less plastic bodywork to crack if you drop the machine. Its performance is about on par with that of some sportbikes.

The 2008 Suzuki SV650 (see Figure 8-10) is a good, all-around standard machine with no bodywork. A lot of experienced riders like this bike, but it's also good for beginners — as long as they're careful until they get used to the power. Check out the specs for the SV650:

Engine: 645cc liquid-cooled V-twin

Seat height: 31.5 inches

Wheelbase: 56.7 inches

Claimed dry weight: 370 pounds

Suggested retail: $5,999

Figure 8-10:
The 2008
Suzuki
SV650.

Photo courtesy of American Suzuki Motor Corp.

Tame sportbikes

If you don't see yourself as a cruiser rider and instead picture yourself as a sportbike rider strafing the apexes of corners on mountain roads, consider a mid-level motorcycle.

But be particularly careful if you decide to go with a sportbike (unless it's one of the small ones, which I discuss earlier in this chapter). A mid-level high-performance machine like the Honda CBR600RR is designed for experienced riders only.

Certain midperformance sportbikes work great for beginners: The Kawasaki Ninja 500R and the Suzuki GS500F combine sleek styling, plenty of power for the novice, and low weight to make a great package for the new rider.

The 2008 Kawasaki Ninja 500R (see Figure 8-11) features a liquid-cooled motor, half-fairing in front for wind protection, and front and rear disc brakes for better stopping power. Here are the specs:

Engine: 498cc liquid-cooled twin

Seat height: 30.5 inches

Wheelbase: 56.5 inches

Claimed dry weight: 388 pounds

Suggested retail: $5,099

Figure 8-11: The 2008 Kawasaki Ninja 500R.

Photo courtesy of Kawasaki Motor Corporation USA.

The 2008 Suzuki GS500F (shown in Figure 8-12) features an air-cooled motor, full-fairing for increased wind protection, and front and rear disc brakes. The specs? Check them out:

Engine: 487cc air-cooled twin

Seat height: 31.1 inches

Wheelbase: 55.3 inches

Claimed dry weight: 396.8 pounds

Suggested retail: $5,199

Photo courtesy of American Suzuki Motor Corp.

Double-duty dual-sports

A great way for a new rider to learn how to ride is to get a small *dual-purpose bike* (also called dual-sport) that can be ridden both on the road and in the dirt. Although I wouldn't recommend taking them on the freeway because they don't have the oomph to get out of the way of an 18-wheeler barreling down on you. These bikes are small, light, and easy to ride. They have a relatively high seating position so you can see in traffic clearly, and they can be taken off-road for some dirt experience, which increases your street skills.

A 250cc or 200cc machine is the best choice. If you decide to go this route, make sure the bike is a street-legal dual-sport machine. It must have lights, turn signals, mirrors, street-legal tires, and whatever else is necessary for you to legally ride it on the street.

Some dirt bikes look like street-legal dual-sports but aren't. For example, they may have taillights and headlights that aren't approved for street use. You can't legally license these bikes for street use. These bikes are called *enduros*. I discuss enduro machines in Chapter 4.

The 2008 Yamaha XT250 is a good example of a dual-purpose machine (see Figure 8-13). Check out the specs for this bike:

Engine: 249cc air-cooled single

Seat height: 31.9 inches

Wheelbase: 53.5 inches

Claimed dry weight: To be announced (the 2007 weight is 238 pounds)

Figure 8-13:
The 2008
Yamaha
XT250.

Photo courtesy of Yamaha Motor Corp. USA

The 2008 Suzuki DR200SE is a smaller machine that's also street legal (see Figure 8-14). Here are the specs:

Engine: 199cc air-cooled single

Seat height: 31.9 inches

Wheelbase: 55.3 inches

Claimed dry weight: 249 pounds

Suggested retail: $3,949

Photo courtesy of American Suzuki Motor Corp.

Chapter 9

Buying a Bike: What You Must Know

In This Chapter

▶ Getting a deal on a new bike

▶ Avoiding a lemon when buying a used machine

▶ Finding a deal and avoiding Internet scams

You've got some cash in your pocket and a spring in your step as you walk into your local motorcycle dealership. You're ready to plunk down cash for a new motorcycle. You've done your dreaming and your homework, and you know exactly what you want and how much you want to pay for it. You're ready to do the deal.

Getting to this point, though, may have taken weeks or even months of research. At one time, you wanted a motorcycle so bad you could taste it. It would have been easy — too easy — to walk into a dealership, look around at the bikes, sit on a few, and then say, "I'll take that one." And that would be fine, since, as a motorcycle owner, you've now joined the motorcycling fraternity. The downside, though, is that maybe emotion would have gotten the best of you, and you would have bought the flashiest bike instead of the one that best fits your needs. Or maybe you would have paid too much. Or maybe the dealership wasn't the best place for you to buy a bike. After all, buying a motorcycle from a dealership should be the beginning of a relationship with that dealership, not the end.

Whether you're buying new or used, the most important research you can do is to first decide what style of motorcycle you want — a touring, a cruiser, or a sportbike — and then decide on a handful of bikes that fit your needs. From there, you need to determine the selling prices of those machines. You also need to decide which of the various dealerships in your area that sells those bikes is best for you. With that research done, you're ready to buy.

In this chapter, you explore the ins and outs of buying a motorcycle, both old and new. You discover how to find a good dealership, how to get a good deal on a new bike, and how to pay for it. Buying new is easy. Buying used, on the other hand, can be tough. Here you discover how to avoid buying a used machine that will require much more work than it's worth, how to negotiate a fair price, and how to avoid getting ripped off. Plus, you get insider tips to make your newly acquired used bike operate like new. (***Note:*** If you're unsure of what type of bike suits you best, head to Chapter 8 first.)

Buying New: Getting on a Bike the Easy Way

There's nothing like the euphoria you feel walking into a dealership that sells various brands of motorcycles, knowing that you're going to walk out as the new owner of one of the bikes. While it may be one of the happiest days of your life, that euphoria can work against you in buying a new motorcycle. Why? Because that euphoria may cause you to pay too much for a motorcycle just because you want it so badly.

If you want to get a deal on a bike, keep your emotions in check and your checkbook in your pocket. Be willing to walk away from a deal if you can't negotiate the price down to a level close to what you want to pay. Also, be firm but polite in your negotiations. After all, you don't want to leave a sour taste in the mouth of the dealership where you'll be returning to buy parts and have service work done.

Ideally, you'll find a dealership that you enjoy going to and that has knowledgeable staff in the sales, service, and parts departments. This should be the beginning of a long and happy relationship for both parties. This section provides tips on finding such a dealer and getting a great bike from it.

Choosing the right dealer

Even motorcyclists with garages full of bikes like to visit motorcycle dealerships to look at the latest machines. They have no intention of buying. They just want to look. A prospective motorcycle buyer also should visit dealerships in the area and look around.

It's important to find a good dealership for several reasons. You want to support a dealership that supports the sport, you want your work done correctly in the service department, you want the right parts when you order them, and you want as little hassle as possible if you need warranty work done. The following sections provide tips on what to watch for when visiting dealerships.

In addition to doing your own research, ask your riding buddies or other riders about various dealerships. Motorcyclists love to talk about anything related to motorcycling and love to give their opinions. You may hear some horror stories about botched jobs at a dealership's service department, but you also may hear praise related to great work and fair prices.

Are the managers and salespeople knowledgeable?

Don't be afraid to chat with the salespeople and managers about motorcycles and motorcycling. Unless they're really busy, at a good dealership, the salespeople and mangers will be happy to talk with you — not only because they're enthusiastic motorcyclists, but also because you may become a customer later.

The manager almost undoubtedly is an enthusiast. However, you may run into some salespeople who don't seem to know much about motorcycling and motorcycles — even the brands carried at that dealership. That lack of expertise is something to make a mental note of, but it shouldn't raise any red flags by itself. Those salespeople could be new to the dealership. And they may not be motorcycle enthusiasts at all, but they sell motorcycles for a job.

When you're ready to buy a motorcycle, if you buy it from that dealership, you'll need to know more about the bike than the salesperson does; the salesperson probably won't be able to answer your detailed questions about the machine. You'll likely find at least one knowledgeable salesperson on the staff, though.

Is the dealership involved in the motorcycling community?

While you're looking around and chatting up the managers and sales staff, find out how involved the dealership is in community motorcycling. Does the dealership sponsor any local racers? Is it involved in any charity rides? Does it serve as a destination of rides? If the dealership does this stuff, it shows that it's part of the motorcycling community and isn't just out to make a buck off motorcyclists. While this stuff isn't critical, it's always best to support those who support the sport.

Is the parts department well stocked?

After you buy a motorcycle, you'll need parts. Check out a dealership's parts department before you buy a bike. Observe and listen. Determine whether the parts people are knowledgeable. See whether they allow customers to step behind the counter to look at the parts microfiche to be sure they're getting the right part. Nothing is more frustrating than ordering a part through the parts department — even something simple, like an oil filter — waiting two weeks for the part to arrive, and then discovering it's not the right part. Be friendly with the parts staff and especially get to know the parts manager. Then they're more likely to go that extra mile to find and order the part you need.

Is the service department well staffed?

If you can get a peek at the dealership's service area, see if there's room around the work areas so that bikes can be pushed around without bumping into things. Note the ages of the mechanics: If they're all very young, maybe the shop has a high turnover rate and it values increasing profits over keeping experienced mechanics. See if education certificates are displayed showing that the mechanics receive training to keep up with the latest motorcycle technology. You'll most likely find a good mix in ages among the mechanics or the dealership probably won't be in business long.

Cutting a good deal

Some people are born hard-nosed negotiators, while others would rather have root-canal surgery than to have to face off with a professional salesperson. But as long as you're willing to walk out of a dealership without a bike if your price isn't met, negotiating is pretty easy.

Okay, one caveat is that you have to be realistic about the price you're willing to pay for a machine. You can't be Mr. Cheapskate and offer half of what a dealer paid for a motorcycle and expect to get it. Plus, some dealerships are very firm about cutting deals — they won't do it. They figure if you won't buy the bike then someone else will at the price that the dealership wants. After all, they don't have the volume that car dealerships have so they can't make the deals that car dealers do and stay in business. Keep in mind that that dealers have other charges related to the bike that are negotiable, such as dealer prep, and some that aren't, like taxes.

But if you're realistic about the amount you're willing to pay, with the idea in mind that the dealership can sell a bike for 15 percent below the Manufacturer's Suggested Retail Price (or even more) and still make a profit, you may go home with your dream machine at a reasonable cost. And with a little research, you may find that the bike you want isn't selling well, in which case you can probably negotiate an even better deal.

Researching price

To get a good deal on a new motorcycle, you need to do research on pricing before you walk into a dealership to buy a bike. After you decide on the handful of bikes that you're interested in, go to the manufacturers' Web sites to find out the Manufacturer's Suggested Retail Price, or MSRP. If you don't have access to the Internet, ask at the dealership. This gives you a base to start from.

If the bike you want is very popular, expect to pay MSRP or more. The dealer knows that if you won't buy the bike, someone else will. On the other hand, if the bike you want isn't very popular, you should be able to get it below MSRP because the dealer wants to get it out of the building. For this reason, having a handful of bikes in mind is a good idea — some may be cheaper than others.

You can research the selling prices of new motorcycles in various ways. You can read bike reviews in motorcycle magazines. Sometimes you'll read that a certain bike is difficult to get and that you can expect to pay over MSRP. Or you may see that a certain bike isn't selling, meaning that you can expect to pay less than MSRP. Also, ask motorcycling friends. They may have a feel for the prices. You can also check the Web sites of dealerships in your state to see what the bikes are selling for. Plus, you can visit local dealerships and see what the prices are on the sales tags.

While you're at the dealership, see if there's a one- or two-year-old model of the bike you want on the sales floor. These bikes are still new and likely will be cheaper than the current model.

Considering other potential costs

When you determine whether you'll likely pay MSRP, below MSRP, or above MSRP, you need to consider the other costs that the dealer will tack on before the motorcycle can roll out the door:

- ✔ **Dealer prep:** This is dealer preparation, also called *setup,* which involves assembly of the motorcycle. The bike arrives at the dealership unassembled in a crate. The dealership must assemble it and put in the required fluids, such as oil. This fee can be $400 or more.

- ✔ **Destination charge:** This charge is also known as the *freight charge.* Here you pay for getting the bike from the factory to the dealership. This fee also can be $400 or more.

- ✔ **Tax, title, and registration:** The government gets this money, but you have to pay it to title and register your motorcycle.

Using your information to negotiate a better price

The full price of a new bike could be MSRP or more plus the following: dealer prep; tax, title, and registration; and the destination fee. This price is the price out the door.

Your goal when walking into a dealership to buy a motorcycle is to walk out the door with your motorcycle at the lowest out-the-door price possible. You need to negotiate. Negotiate the bike price, the dealer prep fee, and the destination charge. Unfortunately, you can't negotiate the tax, title, and registration. But, if you're a good negotiator, you can negotiate a good price on a bike and have the dealer waive the dealer prep charge and destination fee.

You can even try to get the dealer to throw in some accessories to sweeten the deal, like saddlebags and a new helmet. If you can't negotiate a deal that you're happy with, consider walking away and trying your negotiating skills at a different dealership. In fact, after you stand up to head out the door, you may find that the salesperson or manager that you're dealing with is suddenly more likely to come down in price on the bike.

You've probably bought a few cars in your lifetime, so just remember that negotiating to buy a bike works the same way. Although negotiations are usually quicker in a motorcycle dealership, and there's also a lot less pressure to buy. You ask how much they're asking for the bike, you counter with an offer, and they normally say that's too low. Or they may try to steer you to a different machine.

Following are a few additional tips to use to your advantage while negotiating:

- ✔ It's best to go to the dealership at the end of the month or at the end of the year when salespeople and sales managers have to meet quotas. At this time, they're often more willing to deal.

- ✔ A new bike should be pristine. That means that every nick or scratch should reduce the price of the bike.

The bottom line is this: You need to be willing to walk out of the dealership at any time without a new bike. That's what gives you the advantage over the dealership. Realize, however, that it's unlikely you'll get a megadeal. After all, motorcycle dealerships simply don't have the volume to make those kinds of deals, and they can only get limited numbers of the most popular models from the factories.

Financing: But I want that bike now!

If you don't have the cash to pay the out-the-door price for a motorcycle, you have to get a loan. You can get a loan at the dealership, through a bank or finance company, or through a credit union — provided that your credit worthiness is good, of course.

To get a loan, you need a substantial down payment — usually 20 percent or more of the purchase price. Plus, the company that loans you the money probably will require that you have full-coverage insurance on the motorcycle, meaning that if the bike gets damaged, the insurance company will pay to have it repaired. (I discuss motorcycle insurance in Chapter 10.)

Getting financing at the dealership is the easiest way to go. You're already there, and you can get a decision on your loan in minutes. And if the financing is through one of the motorcycle manufacturers, you may be able to take advantage of a special financing deal, such as 0 percent interest the first two years of the loan. So if you can pay off the loan within the first two years, it amounts to an interest-free loan. Generally, though, financing at the dealership incurs a higher interest rate than a loan from a bank or credit union.

If you don't want to get financing at the dealership, you can go to a bank, finance company, or credit union. The credit union probably will offer the lowest interest rate, followed by the bank. The finance company likely will have the highest interest rate, so use it only as a last option. Okay, your last option is to max out your credit cards to buy a bike, but that's not a good idea because of the high interest rate. Besides, you know how difficult it is to pay off credit cards. But if you really want a bike. . . .

At any of these lending institutions, you'll probably have to get a personal loan. You're being lent the money based on your own worthiness to repay the loan rather than on the bike as collateral. Many lending institutions don't accept a motorcycle for collateral.

If you try everywhere and can't get a loan, save some money and buy a used bike, and rebuild your credit so that in a couple years or so, you can buy a brand-spanking-new machine.

Ensuring a safe and successful first ride home

Before you leave the dealership with your new motorcycle, you should have completed a motorcycle safety training course and you need to have insurance and a motorcycle license in hand. Too many horror stories tell of people hopping on their new motorcycle at the dealership and then crashing before they get home.

Familiarize yourself with your bike

Before leaving the dealership, have a salesperson show you how to start the bike and operate all the controls. With some motorcycles, you must hold in the clutch lever to start the bike; with others, you don't. On some motorcycles, the turn signals are operated by a single switch on the left handlebar; on others, a switch on the left handlebar controls the left turn signal, and a switch on the right controls the right turn signal. So, before you drive off the lot, know your controls. Also check the fluids on your bike before you ride off. It's rare, but sometimes when the bike is assembled, the assembler forgets to put engine oil in the machine.

If you're uncomfortable riding your bike home, have an experienced friend ride it home for you. Or you can opt to take it home in a truck or trailer. Who knows? Maybe the dealership will even deliver it for you if you don't live too far away.

Obtain the proper manuals

Besides having the owner's manual that came with the bike, you should consider buying the factory service manual, the factory parts manual, and a general repair and service manual made for your bike.

The *factory service manual* is very detailed and is written for mechanics, so you may find some parts of it difficult to understand. In those cases, the less-detailed *general repair and service manual* should be good enough to walk you through the procedure. The *factory parts manual* is invaluable not only because of its exploded views of how various parts go together (which is extremely useful when those parts are lying around on your garage floor) but also because you can use it as a reference to order parts later from the dealership: You can use the factory part number, ensuring that you get the right part.

Also get a couple spare keys made for your new machine. No matter what you think, you'll eventually lose your keys.

Knowing what to do when you get your bike home

When you get the bike home, read the owner's manual that came with it. This basic manual explains the locations and functions of various controls, tells what fluids to use (such as the type of engine oil), and runs you through the break-in procedure.

The break-in procedure ensures that all the moving metal parts seat and mate properly. Be sure to follow the manufacturer's break-in procedure, which involves such things as not exceeding certain engine rpm limits within a certain number of miles of operating the motorcycle, and changing the engine oil after about 600 miles.

Also consider washing and waxing your bike and lubricating the cables and chains soon after you get it home. Not only does this make your bike shine, but it also gives you the opportunity to check all the bolts to make sure they are tight, and to check the routing of the cables for kinks.

Car people like to put a spray-on rubber or vinyl protectant on their tires to make them shine. Don't put it on motorcycle tires. That stuff is super slippery and takes a long time to wear off. If you get any of that stuff on the part of your tire that contacts the road, you'll crash the first time you take a turn.

Buying Used, Not Abused

We all want a new motorcycle, but we all can't afford it. Of course, the minute a motorcycle is ridden out of a dealership parking lot, it becomes a used motorcycle and drops in value significantly, despite what the owner may think. Very few bikes hold their value. That's great news for those of us who want to get into motorcycling but don't want to spend lots of money to do it.

The bad news is that too many used motorcycles have been, at best, not maintained properly and, at worst, abused. A potential buyer has to know what he or she is looking at, and looking for, when inspecting a machine for possible purchase. That's because when the deal is done and the money is exchanged, the bike is yours.

That said, though, you can find some deals in the used bike market, especially if you're willing to invest some time, money, and elbow grease in making your new machine look, and ride, almost like new. Keep in mind that most riders overprice their bikes when it's time to sell, so unless you really want the bike, don't pay the inflated price. Also, you'll probably have to put a bunch of money into a used bike after you buy it.

But you can get a nice used motorcycle for around $1,500, and a great used motorcycle for $5,000 (compared to $8,000 or more for a new machine). Motorcycling is within reach for anyone with enthusiasm and the ability to sock away a few bucks every couple of weeks for a while.

You can buy a used bike from a dealer, from a private party, or at a bank repossession auction. You pay more at a dealership, but at least you know that the bike has been inspected by professional mechanics, and you may be able to get the dealer to throw a helmet into the deal. When buying from a private party, you need to know what to look for that indicates signs of trouble, and you need to know the right questions to ask.

Old bikes can be trouble

It's tempting to buy an old bike, like a 20- or 30-year-old machine, because it's so cheap. Also, new riders probably figure they will drop the bike a lot while learning to ride, so they don't want to learn on something expensive.

New riders shouldn't get an old bike, for several reasons:

- They're unreliable. One loose wire or bad connection can strand you in the middle of nowhere, and it will be difficult to trace the problem.

- Most dealers won't work on bikes more than ten years old. You would have to be a pretty good mechanic yourself to keep the bike running.

> ✔ Parts are difficult to get, especially if the bike requires odd-sized tires.
>
> ✔ When it's time to get rid of the bike, you probably won't be able to sell it because it's so old.

Stay away from an old bike unless it's supercheap, like 100 bucks, and you plan to ride it only in your yard to learn how to ride.

Asking the right questions

Before you go hunting for a used bike, it's a good idea to know what bike or bikes you want to buy. Do research and have two or three in mind so you aren't locked into just trying to hunt down one particular bike, which may or may not be hard to find. Get all the information you can from friends and off Web sites so you know as much about the bikes as possible. When you find an ad for a bike you might want to buy, make an appointment with the owner to see it.

After you're there, start gathering information:

✔ **Ask to see the title, and then compare the vehicle identification number on the title with the number on the bike.** These numbers absolutely must match. If they don't, then don't buy the bike — you may not be able to get it titled and registered. Also, the bike may be stolen. In some states, the vehicle identification number, or VIN, matches the VIN number on the frame. In other states, the VIN number on the title goes with the VIN number on the motor. Check with your local Bureau of Motor Vehicles title office before you go to look at any bikes, to see how your state handles the VIN on the title.

✔ **Chit-chat with the owner to try to determine whether he or she is a motorcycle enthusiast or just had the bike for cheap transportation.** Chances are, an enthusiast will have taken better care of the bike than a casual rider. Ask if the owner has any maintenance records. If not, find out how often the oil was changed, the chain lubricated, the brake fluid changed, and any other maintenance done. Ask if the fork oil has ever been changed. It's pretty rare for a motorcyclist to change the fork oil, so if you find an owner who has, in fact, changed it every four years or so, you've probably found an owner who has kept the bike in tip-top shape.

✔ **Examine the bodywork.** Is it original? Is it free of scrape marks or cracks? If any body panels have been replaced or there are scrape marks on the bodywork, the bike has been in a crash. Ask about it. A hard crash could mean a bent frame.

✔ **Make sure all the electrical components are working, including the headlight, taillight, and turn signals.** Make sure the controls and switches operate smoothly. Ask when the cables were lubricated last. Make sure the throttle operates smoothly.

✔ **Ask if the bike has a paper, wire mesh, or foam air filter, and ask when it was last cleaned or replaced.** If it isn't difficult to get to, ask to see it. A very dirty air filter isn't a good sign: Dirt may have passed into the motor, which isn't good.

✔ **Find out how old the chain and sprockets are.** Look at the chain to see whether it's clean and lubricated. Check the sprockets to see if they have hooked or bent teeth, which means the sprockets and chain need to be replaced.

✔ **Look for any fluid leaks, such as from the cylinder head or the fork tubes.** If there are leaks, the head gasket or fork seals need to be replaced. Open the gas tank cap and peer inside with a flashlight to look for rust.

✔ **If possible, put the bike up on a centerstand and pull and push the fork tubes back and forth to feel for play in the steering head.** If there's play, the steering head bearings need to be replaced. Do the same with the front and rear wheels, but move them from side to side to check for worn-bearing play.

✔ **Look closely at the frame, even underneath, to see if you find any cracks.** Pay particular attention to the areas around welds. Also try to determine whether all the frame railings are straight.

✔ **Ask for a test ride.** A lot of owners won't do this because so many bikes are stolen that way and because of liability concerns (you may get hurt or even killed). But if you give the owner a deposit to hold while you go for the ride, you may be able to do it. Or you can try to cut a deal with the owner that you will buy the bike with the option of selling it back to the owner for the same price within an hour if you don't like it. If you can't ride it, have the owner start up the bike so you can hear it run. You shouldn't see smoke coming out of the exhaust pipe unless it's a two-stroke machine.

What to look for during a test ride

If the owner lets you take the bike for a test ride, that's great. Take it easy during the ride because it is a new machine to you and you don't know how it handles. For example, if you're used to riding cruisers with heavy steering, you may find that this particular bike steers quickly; if you ride it like you would a bike with a slow-moving front end, you could find yourself in big trouble.

While riding the bike, try to get a sense of whether the handlebars are bent and the frame is straight. Feel how the suspension works. If it's very soft, it could mean you'd need to put money into suspension work. Make sure the bike shifts smoothly. If it's tough to get into second or third gear, for example, that may be a problem. Run it up and down all the gears to make sure they all work. You don't have to go fast to do this.

Listen for any unusual noises from the engine. If you aren't familiar with that particular model, you may need to ask the owner about any usual noises you hear — and hope you get a straight answer.

Make sure the bike feels planted and solid. If it shakes when you turn, the wheel bearings could be shot.

Figuring out and negotiating a fair price

By doing your homework ahead of time — researching bikes on the Internet and talking to friends — you should have a pretty good idea of a fair price for the bike you're looking for. You can glance at prices in classified ads for those bikes, but those prices are generally high. They're asking prices, not selling prices.

After you've inspected the bike you're looking at, you should have a pretty good idea of whether it's worth the asking price — or even the price you researched for a clean, used model of that bike. If it has flaws, such as broken bodywork or worn-out tires, figure that into your negotiations and use those points to try to get the seller to lower the asking price.

Worn-out tires alone will cost you $200 to $300 to replace after you get the bike home. So if the tires need to be replaced, make that a major negotiating point. If the bodywork is damaged, you have another major negotiating point; bodywork is very expensive.

If you negotiate and still feel that the seller wants too much money, walk away from the deal. You'll have other opportunities. Being willing to walk away from the motorcycle gives you the upper hand in negotiations. There will be other machines that you'll want to buy.

Getting the bike home

If you've decided to buy the bike and you want to ride the bike home, you must have completed motorcycle safety training and you must have a license and insurance. (I discuss motorcycle insurance in Chapter 10.) Otherwise, load the bike into a truck or trailer to get it home. Or consider having a friend ride it home for you.

When you get the bike home, it's a good idea to get the factory service manual and the factory parts manual, if they're still available for your machine. Also pick up a general repair and service manual made for your bike. The parts manual is particularly useful because it gives exploded views of how various parts fit together. And it's a great reference for ordering parts from a dealership because you can order by the factory part numbers.

Also get a couple spare keys made. Then wash and wax the bike to make it look as good as possible, and check for any missing or loose bolts. Check the routing of any cables for kinks. Finally, be sure you lubricate all the cables and the chain.

Buying Off the Internet: Deal or No Deal?

The Internet has really been a boon in this information age. You want information about a particular motorcycle? You can probably find it on the Internet. You want to find out how to change the oil or air filter on your bike? Yep, you can probably find that out also. Need parts? You can find them there. In fact, on the Internet you can buy an entire motorcycle from a dealer, a private party, or, unwittingly, a junkyard.

Although you can find a lot of information on the Internet, not all of it is correct. Approach advice cautiously, judging the source. Remember, it's easy to, let's say, embellish when discussing a motorcycle for sale on the Internet. Even so, the Internet allows you to see what motorcycles are for sale not just in your area, but throughout your state and even throughout the country.

If you're thinking about buying a bike off the Internet, consider only machines that you can actually drive to and look at before you hand over cash. Some of the bikes listed on the Internet don't really exist; they're just phantoms to get money from people. Also, if you see the bike that was described as being in "pristine condition," you may find that it isn't in such great shape and isn't worth the asking price. Then you can negotiate the price or walk away.

Buying new: A great way to shop around

The Internet gives you the opportunity to easily and quickly compare prices of new bikes at dealerships around your state. You can shop around by going to the Web sites of the various dealerships or by going to one of the motorcycle-selling Web sites. Probably the biggest is Cycle Trader `www.cycletrader.com`.

Not all dealers sell their bikes at MSRP. In fact, if they want to move some models off the showroom floor, dealers cut the price drastically. You may find it worthwhile to drive across the state, or even to another state, to pick up a bike if you can save $1,000 or more on the purchase price. The dealer may even ship the bike to you.

Just as when buying a bike any other way, do your homework, know the bike well, and be familiar with the going prices. You can try to negotiate with dealers over the Internet, but it's usually not a good idea to try to leverage a dealer by saying you can get the bike cheaper elsewhere. A common response is, "Well, go buy it there, then." Also remember that when you're buying a bike you're starting a relationship with that dealer, so be firm but polite.

Buying used: The deals are out there

Just as in the regular world, the cyber world has a lot of used motorcycles for sale — and a lot of overpriced used motorcycles. You can look for deals at online auction places like eBay or in online classifieds like Cycle Trader or craigslist.

With online auctions, people tend to get carried away with their bidding, or they don't really know what they're buying and they end up paying too much. Don't fall into that trap. Set an upper limit that you'll bid for a bike, and stick to it. If you don't get the bike, you'll have other opportunities. Treat an online classified ad like you would an ad in the paper.

In both cases, ask the seller a lot of questions. If the bike is within driving distance, go look at it. Watch for auctions that end on Wednesday; that seems to be the day when the fewest people bid on things, so selling prices are cheaper. And don't forget to check dealer Web sites to see what trade-ins they may be offering.

Handling the purchase

If you're buying online from a dealer, the dealership will want all its money up front. If you're buying from a private party, the seller usually will want a down payment, or earnest money, within a certain number of days and then the balance when you pick up the bike. If possible, try to arrange matters so that the seller sends you the title when you send the down payment, or try to hand over all the cash at the time you pick up the bike.

The seller will probably want cash because it's too easy to make phony money orders and bank drafts nowadays. The seller may also want to be paid through PayPal, which isn't a bad idea because it offers you some protection.

If you bought a bike from someone who lives far away and you can't go get it, you have no choice but to send the entire amount and hope that the seller is honest and will, in fact, ship the bike to you. This is obviously very risky, and I don't recommend it.

Internet scams to watch for

The Internet is full of scammers; after all, you aren't dealing face to face with people or businesses. So be careful that you don't fall for a scam. If you see a bike for a great price, it's probably a scam. As the old saying goes, if it's too good to be true, it probably is. Sure, when you see a 2-year-old Harley-Davidson for $7,000, you may start drooling, but be realistic. That bike does-n't exist. People have lost thousands of dollars buying bikes on the Internet because they've sent money to scammers who are primarily in Nigeria and elsewhere overseas.

Because a lot of these scammers are overseas, watch for signs in e-mail that the writer's native language is not English. Bad grammar, odd phrasings, and misspelled words are red flags. Plus, if the seller really doesn't know much about the bike, it's a scam for sure.

Also, scammers selling bikes will usually ask you to send a down payment, or all the money, to an escrow account. And they'll probably ask you to do it through Western Union. Don't do it. The escrow account is phony, and you have no recourse through Western Union to get your money back.

If you're selling a bike, you may get e-mail from scammers who will offer to send you a cashier's check and probably will want to have a shipper come pick up the bike. The scammer will give you a check for more than the price of the bike and ask you to wire the extra money back to him or her. Don't do it. The check is phony, and if you wire the cash before the bank tells you the check is phony, which can take 30 days, you'll lose your money.

The bottom line is that you must be very cautious about all sellers and buyers on the Internet. Just delete the e-mail from those folks who appear to be fishy.

Chapter 10

Ensuring You're Insured

....

....

*W*e hate to admit it, but motorcyclists also drive cars and trucks. That means we know a little bit about motor vehicle insurance. For instance, we know that we need to maintain minimum coverage or the police get pretty upset when they pull us over.

Have you ever really looked at your insurance policy? Do your eyes glaze over when your insurance agent starts talking about liability insurance, comprehensive coverage, collision coverage, and uninsured motorist coverage? If you do ignore your insurance policy, and you get all fuzzy-headed when your agent talks, don't worry — you're not alone.

Motor vehicle insurance can be pretty complicated, and it can be even more complicated when a motorcycle is involved. After all, a motorcycle is a special vehicle, and so your bike may have some special insurance needs above what's required by law.

In this chapter, you discover the different insurance coverages. You also find out what's required by law and what special insurance you may want to get to protect yourself if you hit someone or someone hits you. It's important to understand exactly what coverage you have so that when the time comes to call your insurance agent and say, "Oops," you'll know exactly what's covered.

Deciphering Your General Coverage Options

As you probably know, an insurance policy protects you from having to pay money from your own pocket to someone you injure or whose property you damage. It also pays for damage to your own bike. So the first thing you want to do when you get a bike is to get insurance. Besides helping out your wallet in case of an accident, purchasing insurance is the law.

When you meet with your insurance agent about buying an insurance policy, the agent may tell you that state law requires you to have a minimum of $25,000/$50,000/$15,000 (which is sometimes referred to as 25/50/15) in liability coverage in case you hurt someone or damage his or her property. But the agent may suggest that a successful person like you may want to bump that coverage up to 50/100/25 or even 100/300/50.

That's when your eyes glaze over. But it doesn't have to be that way. The following sections show you how to decipher the numbers. These sections also tell you the other insurance options that are likely to be thrown your way. (See the later section, "Paying the Price for Insurance," to find out how much you're likely to pay.)

Paying for others: Liability coverage

By law, you generally need to have two kinds of liability insurance: *bodily injury coverage* and *property damage coverage*. Bodily injury coverage pays if you hurt someone while riding your motorcycle (maybe you crash into a car and injure the driver, or you run over a pedestrian). Property damage coverage pays if you smash up someone's car, bicycle, or other property with your bike. Liability coverage is where the strange numbers come into play, too. I explain all you need to know in the following sections.

25/50/15: Just what does that mean?

When your agent tells you that state law requires you to carry 25/50/15 liability insurance (which, by the way, is the minimum required in many states), the agent is simply trying to tell you the following facts:

✔ Your policy will pay up to $25,000 for each person that you injure, for a total of $50,000 in a single accident. As you may have noticed, those are the first two numbers in the 25/50/15 sequence the agent was telling you about.

✔ Your policy will pay up to $15,000 for any damage that you cause to someone's property with your bike (say, for example, that you smash into the side of someone's car or inadvertently punch a hole through someone's nice white picket fence while you're learning to ride). This payment amount corresponds to the third number in the liability sequence.

A minimum liability coverage amount of 25/50/15 means that your policy will pay up to $25,000 for bodily injury, to a maximum of $50,000, and up to $15,000 for property damage in an accident. So if you hurt two people in a crash, and their medical bills are $25,000 each, you're covered. But if you hurt three people in the crash, and their medical bills are $25,000 each, your insurance will only cover the costs for two of the people. You need to cough up the other $25,000.

Opting for more than 25/50/15

Unless you're really tight on cash, it's best to opt for more than the minimum liability coverage (which, as I mention in the previous section, is generally 25/50/15). In fact, it's best to have at least a 50/100/25 coverage: $50,000 in bodily injury insurance, with a maximum $100,000 per accident, and $25,000 in property damage coverage.

Why? Well, you have to consider several things:

✔ Even though your bike is small compared to a car, station wagon, or 18-wheeler, it can still seriously hurt someone and cause considerable damage to a vehicle. In fact, a motorcycle can total a car!

✔ The price of healthcare isn't getting any cheaper. A person can run up a $25,000 hospital bill in no time. If the bill goes higher than that, you end up picking up the tab. After all, you're liable under the law to make good on the injuries and damages you cause.

✔ Your liability insurance pays for the lost income of the person you hurt as well as for your legal defense if you get sued.

As you can see, the tab for a motorcycle accident can run high pretty quickly.

If you can afford to spend a little more on insurance, another option to consider is an *umbrella liability policy*. Insurance agents generally offer $1 million of coverage relatively cheaply, $125 a year or so, and this protection would kick in after your bike insurance is used up. Plus, this coverage protects you in case someone makes a liability claim against you related to your house or car in addition to your motorcycle. Ask your agent for details.

Protecting yourself: Uninsured and underinsured motorist coverage

So, you've opted for 50/100/25 liability coverage (see the previous section for details), and you're feeling good about being protected if you hurt someone. But wait, what about you? Suppose you're riding down the road minding your own business and some bonehead makes a left turn right in front of your motorcycle, causing a crash. Who pays for your medical bills and for fixing your bike?

If the driver has the minimum amount of insurance coverage required by law, and your medical bills far exceed that amount, you would have to foot the bill for the portion that the driver's insurance doesn't cover. Sure, you can sue, but if the driver has minimum insurance coverage, he or she probably doesn't have any money or assets to sue for. The same is true if your totaled motorcycle is — or rather was — worth more than the driver's insurance would cover for property damage. What do you do now?

The answer is simple: Before you head out on the road, purchase *uninsured and underinsured motorist coverage.* This type of coverage provides you with protection if you were to get hit by an uninsured or underinsured driver or a hit-and-run driver. This coverage picks up the tab for your injuries or the damage to your bike if the driver who hit you has no insurance, or has insurance with lower payouts than what your medical bills and property damage amount to. The policy probably would cover your lost wages as well.

Some states require you to buy uninsured and underinsured motorist coverage. But, if your state doesn't require it, buy it anyway. To find out if your state requires this type of coverage, ask your agent for details. And remember those numbers we talked about earlier: 50/100/25? Here's where you'll see them again, and they mean the same thing except this time you're the person benefiting from the numbers.

In about half the nation's states, the uninsured and underinsured motorist coverage includes both bodily injury and property protection (that is, coverage if your bike gets smashed up). That's where you'll see the 50/100/25 sequence. In the other half of the states, property protection isn't offered as part of the uninsured and underinsured motorist coverage. In those states, the numbers would just be 50/100. The 50/100 means that if you and a passenger are hit by a hit-and-run driver, for example, your insurance policy will pay your medical bills up to $50,000, and your passenger's medical bills up to $50,000, for a total of $100,000. If you opt for collision coverage, which I discuss later in this chapter, you won't need the property protection portion of the uninsured and underinsured coverage if it's offered in your state.

"It's not my fault": Getting to know no-fault insurance

Some states have *no-fault insurance,* where a person's own insurance company is supposed to pay for the injuries that he or she suffers. Motorcyclists are generally exempt from no-fault requirements. But in those states, motorcyclists generally are required to buy *personal injury protection insurance,* which pays for their healthcare if they suffer injuries.

No-fault laws are very complex. So speak with your insurance agent for a full understanding of the law in your state. For example, some states include personal injury protection and property damage protection in their no-fault coverage, and some only include personal injury protection. So if you want property protection you need to speak to your agent before you get in an

accident, or you could end up having to pay to repair your bike yourself. Some no-fault states don't require you to have no-fault insurance, but they still require you to have liability insurance. Also, your state's no-fault policy may cover lost wages and funeral expenses, and it may not.

In addition, all the no-fault states put some kind of limits on what drivers and riders can sue each other for in the case of a crash. Usually you're only allowed to sue if your medical expenses reach a certain threshold or your injuries are severe. Be sure you understand those limits and the limits of your company-provided or purchased health plan so you know that your medical expenses will be taken care of if you're in a catastrophic crash.

Fixing your bike: Collision coverage

Imagine that you're learning how to ride your new motorcycle (happy day, isn't it?). You hop on the bike, twist the throttle, and immediately make a beeline for the nearest tree. "Oh great," you think, "now the front end of my new bike is all smashed up."

Hopefully you thought ahead and bought *collision insurance,* which pays to fix damage caused by yourself or others to your motorcycle. Collision insurance is great for all sorts of situations. For instance, if you smash into a tree, your bike is covered. If an uninsured driver hits you, yup, your bike is covered. If you come out of the grocery store to find your bike smashed up because someone backed into it and then sped off, you're covered.

If you took out a loan to buy a new bike, the loan company probably requires you to have collision coverage. Why? They consider the bike to be collateral. Until you pay off the loan the bank actually owns the bike. Talk to your loan company to find out if it has this requirement because some loan companies don't use motorcycles as collateral.

If you have a relatively new (read: expensive) bike, it's a good idea to have collision coverage. But if your bike is old and only worth, say $500, it may not be worth buying this type of coverage — especially if you opt for a policy that has a $250 deductible. (The *deductible* is the amount of money you have to kick in before the insurance company pays for the rest. Choosing a higher deductible results in a lower premium payment for you.) After all, who wants to spend $250 to fix a $500 bike?

Saving your bike from other damage: Comprehensive coverage

It's a sad fact that motorcycles are stolen. If you don't take the proper precautions, two or three goons can just lift up your motorcycle, throw it in the back of their pickup truck, and drive off. Oh, and some people find it fun to vandalize other people's transportation. (I cover how to keep your bike from getting stolen in Chapter 16.)

If you want to be able to protect yourself, your bike, and your wallet, be sure to buy *comprehensive coverage* for your bike. This type of coverage pays for your bike if it's stolen, or pays to repair it if it's vandalized or burns up. You'll have to pay a deductible, but if you have a newer bike, this coverage will save you money in the longrun. And don't forget that the amount of the deductible you choose determines the premium you pay.

As with collision coverage, it's up to you to decide whether your motorcycle is worth enough to warrant comprehensive coverage. The newer the bike, the more likely it is that you should buy this insurance. Comprehensive coverage is something that you would get in addition to your liability and collision coverage.

Something to keep in mind for both collision and comprehensive insurance coverage is that the motorcycle owner and the insurance company generally have different ideas about the value of the bike when it comes time to pay on a claim. Generally an insurance company will pay for the value of a stock machine that's the same age as yours. So don't expect to get a new bike if your 5-year-old machine burns up. Similarly, don't expect to get enough money to replace the $800 saddlebags you just installed.

To avoid these types of disputes with the insurance company (when you're already flaming mad), figure out the value of your bike and get it straight with your agent before you go and crash. Check out the later section, "Insuring your custom parts and riding gear," to find out how to get insurance for your custom equipment.

Purchasing Motorcycle-Specific Insurance Coverage

In the previous section, I discuss insurance coverages that apply to cars as well as bikes. But, like the people who ride them, bikes are special, and so they have some special insurance needs. Read on for the important details.

Looking after your passenger

One vital area to pay attention to when dealing with insurance is medical coverage for your passenger, who usually will be a loved one, or at least someone you're fond of. *Passenger liability coverage* (which is called *guest passenger liability* by some insurance companies) is a type of coverage you should seriously consider having. It pays for injuries suffered by your passenger in a crash. There have been plenty of cases where a passenger was seriously injured in a crash and sued the motorcycle operator.

Passenger liability coverage is an area where you need to speak with your insurance agent and understand completely what he or she tells you. Why? Because passenger liability coverage is handled differently by different insurance companies. Some insurance companies offer passenger protection as part of its regular liability coverage. Other companies require that you buy separate passenger coverage. And some companies won't cover a spouse as a passenger, which is a mystery to me (and most motorcyclists). So, be sure to know what your policy covers before you carry any passengers.

Insuring your custom parts and riding gear

So you've bought a nice new cruiser and decided to make it your own by bolting on a lot of chrome parts, giving it a splashy paint job, adding great looking, but very expensive, saddlebags, and opening your wallet to buy new custom wheels at $1,000 a pop. Oh, and don't forget that new $800 leather jacket and great $600 helmet that you're sporting. After you've spent that much money, I'm guessing you'd like to protect your investment. But how do you insure that stuff?

Well, here's the scoop: Most insurance companies offer *optional equipment coverage.* This type of insurance pays for the covered parts or gear if they happen to get stolen or damaged. Ask your agent for details, and then decide whether you want to pay the premium or take the chance of losing your expensive gear through theft or a crash.

Finding coverage for your dirt bike

Because dirt bikes aren't ridden on streets, no insurance is *required* to ride them. Also, if you're injured while riding a dirt bike, your medical coverage will typically cover your injuries (unless you were practicing for, or taking part in, a race or other "speed contest," or the coverage specifically excludes motorcycle-related injuries).

A lot of people believe that their homeowner's insurance will cover the theft of their dirt bike if it's stolen out of their garage. Not true. You need to get separate comprehensive or theft insurance that's designed specifically for the bike. You may be able to get liability insurance for a dirt bike (say, for example, you accidentally run over a hunter while you're cruising through the backcountry), but you definitely can't get collision coverage. After all, it's a motorcycle made for riding in the woods and in the dirt. It's going to get dropped and bounced off trees. Insurance companies know the risks, so talk to your agent and shop around, but don't expect to get much coverage.

Know What Your Medical Insurance Will (and Won't) Cover

Suppose you decided not to get uninsured or underinsured motorist coverage (which I explain earlier in this chapter) because you figured that the healthcare plan offered by your employer or union would pay for your medical care if you're hit by a person who doesn't have enough insurance. Well, that may be true. Or it may not be.

In this section, I clue you in to the potential hassles and pitfalls you may encounter by assuming too much on the part of your health insurance carrier. Read the info in this section and then check your policy.

Read the fine print: Finding out if motorcycle injuries are covered

Discrimination exists against motorcyclists, and the health insurance industry is one place you'll find it. For instance, some healthcare plans offered by employers and unions have *exclusions* that spell out what injuries are excluded from coverage. Sometimes these exclusions include motorcycle-related injuries.

Go right now and check your medical insurance policy. Do you see a section that lists the exclusions? Read it carefully to see if motorcycle-related injuries are covered. Can't figure it out? Ask your human resources director. Each year too many motorcyclists fail to check their policies until after they're seriously hurt in a single-vehicle crash, or they're hit by an uninsured driver. Only then do they find out that their medical care isn't covered. Then these motorcyclists have to pay tens of thousands of dollars out of their own pockets.

Congress passed a law a decade ago that barred health insurance companies from discriminating against motorcyclists, horseback riders, skiers, and others when it comes to covering their medical injuries. Congress made it clear that if someone got hurt riding a motorcycle or taking part in other legal recreational activities, their injuries must be covered.

Well, apparently Congress didn't make its intent clear enough. When federal bureaucrats wrote the rules to carry out the law, they said that health insurance companies must provide health insurance for motorcyclists, but they don't have to pay for motorcycle-related injuries. Motorcycling groups are lobbying Congress to close that loophole, and they have bills introduced in both the U.S. House and U.S. Senate. But until that law changes, you need to know what your health plan does and doesn't cover.

Beware of potential lawsuits and the hassles that come with them

Even if your plan covers motorcycle injuries, your health insurance company may consider itself a *secondary insurer,* meaning that it considers the person who hit you as the one having the primary responsibility for paying your medical bills. So, you may have to sue the person who hit you before your health insurance will start paying any bills.

Lawsuits take a lot of time and aggravation, and if you don't have the money to pay in the meantime, bill collectors may continue to knock at your door during the long process. Avoid the hassle. Get uninsured and underinsured motorist coverage (see the earlier section, "Protecting yourself: Uninsured and underinsured motorist coverage," for details).

Paying the Price for Insurance

You would think (or at least hope) that you could simply walk into the office of an insurance agent, plop down some cash, and walk out with an insurance policy that covers your bike. Well, it isn't that simple. Not all insurance companies insure motorcycles, and some that do charge outrageous rates to discourage motorcyclists from seeking coverage from them.

Even more so than with your car insurance, it pays to shop around when you're looking to insure your bike. Some companies are very motorcycle-friendly and offer a variety of coverages, including optional equipment coverage, at reasonable rates. Others don't really want your business, especially if you're a young rider. These companies charge yearly premiums equal to half the cost of a new bike or more. To avoid overpaying, know exactly what coverages you want, and then go shopping.

How companies determine what you'll pay

A lot of people believe that the cost of motorcycle insurance is high, and it can be, depending on a lot of factors. But remember that insurance companies aren't in the business of insuring your bike; they're in the business of making money. So to decide what rate to charge you, they look at what they've paid in claims for riders your age, on your bike, in your area, with your credit. They throw in plenty of other factors as well. Because of all these different factors, I can't give you specific insurance rates for the type of motorcycle you have or are considering buying.

Rate determination is complex, but some facts can give you a better idea of what you can expect to pay to insure your bike. For instance, you'll likely pay more for insurance if you fall into any of the following categories:

- ✔ **You're a young rider.** Young riders tend to pay much more than older riders because of their lack of riding experience.

- ✔ **You have a bad driving record.** If you don't clean up your driving record, you're likely to pay up to three times more than a rider with a clean record.

- ✔ **You ride a sportbike.** If you prefer sportbikes, you'll probably pay more than a cruiser rider. Why? There's a lot of expensive plastic bodywork on those machines.

- ✔ **You have bad credit.** Surprisingly, at least one motorcycle-friendly insurance company uses credit history to help determine the rates that apply to motorcyclists. The company's research shows that riders with poor credit are more likely to make claims.

So, if you're older, you don't ride a sportbike, and you have a good driving record and excellent credit, congratulations! You'll probably get the lowest rate. Even for you, though, it pays to shop around.

Getting insurance relief by being a savvy shopper

If you're a savvy shopper, you can cut your cost of insurance. For instance, get quotes that include deductibles of $100, $250, $500, or even $1,000. The higher your deductible, the lower your premium.

A high deductible may give you a low insurance premium, but if you total your bike be prepared to shell out your deductible amount to replace your machine. If you don't think you can handle the high deductible if your bike gets smashed up, it may be best to have a lower deductible and pay a higher premium. Sure you'll be spending more money on insurance every month, but if the worst happens and your bike gets totaled, at least you can get another one with little cash outlay.

Some insurers also offer discounts for purchasing all your coverage from them. For example, these companies may offer a nice discount if you insure your home, your car, and your motorcycle with them. And some provide a discount merely for being a member of the American Motorcyclist Association or for passing an approved safety training course. When shopping around for insurance, be sure to ask about any discounts available.

In motorcycle coverage, location is key

Several years ago I did research into the cost of motorcycle insurance around the country for riders of various ages riding different types of machines. The results were surprising. For example, a 19-year-old man with a new sportbike in Los Angeles could expect to pay more than $14,000 per year for liability, collision, comprehensive, and uninsured motorist coverage from one company. The minimum coverage required by law would be almost $700. In Indianapolis, on the other hand, that same rider could get _full coverage_ (liability, collision, comprehensive, and uninsured motorist coverage) for less than $1,300 from a different company. The state-required minimum from the same company was under $200.

In contrast, a 45-year-old male riding a big touring bike could get full coverage for as low as $810 in Los Angeles, and the state-required minimum coverage would cost him just $58. In Indianapolis, that same rider could get full coverage for $188 and the state-required minimum for $23.

Now compare those rates to a 36-year-old female rider on a big cruiser. She could get full coverage for as low as $900 in Los Angeles, with the state minimum coverage costing just $82. In Indianapolis, that rider would pay just $207 for full coverage and $23 for the state minimum.

So where you live really has a lot to do with determining your insurance premiums. And so do all those other factors, of course. Before buying a new bike, shop around for insurance. You may find that your dream bike has to remain just that, a dream, at least for a while because the insurance premiums would be more than you can afford.

Chapter 11

Keeping Your Bike in Tiptop Shape

- -

In This Chapter

▶ Surveying the tools you need

▶ Doing routine maintenance work yourself

▶ Allowing someone else to do the work

▶ Prepping your bike for winter storage and spring riding

- -

*U*nlike most car drivers and their cars, many motorcyclists love everything about motorcycling and their motorcycles. Not only do they love riding them, talking about them, and staring at them, but they also love working on them. And you don't need to be a master mechanic to have fun working on your bike. You just need some basic tools and a good service manual. Motorcyclists assume that all their compatriots do their own routine maintenance, and few expect anyone to really do more, so just a little knowledge can get you a lot of respect in the motorcycling world.

People will still respect you even if decide you'd rather take your bike to the shop for maintenance work. After all, what matters in the motorcycling world is that you ride a motorcycle, not that you work on one. However, you'll most definitely lose respect if you try to tackle mechanical jobs that you can't handle. You'll then find yourself having to go to a shop anyway, but this time, they'll be fixing what you messed up.

Although today's motorcycles are complex machines that take a skilled mechanic to cure such things as electrical problems, you can still master the routine work the bike requires. Mastering the routine work, such as changing the oil, lubing the chain, and changing the brake pads, can pay off not only in keeping your bike running at its best but also in saving money that you otherwise would have to fork over to a motorcycle mechanic.

If you're feeling overwhelmed because you don't have a handy bone in your body, don't worry. This chapter gives you a handle on the basic tools that you need to maintain your motorcycle and some of the tools that are available if you want to try to do some more advanced work. This chapter also tells you when it may be a good idea to pay someone else to do work on your bike rather than do it yourself (even if you feel qualified to do it). In fact, if you can afford it, go ahead and pay someone else to do the work even if you can do it yourself. This helps keep the motorcycling industry thriving. Finally, in this chapter you get guidance on how to prepare your machine for long winter storage and how to get it ready to go for the riding season, which starts in the spring.

Toolin' Around: Having the Right Tools for the Job

You don't need to get buckets of tools to perform routine maintenance on your motorcycle — a few tools will do the trick (provided they're the right ones). But you may find yourself acquiring more and more tools as your skill level increases and you tackle tougher jobs. Whether you plan to stick with basic maintenance or tackle tougher jobs, it's always best to have a good mix of tools so that you have one within reach no matter what nut or bolt you want to separate from your bike.

Be sure to get good quality tools. It doesn't do you much good to get cheap ones that don't fit nuts and bolts well or that break, forcing you to head back to the store to shell out more money. It's also best to get screwdrivers with non-slip grips, because your hands will get sweaty and even oily. And while smooth, chrome wrenches aren't a necessity, but they sure feel good when you hold them. Finally, remember not to use American wrenches on metric bolts — they don't fit, and you'll just round off the head of the bolt.

Generally, you want tools that have some weight to them when you hold them. Tools with lifetime guarantees, such as Craftsman available from Sears, are always a good bet because if they break you can get them replaced for free. I have seen sockets crack trying to get off swingarm nuts.

The following sections highlight the basic tools you definitely need for routine maintenance. I also throw in some advanced tools that you may want depending on how much maintenance you plan to do yourself.

Taking stock of the basic tools

If you plan to do any routine maintenance on your bike, you want to make sure that you're prepared with the right tools, which you can buy just about anywhere: Sears, hardware stores, and auto parts stores. The following list outlines the basic tools that you need and some specifics about each:

✔ **Screwdrivers:** A motorcyclist should have both flathead and Phillips screwdrivers. Screwdrivers with magnetized heads are best. And you want to have a variety of sizes so that you're sure to have the right size for the job. The screwdrivers should fit into the slots of your fasteners snugly; otherwise, you could end up wrecking the head of the bolt that you're trying to loosen. In that case, you'll have to resort to a drill to get the bolt out.

Get at least one flathead and Phillips screwdriver in the following sizes: No. 1, No. 2, and No. 3. So you should start out with at least six screwdrivers. Besides getting a variety of sizes in the heads of screwdrivers, you also want a variety of lengths. Motorcycles are pretty compact machines, and some of the bolts that you need to loosen may be in tight, hard-to-reach places. So you're sure to need short screwdrivers as well as long ones.

✔ **Wrenches:** Combination wrenches (see Figure 11-1), which have an open end and a boxed (or closed) end, are a must. Make sure you buy these wrenches in metric sizes if your machine uses metric nuts and bolts (and most do). If you ride an American Harley-Davidson, of course, then you will need American, or SAE, tools. If you get sizes 6 through 22 (in metric sizes) you should be able to loosen and tighten just about every nut and bolt on your bike. In American, start with a set of combination wrenches that are ¼-, ⅜-, ⁷⁄₁₆-, ½-, and ⁹⁄₁₆-inch.

Figure 11-1:
Combination
wrenches.

A good set of Allen wrenches, or hex keys, is also important, because a lot of bikes now use Allen screws or bolts to hold on the bodywork (and in some other places). It's best to get T-handle Allen wrenches (see Figure 11-2) because they give you the leverage you need to apply torque to loosen stubborn bolts. Plus, the L-shaped Allen wrenches sometimes leave little space when you need to put the short end into the bolt so you can put leverage on the long end. The result? You can end up gouging your expensive plastic bodywork.

In metric sizes, get an 8mm, 10mm, 12mm, 13mm, 14mm, 17mm, and 19mm. For American, start with ⁵⁄₃₂-, ³⁄₁₆-, ¼-, and ⁵⁄₁₆-inch. You will need a metric 10mm for your battery bolts on your American bike. You may also need some Torx wrenches for your machine. Start with a T25, a T27, and a T40.

✔ **Ratchets and a socket set:** You'll need some ratchets and a good socket set, again ranging in metric size from 6 through 22 or 24. It's best to get large and small ratchets as well as one or two that pivot at the head so you can get into hard-to-reach places. For American bikes, get sockets in sizes ⅜-, ⁷⁄₁₆-, ½-, ⁹⁄₁₆-, ⅝-, ¹¹⁄₁₆-, and ¾-inch. It's also a good idea to have a ¼-inch ratchet drive as well as a ⅜-inch drive. You'll find that bigger sockets are made for a ⅜-inch drive ratchet. Also, if you get a ¼-inch ratchet and a ⅜-inch ratchet, you know that your ratchet will fit any socket you buy.

You should also get a couple extension bars for your ratchet, such as a 5-inch and a 10-inch for those hard-to-reach places. T-handle sockets aren't critical, but they're definitely fun to have. And like T-handle Allen wrenches, they look cool.

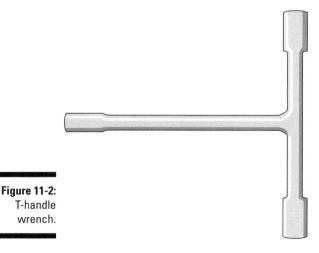

Figure 11-2:
T-handle
wrench.

✔ **Torque wrench:** A good torque wrench is essential. Your owner's or service manual will give the torque specs for all the critical fasteners on your machine. A torque wrench that measures 10 to 80 foot pounds is sufficient for a motorcycle.

Be sure to torque your fasteners back to the manufacturer's specifications after you loosen them. The last thing you want is your brake caliper falling off because you failed to torque the bolts holding them on and they vibrated loose as you happily cruised down the highway at 65 mph.

✔ **Other miscellaneous tools:** Pliers, vise grips, funnels, a spark plug wrench, an oil filter wrench, a battery charger, and a chain breaker (for when you need to replace your drive chain; see Figure 11-3) are also useful. And don't forget a tire-pressure gauge. The cheap, pencil kind work just fine.

When you work on your motorcycle at home in your garage, use the tools that are in the toolkit on your bike. That way you know that if you break down alongside the road, you have the tools you need to fix the problem. While working on your bike at home, you may find that the toolkit doesn't include a proper-sized wrench or screwdriver. In that case, just add one to the kit.

Figure 11-3:
A chain
breaker.

Adding advanced tools to your collection

Specialized tools for motorcycles are available, but I warn you that they can be quite pricey. Do you need them? That's up to you to decide. It depends on how much work you choose to do on your bike. If you like to work with your hands and get a little greasy, you may want to look into investing in these more advanced tools. However, if you prefer to leave the tougher stuff to the pro mechanics at the dealership, feel free to skip this section.

When you do feel ready to buy some of the advanced tools, make sure you weigh the cost of the tool against the number of times you expect to use it, especially if it's a tool that only works on one model of motorcycle. For instance, if you don't plan to ever take the wheels off your bike, there's no need for you to buy a stand or lift. And if you don't plan to change your own tires, and few motorcyclists do on streetbikes, you don't need to buy a tire-changing rig.

Here are some of the advanced tools you may want to purchase:

- ✔ **Front-end and rear-end stands (shown in Figure 11-4):** Sooner or later your motorcycle's tires will wear out. When that happens, the best thing to do is to remove your wheels, take them to a motorcycle shop, and let the mechanics put on new tires. In fact, a lot of dealers offer free installation if you buy the tires from them and bring in your rims. So, when you're in the market for new tires, you're bound to need front-end and rear-end stands.

  These stands lift up the front and rear of your bike. After your bike is raised, you just slide out the axles and the wheels come off. (Don't forget to loosen the big axle nuts *before* you lift the bike. Otherwise, when you put your big ol' wrench on that big axle nut and yank on the wrench to loosen the nut the wheel will spin.) Check out the later section, "Changing your tires," for more info. Front-end and rear-end stands are also useful for when you need to change your brake pads, because the wheels may have to come off to do that.

Figure 11-4:
Front- and
rear-end
stands.

These stands are particularly popular for use on sportbikes that lack centerstands. They attach to your bike and then lever the bike up into a stable position. If you have a cruiser, you may not be able to find stands that will work for your bike. In that case, you need to get a motorcycle jack, which works like a car jack but is designed to lift a motorcycle.

✔ **Lift:** If you can afford it, you may want to consider investing in a full-length motorcycle lift for when you tinker with your bike. A lift (shown in Figure 11-5) makes it a lot easier to get to the stuff that's low and under your bike.

Figure 11-5:
A full-bike
lift.

Saving Some Bucks by Maintaining Your Own Bike

All motorcycles have the same basic routine maintenance needs: oil changes, brake fluid and brake pad changes, chain and battery maintenance, and air filter changes or cleanings. While this is routine stuff, it's also critical because a failure in one of these areas could leave you stranded on the road or could be dangerous to you, the rider.

When armed with the proper tools, a motorcyclist can do all the routine maintenance a motorcycle needs. Not only is maintaining a bike fun, but with shop prices around $60 an hour or more, it also can save some big money. Although some of the maintenance may seem intimidating at first, after you do it a couple of times it will be easy. So don't count yourself out yet. Just take your time, and closely follow the instructions in this section and in your owner's manual and service manual.

Changing fluids

Imagine the innards of your motorcycle engine. There are an awful lot of metal parts scraping together. If you want those parts to last, they must be bathed in oil. Without oil, your motor will turn into a melted heap of fused parts in no time. Even with oil, there's a chance that there are metal shavings being pushed around that have come off the parts that are scraping together. So, frequent oil changes are vital for keeping your motor happy.

While engine oil is the most critical fluid that needs to be changed on a motorcycle, there are other fluids that need attention as well. Most motorcyclists don't change those fluids as often as they should. Fork oil, which helps your front suspension work, is probably the most ignored fluid. But brake fluid ranks right up there. Failure to change those fluids won't lead to disaster like failing to change your motor oil, which can't protect your engine when it is degraded, but it's still important to change them to keep your front suspension and brakes working their best.

Changing the engine oil is an easy task and takes about half an hour. Changing fork oil, on the other hand, is very difficult and may require special tools, so it's best left to professionals. Changing brake fluid isn't very difficult but it's time-consuming, so expect to spend a couple hours at that chore. Or, to play it safe, have it done by professionals. After all, brakes are critical for safety and you want it done right. There's no shame in having a pro do the work; after all, safety should be your primary concern.

Motor oil

Probably the most common routine maintenance done by motorcyclists is the oil change. Changing your bike's oil is relatively easy to do. And it's also empowering: You feel good knowing that you've removed any metal shavings that may be floating around in the old oil when you drain it and that your bike has brand new oil to lubricate its internals.

To change your oil, follow these steps (however, be sure to refer to your owner's or service manual to ensure you do it right):

1. **Park your bike on a flat surface on the side stand, with the bike in gear so that there's no chance you'll bump it and knock it off the stand.**

2. **Loosen the drain plug under the motor with a socket wrench.**

   Don't remove the drain plug. You want it to keep the oil in the motor for now. Loosen it with a wrench and then with your fingers until a little oil starts coming out, and then tighten the bolt up hand tight. You loosen it now, so that you don't have to struggle with it later when the motor is hot. You don't want to burn yourself.

3. **Start your motorcycle.**

   Let the bike run for three to five minutes to heat up the oil and make it thinner. That way, the oil will drain well.

4. **Put an oil catch container under your motorcycle.**

   Make sure that the container you choose is big enough to hold all the oil that will drain out of the bike. Normally, a bike will hold four or five quarts.

5. **Carefully reach under the bike, with a gloved hand, and twist off the drain plug.**

   If you're unlucky, you'll drop the plug into the catch basin as hot oil comes streaming out of your bike. In that case, just fish it out after all the oil drains out of the bike.

   Be careful during this step because the motor is hot. And note that no matter how careful you are, you probably will get some hot oil on your hand. To avoid burns, wear a work glove.

6. **Remove the oil filler cap and tilt the bike straight up off its sidestand so that all the oil can flow out into the catch basin.**

   Tilting the bike upright helps ensure you get all of the oil possible out of the motor. If you leave the bike tilted on its sidestand, oil can remain on the side away from the drain hole.

7. **Remove the old oil filter and install a new one.**

   There will be a gasket on the old filter, so make sure you get that off the bike as well. It usually comes off with the old filter, but sometimes it sticks to the motor.

   When installing the new filter, rub new motor oil on the gasket on the new filter, tighten the filter by hand, and then use an oil filter wrench to tighten it to the bike manufacturer's recommendation, which is usually two and a half more turns.

   It's best to buy an oil filter wrench from a dealership specifically for your bike rather than to try to use a universal one, or even one made for cars. Motorcycle oil filters are usually shoehorned into pretty tight spaces so they're a lot easier to get on and off with wrenches made specifically for them.

8. **Reinstall the drain plug and torque it to the manufacturer's recommendation.**

   Making sure the drain plug is tight is critical because if the drain plug isn't tight enough it could vibrate loose while you're riding down the road, spewing an oily mess onto your rear tire, and the road. That could be big, big trouble.

9. **Using a funnel, pour in the proper amount of oil and reinstall the oil filler cap.**

   You can determine how much oil to add to the bike by consulting your owner's or service manual. Bikes usually hold four or five quarts.

10. **Start up the bike, and look for leaking oil at the drain plug and oil filter.**

    If you discover any leaks, shut off the bike, tighten the part where the leak is, and start the bike again.

Congratulations! Now you're good for another 3,000 to 5,000 miles or more, depending on what your owner's or service manual says.

Radiator fluid

If your bike is water-cooled, you'll have to change the radiator fluid at intervals specified by your owner's or service manual. Usually bikes require a radiator fluid change every two years. This task really isn't that difficult. However, it may be time-consuming to remove the bodywork to get to the radiator. Expect to spend an hour doing this work.

To change the radiator fluid, follow these steps:

1. **Park the motorcycle on a flat surface and put it on the sidestand with the bike in gear.**

   You want the bike in gear so that if you accidentally bump the bike it won't roll off the sidestand and tip over.

Spend now to save later

Do you need to use expensive motorcycle-specific motor oil in your bike, or can you use less-expensive car oil? Opt for motorcycle oil. Really, it's only a couple of bucks more, and it contains more anti-wear additives than car oil; plus it's better for the operation of your clutch, which is bathed in the oil. The question also comes up whether to use petroleum-based or synthetic motor oil. Synthetic motor oil costs more but is supposed to be better for your machine. There's no way for me to prove that, but I always put synthetic motor oil in my bikes. Finally, some motorcyclists may tell you that you can save a few bucks by finding a car oil filter that will fit your motorcycle. Don't take the chance to save a few bucks; buy an oil filter made specifically for your motorcycle. Bottom line: Spending a few extra dollars upfront saves you money in the long run by ensuring a better-running bike.

2. **Remove the radiator drain plug and drain the fluid into a container. Tilt the bike upright to get all the fluid out.**

   Sometimes the lowest point on the radiator is actually a bottom hose. You can unclamp that to drain the radiator instead of using the drain plug, and then you don't need to tilt the bike upright.

3. **Fill the radiator with distilled water. After filling the radiator with water, run the bike for two or three minutes to heat it up, and then drain it again.**

   A lot of motorcyclists skip this step, and you can too, unless you're the type of person who wants to be thorough.

   Don't remove the radiator fill cap because you could get scalded.

4. **Refill the radiator with the proper mix of radiator fluid and distilled water, usually 50/50.**

   You can determine the proper mix of fluids by consulting your owner's or service manual. If your radiator has an expansion tank, put the proper mix of radiator fluid and distilled water in there so that it's between the two level lines marked on the tank. The expansion tank is just like the one on your car, with the same two lines.

5. **Ride the bike around for about 10 minutes and then park it in your garage to let it cool off.**

   After it's cool, check the fluid level in the radiator again and top it off, if necessary.

Fork oil

You should replace your fork oil on the schedule recommended by the bike's manufacturer, normally every two years. (*Fork oil* has nothing to do with your kitchen utensils. It's a special oil that goes in your forks to help the suspension work. When fork oil wears out, the internals of your forks can suffer more wear, and your suspension may feel mushy.)

Many motorcyclists never replace their bike's fork oil, but it really is worth it to keep your suspension in tiptop shape. Because this task can be difficult to do without the correct tools, it's best left to the professionals. However, if you want to tackle the job, expect to spend a couple of hours doing it. And have your service manual handy to help guide you through the steps.

Know what kind of forks you have: a *damping-rod fork* that uses the fork oil for *damping* (controlling how quickly a fork moves up and down) or a more modern *cartridge fork,* which has a cartridge at the bottom of the fork tube to help control damping. The two types of forks require two slightly different techniques for changing the fork oil. Plus, if you have telescopic forks or upside-down forks, you may need to do things differently.

Maintaining the brakes

Brakes are obviously a critical component of any motorcycle, yet they're often neglected by motorcyclists. In order to maintain your brakes properly, you need to change the brake pads and the brake fluid regularly. This section gives you the lowdown.

Changing the brake pads

Changing your brake pads isn't terribly difficult; it generally takes about half an hour. To change them, you just have to follow these easy steps:

1. **Remove the wheel.**

   If you can just unbolt the caliper and pull it away from the brake disc without removing the wheel, that's great.

2. **Remove the pads from the caliper.**

   Some brake pads are held in the caliper with a tension wire that acts as a spring. If your caliper is like this, note the position of the spring before you remove it so that you put it back the correct way. The pads also may have an anti-squeal metal backing. Make sure that comes out with the pad.

3. **Install your new pads.**

   If your caliper has springs to hold the pads, make sure you reinstall those also.

4. **Reinstall the caliper.**

   The only difficult part of changing your brake pads is getting the pads back into the caliper. After all, the new pads will be thicker than the ones you removed, so you'll have to carefully force the new pads back into the caliper to allow enough room for your disc to fit in the caliper. Using a large flathead screwdriver is one way to force the pads into the caliper to create room for the disc.

5. **Reinstall the wheel if you removed it.**

If you wait too long to change your brake pads, the backing to the pads, which is metal, will cut into your brake disc, cutting grooves into it and maybe even destroying it if you let that go on too long.

Changing the brake fluid

Motorcyclists are generally good about changing the brake pads, but many aren't so good at regularly changing the disc brake fluid, which can absorb water over time and become less effective. How will you know? The brakes will feel mushy.

Changing the fluid takes about an hour. Depending on the location of the calipers and how much room you have to reach the front brake lever and rear brake pedal on your bike, changing the brake fluid can require two people.

To change your brake fluid, follow these instructions:

1. **Park your bike on a flat surface, put it in gear, and turn the handlebars so that the front brake master cylinder on the handlebar is as upright as possible.**

   If you need the master cylinder to be even more upright, loosen the bolts holding it to the handlebar and twist it; then snug up the bolts.

2. **Prepare for bleeding the caliper that you're working on.**

   Each brake caliper has a fitting that unscrews to allow brake fluid out. Attach a correct-sized tube to that fitting with the tube running down into a plastic container.

3. **Clean the cap on the master cylinder with soap and water. After removing the cap from the brake-fluid master-cylinder reservoir, pull in the front brake lever (or depress the rear brake lever, depending on which brake you're working on) and loosen the fitting on the brake caliper to allow fluid to bleed out. Then snug up the fitting and release the lever.**

   Don't let the fluid in the reservoir drain down very far. If you do, you'll get air in your system, which results in a spongy feel to the brakes. Also, you want to be sure you snug up the fitting before you release the lever because, otherwise, it will suck air into your system. You want to clean the master-cylinder cap before removing it because you don't want any dirt to fall into the reservoir and contaminate the brake fluid.

   Keep repeating this process of pulling or depressing the lever, loosening the caliper fitting to let fluid out, tightening the fitting, and releasing the lever, keeping the master-cylinder reservoir topped off with fresh brake fluid, until you're confident that all the old brake fluid has been replaced with new fluid.

4. **Replace the brake reservoir cap, reposition your front brake master cylinder if you moved it, and then pump the brake lever to rebuild the pressure in the system.**

   Failure to rebuild the pressure in your brake system will result in having no brakes the first time you need them. Also, dispose of any leftover brake fluid. Brake fluid absorbs water, so you don't want to take the chance that the fluid will get contaminated before you need it again, which will be in a year or two. Finally, if your brakes feel mushy or spongy after you change the fluid, it means you got air in the system and must change the fluid again.

Taking care of the chain

Most motorcycles today transfer power from the motor to the rear wheel with a chain, and that chain requires a bit of maintenance. However, more and more cruisers are being outfitted with a maintenance-free belt to transfer the power. Other motorcycles are equipped with a shaft to transfer the power, which also requires little attention. If you do have a shaft or chain, here's the stuff that you have to take care of: lubing and tightening the chain, and changing the shaft oil at intervals and levels recommended by the motor-cycle manufacturer. I explain each of these in the following sections.

Keeping your chain lubricated

A motorcycle chain, belt, or shaft undergoes tremendous forces as it trans-fers power from the motor to the rear wheel. On a typical motorcycle, this power is transferred from the *front sprocket,* which is attached to the motor, to the *rear sprocket,* which is attached to the rear wheel, by a chain. To stay in good shape, the chain must have lubrication between the links and must be properly adjusted. Also note that when your chain wears out — that is, it stretches to a point where it is too loose and can't be used anymore — your sprockets are worn out also. Also, be sure to get a new front and rear sprocket when you get a new chain.

Lubing a chain is a simple process. Follow these quick and easy steps:

1. **Spray the lube along the top of the sideplates of the chain.**

   It's good to have a flat piece of cardboard under the chain when you do this because chain lube is sticky, messy, and hard to clean up off your garage floor.

2. **Roll the bike forward to lube more of the chain until you have lubed the entire chain.**

   You don't need to lube the rolling pins that roll on the sprockets.

3. **After the chain is lubed, wipe off the excess lube with a rag.**

   You'll end up throwing this rag away because it will be a gooey mess.

Special chain lubes that are sold in motorcycle dealerships are designed to penetrate into the pins and rollers of the chain to keep them operating smoothly. Use a motorcycle chain lube, not motor oil or something else. *Tip:* These lubes are tacky so that they cling to the chain, but because they're tacky, you need to take care when applying them. If you don't wipe down a chain thoroughly after you lube it, you'll get chain lube all over your rear rim, which can take a little bit of effort to remove.

No matter how good the idea sounds, do not, under any circumstances, start the bike, lift the rear wheel, and put the bike into gear in order to spin the rear wheel and chain to lube the chain. You can get seriously hurt if your hand or even a piece of clothing gets caught between the chain and the sprocket. Using this technique is an easy way to lose a finger, all your fingers on one hand, or even your whole hand.

Tightening your chain

You also need to periodically tighten your bike's chain because it stretches with use. To do this, follow these steps:

1. **Loosen the chain adjusters on the end of the *swingarm,* which holds the rear wheel axle, and loosen the axle nut; then lift the rear of the bike using a rear-wheel stand.**

   If your bike has a centerstand, that would lift the rear wheel off the ground also.

2. **Adjust the locknuts on the chain adjusters until marks on the adjusters line up with marks on the swingarm.**

   For example, if one side is set on the third mark from the rear, the other side should be also.

3. **Set the bike down, and then measure the chain play at the middle of the chain, along the bottom, and between the front sprocket and the rear sprocket.**

   When the chain is tightened appropriately, you should see about three-quarters of an inch to an inch of play. Check your owner's manual or service manual for direction.

4. **Tighten the chain adjuster locknuts and the axle nut to your bike manufacturer's torque specs as found in your owner's or service manual.**

Changing your shaft oil

If your motorcycle has a shaft drive — that is, the power is transferred from the motor to the rear with a shaft — you'll need to check your shaft oil level and change it at intervals specified in your owner's manual. For example, your manual may tell you to check it at 8,000 miles and change it at 15,000 miles or 24,000 miles.

Changing the shaft oil is simple. Just follow these steps:

1. **Ride the bike around to heat up the oil already in the bike.**

   This step isn't absolutely necessary but the oil will drain out better if it is heated up.

2. **Put the bike on the centerstand, or put a block of wood under the centerstand so that the bike is straight up. Then take a rag and clean around the filler cap and the drain plug on the shaft housing at the rear wheel.**

   You want the bike upright so all the oil drains out. And you want to clean around the filler cap and drain plug so that no dirt gets into your new oil.

3. **Place a container to catch the oil under the shaft housing, and then remove the filler cap and drain plug to drain the oil.**

   You won't have much oil in there so you don't need a big catch basin. In fact, you may only have about 4 or 5 ounces of oil involved. You can dispose of this oil like you would your transmission oil — take it to be recycled. It's okay to mix the oils.

4. **Inspect your drain plug gasket for any cuts.**

   If the drain plug gasket is damaged, replace it. It's a good idea to replace it anyway for peace of mind so that you don't develop a leak.

5. **Reinstall the drain plug gasket and drain plug. Torque to the manufacturer's specs. Use a funnel to pour in the proper type and amount of hypoid gear oil.**

   Your owner's manual will specify the proper type — that is, the weight of the gear oil you need — and the proper amount. You can get what you need at a motorcycle dealership. The proper torque should also be in your owner's manual. If not, it's in your service manual, if you bought one.

6. **Replace the filler cap and go for a short ride. When you return home, check for leaks.**

   If you have a leak it's probably because of a bad gasket.

Maintaining the battery

Getting stranded on a motorcycle because of a dead battery isn't much fun. After all, you can't just ask some guy in a car to jump your battery for you. So a routine inspection of the battery every month will help keep you from being stranded.

Here are the things to check when inspecting your battery:

✔ **The electrolyte level:** Make sure the electrolyte level is between the upper and lower line markers on the side of the battery. If it's low, bring it up to the proper level with distilled water.

- ✔ **The cables and connections:** Make sure these parts aren't damaged or corroded. Look for cuts or splits in the insulation on the wires, and white, powdery corrosion at the connections. You can spray the connectors with a special electrical cleaner available at auto parts stores to clean them, or use a tiny piece of rolled-up fine-grain sandpaper.

- ✔ **The terminals:** Check these to be sure they aren't corroded. If they are, wipe them off with an old toothbrush or some fine-grain sandpaper.

- ✔ **The casing:** When inspecting your battery casing, be on the lookout for cracks. If there's a crack in the case, get a new battery.

- ✔ **The battery vent tube:** Make sure this tube isn't kinked. You should be able to thread the vent tube through the bike almost straight down so it exits under the bike.

You can clean the top of the battery (or the entire battery for that matter) with a solution of water and baking soda. You want the battery clean so that when you take the battery filler caps off to top off the electrolyte with distilled water you don't get any corrosion or dirt in the battery, which would make it lose its charge faster. If you haven't ridden the bike in a couple of weeks, be sure to charge the battery. Get a charger made specifically for a motorcycle battery — that is, a 1-to-2 amp charger — and then charge the battery for 8 hours or so. You should charge the battery once a month when in storage.

Cleaning the air filter

A clean air filter is critical for the operation of your motorcycle. You need good air flow for your motor to work properly, and you don't want any dirt getting past your filter into your motor, where it can do some expensive damage. Fortunately, you don't need to inspect the air filter very often. You can probably inspect it every six months or every year, depending on how dusty your riding conditions are.

Unfortunately, getting to the air filter can be a hassle on some motorcycles. In fact, sometimes it requires removal of the gas tank. Some filters are located under the seat and some are accessed on the side of the machine. Check your owner's manual for instructions on how to remove and reinstall your air filter.

After you remove your air filter, you have two options:

- ✔ **Clean your filter:** If you have a paper filter, you can blow compressed air through it from the inside to clean it. If you have a foam-and-mesh filter, you have to clean it with dish soap or another cleaning solution, let it dry, and then oil it with air filter oil, which is available at your local motorcycle dealer. When visiting the dealer, you can also pick up a special cleaning solution for your air filter if you want.

> ✔ **Buy a new filter:** All air filters are shaped differently, so be sure you buy one that's made specifically for your machine. Ask your motorcycle dealership parts department for the correct one. A new stock paper filter will cost about $25. A wire-and-mesh air cleaner will cost double that amount.

Which is better, paper or mesh? If you ride in really dusty conditions, it's better to get a mesh filter you can clean frequently. Otherwise, you can use a stock filter and may need to only change it every three or four years.

Changing your tires

Sometimes what seems like a simple job isn't so simple. Take changing a tire, for example. If you prefer to change your own tires you can, but be aware that it can be a real chore. It may also involve expensive tools. On the other hand, changing your bike's tires can empower you and truly connect you to your bike and the whole experience.

Removing the wheels

Removing your bike's wheels, which is the first step in changing your tires, is a relatively easy task unless you have a big touring rig like a Honda Gold Wing. This type of bike is very heavy and difficult to get off the ground. And because of the weight, it's difficult to keep steady off the ground.

To change your bike's front tire, follow these steps:

1. **Loosen the axle nut.**

   You must do this while the tire is still on the ground. If you have the tire up in the air by lifting the front end of the bike with a stand, or even the centerstand if your bike has one, the wheel will just spin as you try to loosen the axle nut.

2. **Loosen the bolts on the bottom of the fork leg.**

   You don't need to take the bolts out, but you do need to loosen them so that they almost come out.

3. **Lift the front end of the bike up.**

   It's best to use a front-end stand to lift the front end of the bike off the floor so that you have enough room to drop the wheel down, allowing the brake discs to come out of the brake calipers. Make sure the bike is held up securely by the stand. It should be stable, not wobbly.

4. **Take the axle nut off, hold onto the wheel, and pull the axle out from the fork legs and the wheel.**

It's best to hold the wheel rim at the top instead of putting your hand under the wheel because if you aren't strong enough to hold the wheel up with one arm you'll smash your hand when the wheel hits the floor.

When you're ready, you can install the front wheel by reversing the procedure. It's a good idea to wipe the old grease off the axle and then apply a coat of high-temperature grease before reinstalling the axle to keep your wheel turning smoothly. Also, you may need to pry apart the brake pads in the calipers with a big flathead screwdriver to make room for the brake discs to slide in. Finally, pump the brake lever a few times to make sure you have the proper pressure in the brake lines.

Removing the rear wheel of a bike is much like removing the front, with a couple additional steps:

1. **Take the cotter pin out of the axle that keeps the axle nut from turning and then loosen the axle nut.**

   You don't necessarily have to do this before lifting the rear of the bike off the ground, but you may as well do so to keep your technique for changing the front and rear wheels as similar as possible.

2. **Loosen the chain adjusters on the swingarm.**

   To do this, just loosen the bolts on the chain adjusters.

3. **Lift the rear of the bike up using a rear-end stand or a jack.**

   Make sure the rear end is held up firmly. The bike should be stable.

4. **Hold the rear wheel firmly and pull the axle out.**

   The rear wheel is big and heavy, so be sure you have a firm grip on the wheel.

5. **Push the rear wheel toward the front of the bike so that you have a lot of slack in the chain. Pull the chain off the rear sprocket and move it to the side.**

   You may be able to hang the chain on the end of the swingarm.

6. **Drop the rear wheel out of the swingarm.**

When you're ready, you can install the rear wheel by reversing the procedure. Be sure to put new grease on the axle. And remember that you may need to pry apart the brake pads in the caliper to accommodate the brake disc. Be sure to pump the rear brake lever a few times to make sure you have pressure in the brake.

Taking the old tires off and putting on new ones

You can try to get your tires off the rims with tire irons, but that's tough with big tires with short sidewalls. You also can buy a tire-changing rig, but they're expensive (hundreds of dollars) and would take up a lot of room in your garage. And, really, you probably won't be changing your tires that often to warrant the purchase. But if you do want to change your own tires, you'll need a bead breaker that costs about $75, a pair of tire irons that would run you about $30 each, a wheel balancer for about $200, a valve core tool (for removing the valve core) for $4, a wheel crate for $10, and wheel weights for about $15. You also need a spray bottle with a solution of warm water and some dishwashing liquid.

If you don't have a front-end or rear-wheel stand, it really isn't a good idea to improvise a way to lift your bike up when removing a tire. Sure, you could try using a car jack, but think of the damage to the bike if it slips off the jack, especially after you have the front or rear wheel off. Instead, take the bike to a dealership to have the tire changed.

After you have your wheel off the bike, follow these steps to change the tire:

1. **Using your valve core tool, take out the valve core where you fill the tire with air.**

   This step will allow all the air to get out of the tire.

2. **Place the wheel sideways on your wheel crate.**

   Make sure the brake disc isn't touching the crate because discs bend easily and you'll be putting pressure on the wheel in the next step.

3. **Use your bead breaker to push the bead of the tire down away from the rim.**

   You need to move in small steps all the way around the tire to break the entire bead from the rim. Be careful that you don't mar your rim with the bead breaker during this process.

4. **Flip the wheel over and break the bead on the other side.**

5. **Take your spray bottle with the mixture of water and dishwashing liquid and spray the rim where you just broke the bead as well as the tire bead.**

   Spraying in this way will make it a lot easier to get the tire off the rim. Don't use a spray lubricant or any other liquid that won't dry away.

6. **Wedge a tire iron between the tire and the rim, and then lift the tire bead. Use a second tire iron to lever the bead up over the rim on the left and right sides of your first tire iron. Continue around the entire rim.**

   You can use *rim protectors* to protect your rim from tire iron damage when you lever the bead of the tire up over the rim. Or you could use a little strip of duct tape.

7. **Repeat to get the second bead off the rim.**

8. **Install a new tire by reversing the process.**

   After the tire is on the rim, reinstall the valve stem core and inflate the tire. The tire will make a loud pop sound as each bead seats. If it doesn't, deflate the tire and try again.

9. **Balance the new wheel.**

   To balance a wheel, put the wheel on your tire balancer and put a bit of weight on the rim on the opposite side of the valve stem. Then give the wheel a little spin. Let the wheel stop, and then spin it again.

   If the weight is too heavy, it will be at the bottom when the tire stops spinning. If that's the case, add less weight. If the weight is too light, the heaviest part of the wheel will always wind up at the bottom. The key is to get the right amount of weight on the wheel so that you can move the tire one-quarter turn and stop it in place four times and the wheel will stay in place each time.

Hiring a Pro to Do the Work

If you can do some of the minor motorcycle maintenance work yourself (see the section, "Saving Some Bucks by Maintaining Your Own Bike," earlier in this chapter), you can save some money. However, you really need a mechanic for some of the more difficult tasks. For example, if you have a big cruiser or touring bike and you can't find a front-end or rear-end stand that will work for changing the tires, you'll likely want a mechanic to do the entire tire-changing job.

Another area where you'll probably want to pay a dealer to do the work is when dealing with suspension components. Replacing the fork oil can be a tough job even with the proper tools, so it's best left to the pros. And while you're having the front fork oil changed, you may as well have your rear shocks rebuilt (if they're actually rebuildable).

In fact, you may decide right off the bat that you aren't mechanically inclined and want to have a shop do all the work, even the routine maintenance. And that's okay. If you're considering hiring a professional mechanic to work on your bike, this section can help. Here you can find info on the pros and cons of using a professional and how you can find a good mechanic.

The pros and cons of using a professional

Just like most decisions in life, if you want to take your bike to a mechanic, you need to weigh the pros and the cons before you make a decision. After all, having the work done in a shop has its clear advantages and disadvantages.

The following are some of the pros of having a mechanic work on your machine:

  ✔ **You know that the work will be done right.** Professional mechanics typically are skilled and can handle all types of work, particularly the more difficult motor work. (**Note:** If your bike needs motor work, I highly recommend that you use a mechanic. Why chance blowing up your motor to save a few bucks?)

  ✔ **You have a guarantee.** A dealership or repair shop will guarantee its work, usually for 30 days.

  ✔ **You have all the service receipts, which is important if you ever decide to sell the bike.** A bike is easier to sell when you can prove to prospective buyers that it was well maintained.

Unfortunately, using a mechanic has some downsides as well. Here they are:

  ✔ **You're at the mercy of the dealer concerning when he can get the work done.** For instance, you may take your bike into a shop and not get it back for a week or two (or even more).

  ✔ **You have to arrange transportation back from the shop while you leave your bike, and then back to the shop to pick up the bike when the work is finished.** You can avoid this if you haul the bike to and from the shop in a truck or trailer.

  ✔ **You're paying for labor costs that you wouldn't pay if you did the work yourself.** With labor costs running $60 to $75 per hour or more, you can save $120 or more in labor cost by doing a 2-hour job yourself. That's why it's cheaper to take just the wheels in to get your tires changed than to take the whole bike in.

Finding a good shop

If you decide that you need to use a mechanic, make sure that you use a reputable one who will take care of your bike and not take advantage of you. So how do you decide which mechanic is best? I suggest you first ask your fellow riders; they can easily tell you who they take their bikes to.

Ask them what kind of work they've had done on their bikes, how much it cost, whether they thought the work was done right and the cost was reasonable, and how long it took to get the work done. Ask if they believe there's a certain mechanic you should ask for by name.

After you have a couple of referrals from friends or fellow riders, make sure you do the following as you make a decision:

✔ **Visit various dealerships.** First, take note of how the staff treats you. Obviously they should be polite, friendly, and easy to deal with, but don't forget that the service people should be very knowledgeable. Try to get a sense of how well the service manager knows your model of motorcycle by chatting about your problem and asking what the problem may be. By now you know a little bit about your machine so you may be able to tell by what the service manager says whether he or she knows about your bike. For example, if you have a fuel-injected machine and the service manager talks about the carbs, that's a red flag.

Also take a look at the service area. See if it looks neat, and then try to get an idea of whether the workers look like they know what they're doing. Do they look methodical, with few wasted movements? Or are they stopping a lot to talk, contemplating, and spending time walking across the shop to get various tools? Time is money — yours.

✔ **Remember that you aren't limited to dealerships that sell the major brands of motorcycles.** A lot of little repair shops out there (that don't sell motorcycles) are just as good, or even better. In fact, if you have an older bike, you may have no choice but to patronize a repair shop. Why? Because a lot of dealerships won't even work on bikes that are 10 years old or older.

✔ **If you're a sportbike rider, you may want to seek out a specialty shop that works only on sportbikes.** These specialty shops know the machines well and can handle the performance enhancements you want. Many times local racers run sportbike repair/performance shops. Ask around at the local racetrack on race day; the racers can steer you to the right people.

✔ **Sometimes you don't get any clear advice from your riding buddies and you just have to take a chance on a shop.** For instance, you may have to go to the closest shop to your house or one you pick out of the telephone book based on its ad. That's fine, too. Based on your first experience with that shop you'll decide whether to go back again, and whether to recommend the shop to friends.

After you find a dealership or shop you like, stick with it even if prices may be cheaper at another place. It's worth it to pay more to patronize a shop where you're comfortable with the work and the people.

Handling Special Maintenance in the Winter and Spring

Hard-core motorcyclists ride year-round, even if they live in the Snowbelt. In Michigan, for example, there's an organized ride that begins each year at midnight on January 1. Now that's dedication to the sport! However, not all motorcyclists like winter riding. And in fact, riding in the winter's icy and snowy conditions may not be the smartest choice for a beginning rider. So in late fall, when temperatures start to take a dive, many motorcyclists tuck their bikes away for the winter. And then, after what seems like forever, they get to pull their bikes out in the spring to begin another riding season.

You can't just park your bike in the winter and then start it up in the spring and expect it to go. Unless you want to deal with some time-consuming and possibly expensive problems in the spring when you try to start your bike, you need to properly prepare it for winter storage.

This section discusses those maintenance steps you need to take to prepare your bike for the winter hibernation and for the riding season in the spring.

Preparing your bike for winter storage

Carefully preparing your motorcycle for winter storage will save you a lot of headaches and expense when spring comes and you want to ride. If you don't take the proper steps, spring will find your carburetors all gummed up and not working and your battery dead.

It's best to store your bike in a garage away from the elements. If you don't have a garage or a buddy who will let you store your bike at his or her place, some dealerships will store your bike in the winter for a monthly fee. You can also use a self-storage business if the company allows vehicles to be stored in the storage units. Some don't. Finally, you can keep the bike outside with a motorcycle cover over it.

To properly store your bike for the winter, you need to follow these steps:

1. **Fill the gas tank with gas, and then add a fuel stabilizer.**

   This step will keep the gas from going bad and creating a varnish in your carburetors that's time-consuming to clean out. You can get fuel stabilizer at any auto parts store. Filling the tank will keep condensation from getting water in the gas.

2. **Start the bike and run it for three minutes to get the old gas out of the carburetor and the new gas with the stabilizer into it.**

   This will ensure that the small orifices in the carburetor won't have the old gas in them that would harden, blocking the passageways and requiring cleaning in the spring.

3. **Remove your battery so your bike doesn't drain it.**

   Charge the battery overnight every month. It really doesn't matter where you store the battery. Just be sure it isn't near fire or something very hot, since it could explode. And don't put it where kids can get to it and possibly get burned by the battery acid.

4. **Change the oil and filter.**

   This ensures that everything is fresh for the winter and contaminants don't cause any problems.

5. **Check your radiator coolant to make sure you have enough to withstand the cold winter temperatures.**

   The radiator fluid level should be between the two lines on your plastic fill tank, just like in your car.

6. **Put the required amount of air in the tires.**

   You can figure out how much air to put in your tires by looking to your owner's or service manual. You don't want your tires to be low on air because they can develop a flat spot from sitting in one place for several months.

7. **Clean the bike thoroughly and wax it.**

   This keeps dirt and other grime from possibly permanently etching itself into your bike. Plus, when spring comes you won't have to give your bike a thorough cleaning.

8. **Wipe or spray your cables, engine cases, exhaust system, and bodywork with protective lubricants.**

   This cleaning will keep the plastic parts from cracking and will keep any dust or other grime that may get on the bike while it's stored from making your bike a permanent home.

   Be sure to use the proper spray for the surface you want to protect. Some sprays aren't good for plastic, for example. You can get special lubricants at motorcycle shops to clean the windscreen. Other lubricants may damage it. Read the labels on the products for what the product is made for, and what it cautions against.

9. **Cover your bike with a bike cover.**

   If you don't have a bike cover, use an old blanket or a sheet. This just helps keep the bike clean and keeps dust and possible grime from getting into hard-to-clean places.

10. **Go into the garage every week or so during the winter, uncover the bike, and just look at it.**

    This step will be the one to help you get through the winter.

Getting your bike ready for spring riding

If you prepped your bike properly for winter storage, there isn't a whole lot you need to do to ride in the spring. The most important things you need to do are change the oil again and install the fully charged battery. Then you're all set to go for a ride.

If you didn't prep your bike properly for winter, you need to do the following:

- ✔ Drain the gas tank and put in new gas.
- ✔ Have the carburetors cleaned (they probably have varnish in them and are clogged up).
- ✔ Change the oil and filter.
- ✔ Buy and install a new battery.
- ✔ Check the tires to be sure they have enough air.

After taking care of these tasks, you, too, are ready to ride.

Chapter 12

Customizing: How to Make Your Bike Your Own

In This Chapter

▶ Discovering the most common cosmetic improvements

▶ Making your machine perform better

▶ Finding parts and good deals on the Internet

We motorcyclists like to think that motorcycling is all about individuality. Okay, maybe a lot of us wear the same black leather jackets, the same chaps, and the same black boots. But we are all individuals, and a lot of us like to reflect that individuality in the machines we ride. Something as simple as a well-placed sticker can set one bike apart from another and reflect the personality of the rider.

Most riders aren't satisfied with just slapping a sticker on the bike's bodywork, however. In this chapter, you discover some of the changes that you can apply to your machine to make it your own. These changes include cosmetic ones to make your bike look just the way you want it to look, or performance improvements to allow it to handle well and stop and go better. Making these improvements can be expensive, so I show you where to get deals and check out the real cost of making changes.

Cosmetic Improvements for the Look You Want

You can make a lot of changes to your bike to personalize it without spending gobs of money. New turn signals, mirrors, handgrips, a smoke windscreen, footpegs, custom gas caps, and a custom seat are just some of the items you may try.

Other changes, which start to get pricey, include various carbon-fiber parts for sportbikes (such as fenders) or various chrome parts for cruisers. However, be aware that a lot of chrome can make your bike heavy and can slow down the handling.

You can also find fender-eliminator kits that eliminate your stock rear fender and give the rear of your sportbike a sleek, roadracer look. In fact, if you want to go all out, you can get a paint job and have stickers made to make your machine look just like your favorite roadracer's bike.

Whether you have a new or used bike, you may want to paint and customize it to reflect your personal style. That's great, because it's all a part of motorcycling. But remember that no matter how much you like the paint job or all those great chrome accessories, most prospective buyers won't share your aesthetic taste when it comes time to sell. In fact, they'll probably want to customize the bike themselves. So if you do customize your machine, keep all the stock parts. Then, when it's time to sell, bolt the stock stuff back on to sell the bike, and sell the accessories separately. You'll get more money that way.

New paint

A full paint job can cost between $1,000 and $5,000 or more, depending on how many body panels are involved and how complicated the pattern is. If you aren't prepared to shell out that kind of cash, just get the gas tank painted — maybe you want a skull, a rose, or some other item on the top of the tank. This touch is a lot cheaper, and you can repaint the tank to the stock colors when it comes time to sell.

Shop around for painters, because you'll find differences in prices. Be sure to check out examples of their work. And remember that the more famous the painter is, the more expensive his or her work will be. Of course, you can get a lesser-known painter to do just as good a job. Consider, too, seeking out someone who's experienced in painting bikes instead of choosing someone who primarily paints cars.

New pipes, wheels, and saddlebags

Usually the first thing riders do to their bikes is change the exhaust pipe. They have different reasons for doing so — they want a deeper, throatier sound, or they just don't like the look of the stock exhaust. Of course, they may have another motivation: They may have smashed it in a crash.

Whatever your reason, be sure the new pipe meets federal sound requirements. Why? Because more towns are cracking down on loud pipes. And loud pipes aren't worth getting a ticket over or being the cause of a bike ban in town.

To get around federal sound limits for exhaust systems, pipe makers stamp on their pipes phrases like "For off-road use only" or "For competition use only." Doing so is quite funny, really, because a lot of those pipes are made for cruisers that would never go on a racetrack or off road.

The motorcycling climate is changing, however. Loud pipes increasingly are being seen as uncool and as a risk to all motorcyclists' freedom to ride where they want, when they want. So, don't buy a pipe that says "For off-road use only" or "For competition use only," because you may not be able to ride your bike in some towns — and if your city or state requires safety inspections, you probably won't pass. (I go into more depth on the sound issue in Chapter 2.)

 Keep in mind that a loud pipe isn't necessarily a more powerful pipe. In fact, you could experience a loss of power and reduced throttle response by getting a louder pipe. After all, your stock pipe was made specifically for your motorcycle. In the aftermarket world, compromises sometimes must be made to ensure that pipes fit a lot of different bikes.

You can also get custom wheels to give your bike a really sharp look. Most of the time, these wheels are lighter than stock, which improves handling. But be forewarned that custom wheels can cost $750 to $1,500 each.

Hard saddlebags that look like they came stock with the bike are a nice option, but they can set you back $500 or more. You can get leather bags for much less.

Performance Improvements for Your Machine

If you want to make major changes to your bike, spend the big money on performance improvements. After all, you bought the bike to ride. Well, okay, you also probably spend a lot of time in your garage just looking at your bike. Yes, that's another thing that separates car people from bike people. How many car people do you know who can spend hours in their garage just staring at their car? Not many. Bike people do it all the time.

 Most performance improvements will make you a better rider because they also make the bike easier to ride. So while your riding buddies are spending thousands of dollars on paint, chrome, and accessories, you'll be spending less on your performance improvements — and you'll be smoking them on the road.

You don't need to do a whole lot to your bike to make it perform better. In fact, if you have a new bike, you need to do very little — at least, right away. Modern bikes, especially sportbikes, are good straight from the factory. If you'd like, you can make some upgrades to cruisers almost immediately, such as improved brakes or motor work.

In this section, I cover the various types of improvements that you can consider to make your machine your own or to make it perform better.

Suspension: Improving the ride

There's no question about it: The best place to put money is in your suspension. If you improve the suspension in the front forks and the rear shock(s), you'll be amazed at how much better the bike handles. The performance improvement makes sense because bikes from the factory come with the suspension components set up for a mythical rider who probably weighs 160 pounds or so. If you weigh more or less, the suspension isn't tuned for you.

Some outfits can revalve your front forks and install springs to set up the suspension for your weight and riding style. You need to talk to the mechanic in person, on the phone, or on the Internet so he or she can get all the details needed from you to correctly set up your forks. Of course, you'll also have to give them your forks. You can buy the components to do the job yourself, but you have to be a pretty skilled mechanic and you may need special tools to do it.

A new rear shock or shocks will greatly improve your ride as well. Even better is the fact that aftermarket shocks have a lot of adjustments, which means that you can fine-tune them. Again, contact the shock maker to be sure the company has all the details it needs to set up the shock correctly for you and your riding style. When you get your shock, don't fiddle with it. Even experienced motorcyclists can become befuddled with all the adjustments that are available on a good aftermarket shock. Learn all you can about adjusting the shock before you even attempt it, and take copious notes every step of the way so you can put it back the way it was, if you need to.

Brakes: More stopping power

You always need to stop on a bike. And sometimes you need to stop fast. Are your brakes up to it? If not, you can make some changes to keep yourself out of trouble when it's time to hit the binders hard. Brake upgrades range from simply changing the brake pads to replacing all the brake components. All you have to decide is how much stopping power you want — and how much money you're willing to spend.

Besides the pads, you can change the discs by increasing the diameter to give the pads more area to grip. Sportbikes with massive brakes have 330 mm discs. That's about 13 inches. For a great combination, add braided-steel brake lines if you have rubber ones on your bike, and upgrade your brake calipers. You can get four- or six-piston calipers, but four should be plenty.

A lot of motorcyclists keep their stock brake systems but immediately replace the rubber brake hoses on their bikes with steel-braided lines. This upgrade does away with any mushiness the motorcyclist may feel when the rubber hoses flex under pressure. The steel-braided lines don't flex and provide a firm feel. You can also replace your brake master cylinder and front brake lever.

If you're going to go all out — that is, you want to change your brake lines, calipers, rotors, master cylinder, and brake lever — it's cheaper to buy a complete brake system made for your bike. Plus, then you know you'll be getting exactly what you need. Price? Try $1,500 to $2,500.

The seat: Riding in comfort

Most stock seats are great, but they aren't all great for everybody. If your seat isn't quite as plush as you'd like, don't worry. Aftermarket manufacturers feel your pain and have come up with some nifty, more comfy seats that bolt right on. A new seat won't improve the performance of your bike, of course, but it will dramatically improve your riding experience.

A wide variety of seats are available, especially for cruisers. You can get single seats, or seats made for the rider and a passenger, or seats with colored piping or other designs to fit your bike. So a long-distance ride doesn't have to be a pain in the seat. Expect to pay around $250 or more.

Cheaper alternatives do exist. For example, companies make gel pads that attach to your seat to soften the ride, and you can also buy sheepskin covers and other add-ons. So if you can't afford to buy an aftermarket seat, explore some of the other alternatives.

Tires: Choosing between stickier or longer lasting

At some point, you'll need to change your tires. Then you'll have some choices to make. Do you want a long-lasting tire or one that really sticks to the road when you lean way over? You can't have both. To be long lasting, a tire needs hard rubber. But a tire with a lot of grip is a soft tire.

You also have to make sure that you get the right-sized tires for your bike. The best thing to do is to get tires that are the same make and size as the ones that are already on the bike. But if your bike came with long-lasting tires and you want something sticky, you have to know what tires will fit. Fortunately, the tire manufacturers have fitment guides on their Web sites to show which of their tires fit which bikes.

Tires have important information on the sidewall that you need to know how to decipher. This information is a combination of letters and numbers. For example, a tire may have this on its sidewall: 130/90 WR 17. Here's what that means:

- ✔ 130: The tire is 130 mm wide, or 5 to 5.10 inches.

- ✔ 90: This number is the aspect ratio of the tire, which is the ratio between the height of the tire and the width. In this case, the tire is 117 mm tall, or 90 percent as tall as it is wide.

- ✔ W: This letter is the speed rating, or the maximum speed a tire can handle for a sustained amount of time under its recommended load capacity. W is 168 mph. The ratings range from Q, which is 99 mph, to Y, which is 186 mph.

- ✔ R: This letter means that the tire is a radial tire, or has a radial construction. A B means the tire is a belted bias tire.

- ✔ 17: This number is the size of the rim, which is 17 inches in this case.

You'll also notice on a tire the maximum air pressure, which could be, say, 45 pounds per square inch (psi). Don't fill the tire to that maximum unless you'll be carrying a lot of stuff. The manufacturer's recommended pressure is usually more like 32–36 psi. If the tires came on the bike new, you can get the recommended pressure from your owner's manual. If the tires aren't stock, you can get the recommended pressure from the tire manufacturer's Web site. The tire also notes the maximum load the tire can handle, such as 500 pounds.

Would you like to know when the tire was made? Well, you're in luck because that information is on the sidewall as well! This information is useful because you don't want to buy tires that are four years old. You'll find on a raised area four numbers, something like 1008. That means the tire was made in the 10th week, or March, of 2008.

Finally, you'll see a directional arrow that shows which way the tire should rotate when it's mounted. When mounting tires, or having them mounted, be sure that these arrows are pointed the correct way. Tires are designed to work in the rain or in wet conditions if they're mounted the correctly.

Motor work: How fast do you want to go?

When most people think about improving motorcycle performance, they usually think about beefing up the motor. However, the fact is that most people can go faster by learning how to ride better and smoother. (I cover performance-riding schools in Chapter 3.) Besides learning to ride better, if you want to go faster, you can improve your suspension. After you do that stuff, then you can consider building a more powerful motor.

Here's the problem: To make a lot more power, you need to spend a lot more money. After all, building a better motor involves more than just putting on new cylinders and throwing in bigger pistons (although that's a fairly easy upgrade if you want make your Harley-Davidson 883 a 1200cc machine).

Consider this: To make big power, you probably need hotter camshafts, bigger pistons, a high-compression head, bored-out or different (meaning bigger) cylinders, bigger carburetors, a new exhaust system, probably stronger connecting rods, and more. So to boost your horsepower by 25 percent or so, you could end up spending $5,000. Is it really worth it? Only you can decide. Let's say you want a smaller power boost, perhaps 10 percent. Depending on your machine, that boost could cost $1,000 to $2,000. Again, is it worth it? Besides the cost, your motor will be less reliable.

If you decide on motor work, you have to pay for all the parts at once and have them installed at one time. What you want done to your bike may be so common, such as bigger pistons and high-performance camshafts, that there's a kit available for purchase.

You need to find a reputable motor-building shop to do the work so that your motor doesn't explode shortly after you get it built. If you're serious about getting a motor built, go to your local roadrace track and ask around. The racers know who the good engine builders are. Or ask the motorcycle competitors at the local dragstrip. In fact, the dragstrip would also be the place to go to ask about good motor builders for cruisers.

Finding Deals on the Parts You Need

You're all set to create your masterpiece of a motorcycle with aftermarket parts and accessories. From researching what you want at the dealerships, in motorcycle magazines, and on the Internet, you have a pretty good idea of what the retail prices are. So you do some quick math in your head, add up the price of all the parts, and suddenly your dream machine is going to cost you a lot more than you thought.

Hey, no one said that motorcycling was cheap. But, luckily, there are ways to cut your costs and get the look and performance you want without having to take out a second mortgage. The key, like in buying anything else, is to shop around and look for deals.

These days, the Internet makes finding deals a lot easier because you aren't stuck just looking exclusively in stores in your area. And parts manufacturers and others often have Internet-only specials on their Web sites. These items are sold at a sale price online only. Dealers also often unload old stock this way. Deals are out there. You just need to find them.

Getting deals on the Internet

Customizing your bike can be expensive — very expensive. So, when you can, buy your parts from a local dealer. You should shop this way for two reasons:

- ✔ You'll be supporting your local bike shop and its support of the sport.
- ✔ If you have a problem with the accessory, you can take it back.

But sometimes the dealer can't get what you want, or it's just too expensive. That's when you need to shop around on the Internet.

Just about anything imaginable is available for your bike if you look hard enough for it. And the Internet has made shopping very easy. Not only can you check out the Web sites of the manufacturers of the parts you're looking for, but you can also go to big mail-order houses. You can even find used parts that may suit your needs.

The problem with buying on the Internet, though, is that it can be a hassle to return a part if it doesn't fit. Or, if you aren't careful, you can get ripped off. Scams are more likely to happen if you're dealing with a person across the country than if you're dealing with a reputable store.

So, after you've decided on all the great stuff you want to buy and you've picked up what you can from your local dealer, it's time to sit down at your computer and use your favorite search engine to find what you need. Suppose you're looking for some nifty leather saddlebags so you can carry your stuff. Just type into your search engine "motorcycle saddlebags," and you'll find zillions for sale. The process is like magic, really.

Now you can simply read the descriptions of the products to find exactly what you want and look for the best price. You have a wide variety of sources to buy from, including leather stores, motorcycle dealerships, and big mail-order houses. When you go to these various Web sites, look for a button to click that says something like Closeouts, Specials, Internet Specials, or Blowouts. Always look there first for the item you're looking for. This section is where the deals are.

eBay: Deals are there, too

eBay, the great online auction site, used to be a great place to get very good deals on used motorcycle parts sold by people around the country. Granted, you had no way to tell whether the parts you were buying were stolen, but that was a chance you took. (Some people won't buy parts off eBay because they don't want to support the theft of parts in any way.) And you also faced the chance of getting ripped off; however if you used PayPal, you could get some protection.

You can still find some great deals on eBay, but it seems to have a lot fewer private sellers than it did in the past and a lot more stores. Stores have discovered eBay as a way to reach consumers nationwide, and they don't really offer good deals on a lot of the products. But big mail-order houses also use eBay as a way to sell off their overstocked items, so you can get some really good buys this way. Some individuals also sell used items on eBay.

Sometimes to find good deals you need to be creative, though. For example, if you're looking for motorcycle saddlebags, try typing in what you are looking for in various ways: *saddlebags, motorcycle saddlebags, motorcycle saddle bags,* even *saddle bags.* Sometimes sellers misspell what they're selling and don't catch the mistake.

Making sure the part is worth the price

Be a savvy shopper. Check out the prices of what you're looking for at dealerships in your area, and use the Internet to compare prices. Don't buy the first set of saddlebags you come across when searching on a search engine; you're sure to find the same thing cheaper elsewhere. You may have to take a little time, but it could save you a bunch of money.

You probably won't find deals on some items, though. For instance, aftermarket wheels are always full price. You may be able to find used wheels from private dealers or salvage yards, but you're taking a chance that the wheels have flaws, such as cracks, that could cause them to explode while you're riding down the road.

Ultimately, though, a part is worth what you're willing to spend for it. If you really, really want it, and it will make your bike look great, then go for it. Spend the cash.

Deciding whether a combination of parts is worth it

The great thing about customizing your motorcycle is that you don't have to do all the improvements at once. You just add bits as your budget allows. For example, at first you can add relatively inexpensive items, such as saddlebags, new hand grips, new levers, and new mirrors. Then you can make suspension upgrades and put money into the brakes. You can do this over several years.

But if you want it all, and you want it now, it may be a good idea to figure out your total cost and see if it may be cheaper to just have a custom machine built for you. That way, you get the paint job, the motor, the suspension, and all the accessories you really want. The downside? You need the money up front, and that could be $25,000 to $50,000 or more.

Keep in mind that aftermarket accessories and custom paint jobs can be difficult to insure. Some companies will insure them, however, so make sure you and your agent agree on the value before you need to file a claim. I discuss insuring accessories in Chapter 10.

If you don't have a lot of money to spend right now, you'll have to add on bits here and there and do performance work over the years. Only you can decide whether the improvements are worth the cost. Remember, at resale time, you won't get back nearly the amount of money you sink into the machine. In fact, you may actually lower the value of your bike. But you'll sure have fun riding it before you decide to sell it — if you ever decide to sell it.

Part IV
Let's Ride!

The 5th Wave — By Rich Tennant

"I know it's not as exciting as motorcycling, but this might be the time to take up meditating as a past-time."

In this part . . .

Now you're ready to ride . . . or are you? Good motor-cyclists don't just hop on their bikes and go. They follow certain rituals to be sure they're mentally and phys-ically ready to ride and that their bikes are in good shape. In this part, I cover some of the mental and mechanical preparation you should go through any time you ride.

I also show you how to handle a flat tire on the street, a stuck throttle, and the best ways to cross railroad tracks safely. In addition to other beginner tips, I introduce some advanced riding techniques that help you be the best rider possible.

After you're a bike pro, you're ready to figure out where you want to go. Your adventure is only limited by your imagination. So in this part, I give you tips on how to plan a spectacular trip, whether it's for two days or two weeks. I also reveal what you need to take on your trip to be pre-pared for just about anything.

Chapter 13

Preparing to Hit the Road

Motorcycling is an active sport that requires a rider to make a lot of split-second decisions and give the machine precise inputs to ensure that it does what the rider wants it to do. Liken riding a motorcycle to flying a jet fighter: You need clear thinking, precise control, and complete confidence in your machine and your safety equipment to do whatever you need it to do.

Just as a jet fighter pilot wouldn't fly with a hangover, while sick, or with a lack of confidence in his or her equipment, neither should a motorcyclist. Unfortunately, many do. Pilots go through a preflight ritual to make sure that everything is up to snuff before they climb into the cockpit and take off. A motorcyclist should also.

In this chapter, you explore what it takes to prepare for a motorcycle ride, whether you're a rider or a passenger, and whether you plan to go across the block or across the country. Here you'll discover what you need to think about mentally and physically to prepare for the ride, what to examine before you put on your jacket and other safety gear, and what to look at when doing a safety check of your motorcycle. If you do this a few times, you'll develop your own preride ritual that will help you stay safe on the road.

Judging Your Mind and Body

Riding a motorcycle is great fun, but it's also serious business. Think about a motorcycle. You have only two tires, and those two tires have only a small area touching the road. A motorcycle can easily fall over if you aren't careful.

And you have to be careful every time you ride, especially if you're a new rider. Your mind has to process a lot of different information constantly, and you have to decide how to manipulate the controls of your machine based on that information. A clear mind is required to be able to do that — and do it quickly, when necessary.

For example, that small part of the tire that comes into contact with the road is called the *contact patch*. You need to be able to accurately judge how much traction that contact patch has every second you're on a motorcycle. A fuzzy head could cloud your feel for the traction, which could lead to a crash.

You have to be physically prepared to ride as well. After all, riding a motorcycle takes a lot of body movement. So before you ride, evaluate both your mind and your body.

Getting mentally prepared for a ride

You don't need a crystal-clear head every time you ride, but if you aren't crystal clear, be sure to ride accordingly by slowing down and being extra careful. Here's what you should do to get ready mentally for a ride:

- **Get a good night's sleep the night before.** You don't want to hit the hay at 1 a.m. and then get up at 4 a.m. for a long day of riding. Being groggy can be dangerous.

- **Don't ride drunk or under the influence of drugs.** 'Nuff said.

- **If you're angry, it's a good idea to calm down and relax before you go for a ride.** Being angry may make you twist the throttle a little harder than you should, or go a little faster, or take chances you otherwise wouldn't.

- **If you're worried about something, be honest with yourself before you get on your bike.** For instance, be honest about whether a ride would clear your head and make you forget about your worries, or whether you would spend so much time worrying that you wouldn't concentrate on your riding. Riding takes a lot of concentration, so you can't be thinking about something else and riding at the same time.

- **Be excited about the ride.** If you feel that the ride may be a chore, take your car.

- **Use your best judgment.** If you feel like you shouldn't ride your motorcycle, even if you can't explain why, don't.

Making sure your body is saying "Let's go!"

Much of motorcycling is mental, but you can't ignore the physical aspects of the sport. A lot of movement is involved. You're shifting with your left foot, braking with your right foot, manipulating the clutch with your left hand, using the front brake with your right hand, and shifting your body on the seat of the bike. Plus, you're turning the handlebars, raising and lowering your upper body, and even standing up on the footpegs sometimes. Unlike when driving a car, a lot of physical activity is involved when riding a motorcycle.

When you know you're mentally prepared for a ride, you need to determine whether you're physically prepared. Ask yourself these questions:

- ✔ **Am I feeling too sick to ride?** If you're really sick, don't ride. If you're only a little sick, judge whether your balance is affected. Being able to balance your motorcycle and keep your balance in sharp turns is critical for a safe ride. If your ears are plugged or you have trouble hearing, don't ride: Your balance may be affected, and you need to be able to hear what's going on while you're on the road.

- ✔ **Am I fully hydrated?** If you're dehydrated and head out on a long ride in the hot sun, you can get very sick very fast, and you may not even be able to make the ride home.

- ✔ **How's my eyesight?** When is the last time you had your eyes examined or your glasses prescription changed? You need good eyesight to ride because you'll be looking for dangers far down the road. If you're an older rider, a check-up is even more important.

- ✔ **How's my night vision?** Some people have a lot of troubling driving a car at night, let alone riding a motorcycle at night. If you have bad night vision, don't chance riding at night.

- ✔ **Do I have aches and pains or stiffness in my muscles?** Minor aches and pains or stiffness are no problem. But if it hurts to move your back, to pull in the clutch or brake lever, or to move your foot to shift, you may want to put off riding until later.

- ✔ **Am I dressed for the weather?** Are you wearing the proper gear if it's hot, cold, or raining? If it's hot outside, will your trip be so long that you'll be riding at night when it can get cold? If so, you need to bring some cold-riding gear. (Check out Chapter 17 for more on dealing with weather on a trip.)

Checking Your Riding Gear

Car drivers have a big safety cage and a lot of metal surrounding them — not to mention airbags — to help protect them in a crash. A motorcyclist has, well, a helmet, a jacket, gloves, pants, and boots. Since that's all you have for protection, you have to be sure to inspect all that safety gear before every ride.

The inspection doesn't take long. It should just be a quick, thoughtful look at each piece of safety gear. *Thoughtful* is the key word here. If you do crash, you want as much protection as possible. And you don't need a jacket with splitting seams that will explode on impact with the asphalt. Performing this inspection may help save you from serious injury.

You'll feel better knowing that your gear is in good shape when you throw your leg over your motorcycle. The following sections tell you exactly how to perform your gear inspection.

Determining whether your helmet is in top shape

You need to consider several things about your helmet before you go for a ride. Fortunately, you need only a couple of seconds to check it out and make sure it's ready to protect your noggin. Here's what to do:

✔ Consider how old the helmet is. Is it nearing five years old? Sure, you can still wear it, but to be on the safe side, it's time to buy a new helmet. Even exhaust fumes from other vehicles on the road can begin to break down the protective lining in a helmet after five years.

✔ Check for deep gouges in the helmet that may compromise the helmet's integrity.

✔ Make sure the chin strap and D-ring fastener are secure.

✔ Determine whether the faceshield is clean and operating properly. If you wear a smokeshield during the day and think you may be riding at night later, take a clear shield with you so you can swap it out when it starts to get dark.

Examining your jacket, pants, and gloves

When taking a look at your jacket, make sure that all the zippers are functioning properly and that the seams aren't splitting anywhere. If the jacket has built-in protective armor, make sure the armor is in the right place. For example, make sure the elbow armor hasn't twisted sideways or dropped down so that it's no longer protecting your elbow.

Also, be sure the jacket is comfortable. Maybe you bought it several years ago and, well, I'm not going to say you gained weight, but maybe the jacket has shrunk. If the jacket is uncomfortable to wear now when you hop on the bike, it may be brutal to wear a couple hundred miles down the road. And it offers absolutely no protection if you aren't wearing it. So, if you need to, buy a new one. Picking out a new one is fun, anyway, and you have a great excuse to do so.

Examine your riding pants like you do your jacket: The seams should be in good shape, the zippers should function properly, the padding or armor should be in all the right places, and the pants should be comfortable. If the pants are too tight, they'll hamper your movement on the motorcycle. Get a bigger pair if necessary.

Your gloves also should be comfortable and show no signs of tearing at the seams. If they're old gloves, maybe you've almost worn through the leather in the palms. Time to get a new pair that has plenty of protection.

As you may have noticed, comfort is turning into a mantra here. Your boots should be comfortable also: The seams shouldn't be splitting; the soles should be securely fastened to the boot; and all the protective stuff, like toe sliders (if your boots have them), should be attached.

When you're looking over your riding gear, don't forget to consider what you wear under it. T-shirts are popular because you can soak them in cool water if you're riding in the hot sun. Some riders like to wear bicycle shorts instead of underwear for comfort and to avoid chafing. Finally, don't forget a bandanna, to keep the back of your neck from getting sunburned and to soak in cool water when it's hot outside.

Performing a Bike Preride Inspection

If you want to have a safe ride, you have to be sure that your motorcycle is in great shape. Doing an inspection takes just a few minutes. You just need to be methodical and know what you're looking for. The first few times you inspect your bike, it may seem like it takes a long time. But the more you do it, the faster you'll be able to complete the task without compromising your safety.

Performing an inspection before every ride points out little problems that can turn into some major ones through neglect. Some of these problems can even be deadly. Plus, this type of inspection helps you keep up with the routine maintenance of your machine, which will keep it running strong. Maintaining your bike is important not only for your own safety, but also for the value of the bike, if you ever decide to sell it. (Check out Chapter 11 for more details on maintaining your machine.)

Taking a look at the tires

The tires really are the most important part of your motorcycle. So, don't skimp when you buy them. And be sure to inspect them regularly to make sure they stay in tiptop shape. Look for these points during a preride inspection:

✔ **How's the tread?** Is there a lot of meat left to the tire, or is it almost bald? Remember that the contact patch that actually touches the road is very small, so you need good tread. Why? Good tread translates into good traction, and good traction means that you have a much better chance of staying upright on your ride.

✔ **How's the air pressure?** Make sure the tires have the pressure that the manufacturer recommends. Having the wrong pressure affects both the feel of the bike and your ability to judge the tires' traction on the road. And if that doesn't convince you, maybe this will: The wrong tire pressure will wear out your tires faster.

✔ **Have you picked up any nails or other sharp objects from the road?** When examining your tires, make sure no nails, bolts, or anything else is sticking in the tire and causing it to lose air. Remove any big or sharp stones from the tread as well.

✔ **How old are your tires?** Do they look dried out and have cracks in the sidewalls? If you've had your tires for three years or more, consider replacing them because they may be hard and not work as well as they should.

Besides checking your tires, take a look at the wheels they're mounted on. Make sure the spokes are tight if you have spoked wheels; if you have cast wheels, check for cracks. Make sure the sire is seated properly on the rim.

Assessing the lights and turn signals

Too many motorcyclists fail to check their lights and turn signals. These folks ride away with broken taillights or highlights until the police pull them over. Operating lights and turn signals aren't just the law; this equipment is important for the safety of the motorcyclist. Here's what to check:

✔ **Operate your turn signals to be sure that all four are working properly and flashing at the correct rate.** If they're flashing slowly or they look weak in brightness, charge your battery. Make sure that the lenses aren't cracked and that they're fastened securely.

✔ **Make sure that the high beam and the low beam of your headlight is working.** You don't need to do this every time you ride, but do periodically check to make sure that your headlight is adjusted properly. After all, you don't want it to be blinding the drivers of approaching vehicles. Make sure your headlight lens isn't cracked as well.

✔ **Make sure your brake light is functioning properly.** To do this check, stand on the side of the bike and press the foot break lever and the hand brake lever while you hold your other hand near the brake light. You'll see the light on your hand when the brake light is working. Make sure your taillight lens is securely fastened.

✔ **Check your horn.** You want to be able to signal your presence if someone tries to cut you off.

Ensuring that the oil and other fluids are at the proper levels

During this part of the inspection, you need to check the fluids in your machine to make sure that they're at the proper levels. You need to check the following fluids:

✔ **Gas:** Without gas, you aren't going anywhere.

✔ **Engine oil:** Not having enough oil in your crankcase can cause some real problems down the road.

✔ **Brake fluids:** Make sure that these fluids are at the correct level in the front- and rear-brake reservoirs. As you know, brakes are critical components. You don't want to take any chances here.

✔ **Radiator fluid:** It's important to ensure the proper amount of fluid in your radiator.

Check for any leaks in these areas because they could be a sign of trouble. For example, if you have brake fluid leaking from your caliper onto your break disc or fork oil leaking from a failed seal onto your brake disc, you won't have any stopping power.

Exploring the condition of the chassis and other structures

Make sure your chassis doesn't have any cracks, especially around welded areas, and be sure all your bolts and fasteners are tight. Replace any that are missing. You don't want to be riding down the road and have bodywork or other stuff fall off at 55 mph.

The chain should be adjusted properly and should be lubricated. (For more on adjusting your chain, see Chapter 11.) Sit on the bike, pull in the front brake lever, and press down on the handlebars to be sure that your front suspension is working properly without sticking or leaking at the seals.

Turn the handlebars from side to side to make sure that they aren't sticking. Similarly, check your brake and clutch levers, your brake pedal, and your shifter to check for sticking. Also check your throttle because a sticking or stuck throttle could be trouble. Check your various cables to determine that they're in good shape and that they operate smoothly.

Carrying Passengers and Other Stuff

A motorcycle is a complicated, finely tuned machine that has a lot of components working in unison to give you a safe ride. If you add something new to the mix, like a big passenger on the rear of the seat or a small bag on the gas tank, the bike's delicate balance can be upset.

So if you plan to take a passenger on your ride or plan to carry stuff, whether a little or a lot, you need to add some tasks to your preride checklist. Again, these points don't take very long to check, and if you're carrying the same passenger all the time, you need to go through this inspection with the passenger only once. However, you definitely need to do this stuff to ensure a safe ride. And as with everything else in your preride checklist, this part of the inspection will become second nature after you do it a few times.

Understanding that the passenger is a rider, too

Before you take someone for a ride for the first time, you need to teach that person how to ride as a passenger. After all, you don't want the passenger leaning right in a turn when you and the bike are leaning left. That could force you to ride in a straight line, straight off the road.

Take a few minutes before a ride to talk with your passenger. Explain the importance of hanging on snugly, breathing normally, and keeping his or her body in line with yours, whether you're riding in a straight line or going through turns. Tell the passenger to look over your shoulder on the side of turns instead of looking on the outside. This will help him or her maintain the correct body position.

Start out slowly with a new passenger, and make all of your actions, such as accelerating, shifting, and braking, smooth. You certainly don't want your passenger falling off, and you don't want that person's helmet constantly banging into the back of yours. Don't try to show off or scare the passenger: Riding like this is dangerous and just asking for trouble. Plus, your machine will act differently with the added weight, so you need to get the feel for that.

If you can, adjust your rear shock to make it stiff to account for the extra weight you'll be carrying. This adjustment will keep the bike level, which is important to make sure that the bike steers as it should. It also keeps your headlight pointed in the proper direction.

Considering the effects of carrying stuff

If you plan to carry stuff on your trip, think about it a minute before you go. As when carrying a passenger, carrying a lot of stuff on your bike adds weight and makes it perform differently. You also need to distribute the weight evenly on the bike so that it doesn't disrupt the normal tracking of the wheels on the machine and how the bike operates.

Be mindful of how you attach bags or other items to your bike. You need to avoid having straps come loose and getting caught in the wheels or chain. And you need to stop the bag on your gas tank from hampering your ability to turn the handlebars. (I cover carrying things and packing in Chapter 17.)

Thinking About Your Ride Before You Leave

One of the joys of motorcycling is that you can just hop on your bike and go. But you need to put at least a little thought into it. After all, you do need gas money, don't you? Maybe not, but it's a good idea to carry some. (You can read about things to take on a ride in Chapter 17.)

Also, you must think about whether you're heading out on your own or whether you'll be riding with a handful of buddies. Or perhaps you'll be taking part in an enormous ride, like a Christmas toy run involving hundreds of motorcyclists. If you're going on a group ride, give a little thought to how to do it properly to make sure you and your fellow riders stay safe. For example, consider these pointers:

✔ **Don't get sucked into riding over your abilities when riding in a group.** Some riders like to show off and try to sucker you into keeping up with them in fast turns or long straights. Let them go. Riders have more respect for other riders who play it safe and know their limits than they do for riders who ride over their heads and crash.

✔ **If you're riding in a group and you come to an intersection and a rider is far behind, at least one rider should wait at the intersection so the trailing rider doesn't get lost.** The idea is that the rider who waited at the intersection knows which way the other riders turned, and can follow. So even though individuals in a riding group can get separated by several miles, they still all end up at the same destination.

✔ **If you don't feel comfortable riding in a tight, staggered formation with a group, don't do it.** Either ride at the back of the pack or give the group a 10- or 15-minute head start. If you don't mind riding in a staggered formation, leave at least a two-second gap between you and the bike in front of you.

✔ **Show up for the ride on time and with a full tank of gas.** Nothing annoys riders more than having to wait around for a riding buddy who shows up late — or worse, shows up late and then has to get gas.

✔ **Obey all traffic laws.** Don't get off your bike and block traffic at an intersection so that the group can get through. And don't run a red light to stay with the group. If some riders get separated from others because of a traffic signal, they'll catch up.

✔ **If you don't know basic hand signals, get them straight with other riders in the group before you head out on the group ride.** For example, many riders hold their left arm down to signal others to slow down, point at road hazards to be avoided with a finger or a toe, and hold one finger in the air when the group should ride single file instead of in a staggered formation.

✔ **Have a Plan B in case you do get separated from the group.** Know the destination for the ride, and head there.

Chapter 14

Street Survival: Staying Safe

In This Chapter

▶ Understanding how motorcycle accidents happen
▶ Mastering maneuvers to keep you safe
▶ Exploring safe ways to navigate different kinds of corners

*B*ikers have a saying that there are two kinds of motorcyclists: Those who have crashed, and those who will. Although this sounds like a fatalistic statement, it's true. The key to staying safe is reducing risk. And you do that by learning everything you can about riding a motorcycle safely.

If a motorcyclist gets into a crash, 99 percent of the time, the motorcyclist likely could have avoided the crash. For example, I have been riding motorcycles for more than 35 years, and have dropped a motorcycle on the street only once. I got hit by a drunken driver in 1981. But if I had been checking my rearview mirrors more frequently, I would have seen that drunken driver barreling down on me. I could have avoided the crash by simply accelerating out of the way.

In this chapter, which is meant for beginner as well as veteran riders, you explore research on how motorcycle crashes happen so you can avoid falling down. You discover riding techniques for staying safe, including keeping your eyes moving to look for dangers around you, accelerating quickly to get out of a car's way, braking quickly so you don't hit a skunk or some other obstacle, and swerving, passing, and cornering. Armed with this info, you have a solid base for many accident-free miles on the road.

"Officer, 1 Never Saw the Motorcycle!": How Accidents Happen

Motorcycle crash statistics are sobering. Of course, many more people are injured or killed in car crashes, but many more people drive cars than ride motorcycles. The number of motorcycle crash fatalities each year has been going up for about the past decade. Granted, more motorcycles are taking to the road now than before, but even one motorcyclist fatality is one too many.

According to the National Highway Traffic Safety Administration, 4,810 motorcyclists were killed on the nation's roads in 2006. This figure is a 5 percent increase over the number killed in 2005. And it marked the ninth straight year that motorcyclist fatalities went up. The trend looks like this:

2006: 4,810 fatalities

2005: 4,576 fatalities

2004: 4,028 fatalities

2003: 3,714 fatalities

2002: 3,270 fatalities

Groundbreaking motorcycle crash research done a quarter-century ago (which I discuss later in this chapter) has provided valuable insights into the contributing factors of motorcycle crashes. The motorcycling community has learned a lot from it and has taken steps to improve safety where it can.

The Hurt Report

In January 1981, the National Highway Traffic Safety Administration, part of the U.S. Department of Transportation, published a landmark study called "Motorcycle Accident Cause Factors and Identification of Countermeasures." Over the years, this remarkable study has come to be known as the Hurt Report, after lead researcher Harry Hurt, who, at the time, was with the Traffic Safety Center at the University of Southern California in Los Angeles.

Hurt and his team conducted an in-depth study of every motorcycle crash in the Los Angeles area over five years. Specially trained researchers actually went to the scene of the crash and gathered detailed information. At the end of the five years, they analyzed the data, crunched the numbers, and released the important findings.

So what did Mr. Hurt and his team discover? Put another way, what do motorcyclists need to know to avoid crashes? In a nutshell, the team found that the most common motorcycle accident involved a car driver violating the right-of-way of the motorcyclist at an intersection: The driver turned left in front of an approaching motorcycle because the driver simply didn't see the motorcyclist.

To avoid this common crash, motorcyclists must be conspicuous in traffic. Consider wearing bright clothing, and be sure to position your bike in traffic so drivers can see it. Also make sure your bike isn't riding along in the driver's blind spot.

At the time of the Hurt research, motorcyclists also had the option of turning their headlights on or off. No longer. On today's bikes, the headlights come on automatically when the bike is started, making motorcycles more noticeable.

Riders can take other steps to protect themselves, too. The Hurt Report found that motorcycle riders with the following characteristics were over-represented in the data:

 ✔ Inexperience

 ✔ No motorcycle safety training

 ✔ No motorcycle license

 ✔ Little or no protective safety gear

 ✔ Poor skills at handling the motorcycle to avoid the crash

So what's the lesson to be learned from this research? To increase your chances of staying safe, sign up for motorcycle safety training, wear protective safety gear (including a helmet), and practice various riding techniques, such as quick stops and swerving, for avoiding a crash.

Use caution on the road: Slow down when approaching intersections, cover the clutch and front brake levers with your fingers, and cover the rear brake lever with your foot to reduce reaction time in case you're forced to stop quickly to avoid a crash. Most important, be extremely careful riding until you get more experience with your bike.

Fatal single-vehicle motorcycle crashes

In October 2001, a report sponsored by the U.S. Transportation Department and published by the National Center for Statistics and Analysis outlined some interesting findings related to single-vehicle motorcycle crashes from 1975 through 1999. More than 38,000 motorcyclists died in single-vehicle motorcycle crashes during those years. Called "Fatal Single Vehicle Motorcycle Crashes," the report analyzed information from the federal Fatality Analysis Reporting System, which is essentially a database of various information collected about all fatal crashes around the country.

So what did this analysis find? See for yourself:

 ✔ More riders 40 years old and older are getting killed.

 ✔ Most of these fatal single-vehicle motorcycle crashes happened on rural roads.

 ✔ Drunken riding was a major problem.

 ✔ Half of the riders died when they failed to negotiate a turn or curve.

New study on the horizon

Much has changed since the Hurt Report: More cars are on the road, SUVs have become popular, bikes are more powerful, and so on. The federal government has funded a new multimillion-dollar study into the causes of motorcycle crashes. The study will get underway in 2008. When completed, it will offer new insights into motorcycle crashes and how to avoid them.

Until this study is completed, however, you need to rely on the former research for insights. Analysis of the Hurt Report offers a lot of simple things a motorcyclist can do to help avoid a crash.

Some other preventative measures, however, are more difficult and very expensive. For example, how do you teach car drivers to make a conscious effort to look for motorcycles on the road? Most drivers are looking for approaching cars when they're preparing to pull away from a stop sign at an intersection, so they may not see a motorcycle. The car driver's excuse, "I never saw the motorcycle," is way too common. Fortunately, some states are now teaching new drivers about watching for motorcycles in driver's education classes. Some states also have "Watch for Motorcycles" public safety campaigns. But we still have a long way to go in this area.

The federal government is stepping up its efforts, however, through the U.S. Department of Transportation. (By the way, U.S. Transportation Secretary Mary Peters is an avid motorcyclist.) The federal government is launching programs to accomplish the following:

- ✔ Conduct a motorcycle crash causation study

- ✔ Develop national standards for motorcycle safety training for beginning riders

- ✔ Help road planners, designers, and engineers design, build, and maintain roads with the safety of motorcyclists in mind

- ✔ Promote "Share the Road" campaigns in states and communities around the nation to educate drivers to share the road with motorcyclists

- ✔ Almost two-thirds of the riders were speeding when they crashed.

- ✔ Almost 60 percent of the crashes happened at night.

- ✔ Fewer than half of the riders killed were wearing a helmet.

- ✔ Almost a third of the riders didn't have a motorcycle license.

You can take away some lessons from this research: If you're an inexperienced rider, even if you're over 40 years old, be very careful while riding. Be extra careful while riding in the country. Don't drink and ride. Know how to safely navigate turns and curves. Obey the speed limit. Be extra careful riding at night. Wear a helmet. And get a motorcycle license.

Developing Your Safety Skills

Riding a motorcycle is a lot more intense than driving a car because you have to watch for so much on the road — and you need to do so much more on the bike. After you've been riding a while, most of what you do is second nature, like shifting, accelerating, and braking. But until that time comes, pay attention to what you're doing and stay alert.

If you're a new rider, it's good to develop good riding habits early that will stay with you the rest of your life. If you're an experienced rider, whether you want to admit it or not, you have some bad habits that you need to correct. Both beginners and veterans can benefit by practicing the basics, which include constantly scanning the road for dangers, making frequent head checks to see the traffic around you, maintaining proper lane position, and more.

When you have the basics down and are better aware of what's around you, you can work on skills to keep you out of trouble, such as accelerating quickly, making fast stops, swerving, and executing safe passes. With these basics mastered, you can hit the road with confidence, knowing that you have the skills to stay safe and enjoy the ride.

Scanning, head checks, and more

To be safe riding a motorcycle, you need to scan the environment around you looking for dangers. And really concentrate when you look. You can too easily get complacent and make quick glances without your brain really absorbing what your eyes are seeing.

To scan, look ahead of you to see what's far down the road as well as what's immediately in front of you. Look at what's ten seconds ahead, what's five seconds ahead, and what's immediately around you. Do you see intersections? Traffic signals? Stopped traffic? Slippery manhole covers? Do you see a bicyclist who may suddenly turn in front of you? Make note of it and be prepared to act.

Also be aware of traffic on either side of you, and know what's happening behind you. Constantly glance at your rearview mirrors and make head checks to your right and left to look into your blind spots. Whew, the road has a lot of activity going on all the time, and you're executing a lot of movements and making a lot of decisions while scanning. But if you keep it up, this practice will become a great habit and will help keep you safe.

Lane position is vital

A key element for staying safe on the road is the position of your motorcycle in the traffic lane, and changing that position based on what's happening around you. Remember, you have just as much right as a car driver to use the entire traffic lane, so use it to your advantage. Your goal is to be able to see traffic and other things around you (and at the same time ensure that traffic sees you).

Normally, the best place to be on your motorcycle is slightly left of center in the traffic lane, where the car driver in front of you can see you in his or her rearview mirror. Generally, riding in the center of the lane is not a good idea because that's where oil and other stuff leaking from cars and trucks end up. But being as near to the center as possible helps the drivers in front and back of you see you, and it also gives you a little extra room if a car driver from one of the sides decides to encroach in your lane. You've already figured out what you would do if that happens, haven't you?

Of course, you don't always want to be in that lane position. For example, if you plan to pass a vehicle in front of you, you need to get in the far-left portion of the lane so you can see whether any oncoming traffic is coming far down the road. Or maybe you need to exit a freeway on an off-ramp that's on the far right side of the road. Then you need to be in the far-right portion of your lane so you can set up your lane changes to get over to the off-ramp. When negotiating turns, change your lane position to set yourself up to make the turn or curve safely.

Just as you learned long ago in your driver's education training, keep a two-second cushion between you and the vehicle in front of you. You need time to react if something goes wrong on the road.

Not all car drivers follow the two-second rule, of course, so sometimes a car will tailgate you. What do you do? The best thing to do is get out of the way. Change lanes if you're on the freeway, or let the car pass if you're on regular roads.

Always anticipate what could go wrong, such as a car turning left in front of you or a big rig changing lanes into you on the freeway. Have an escape plan before it happens. A lot of motorcyclists play a game called "What If." They imagine, "What if that car turns in front of me?" or "What if that dog runs out into the street in front of me?" Then they form a plan to avoid a crash, in case they need it.

Quick acceleration without laying a patch

Sometimes you need to squirt out of a car's way or get on the gas to get away from that pesky mutt that just decided to dart out from his yard to try to snack on your leg.

If you're cruising along, just rolling on the throttle to accelerate may not give you the oomph you need. Then again, it may, so you should know the power characteristics of your machine. If it does, great! But if it doesn't, you'll have to act fast.

Simply shift down a gear and roll on the throttle smoothly. Don't just twist the throttle wide open, or you could end up spitting yourself onto the asphalt. You don't have to twist the throttle at a snail's pace, but you don't want to just snap it wide open, either. Be smooth. In fact, make that your mantra for just about everything you do on a motorcycle: Be smooth.

If you're downshifting and gassing it to change lanes to get out of the way of a big car barreling down on you, don't forget to make a head check and scout out the traffic around you to be sure your maneuver is safe.

Quick braking: No, you won't flip over

One of the biggest myths in motorcycling, which some motorcyclists swear is true even today, is that if you use the front brake of your motorcycle quickly, you'll end up flipping yourself over the handlebars. Some motorcyclists use this myth as an excuse for why they use only their rear brakes — and it also explains why it takes them forever to come to a stop.

The fact is that most of a motorcycle's stopping power comes from the front brake, especially on high-performance machines with large dual disc brakes on the front. In fact, the stopping power for a motorcycle is something like 70 percent for the front brake and 30 percent for the rear.

If you think about the dynamics of a motorcycle, this makes sense and also explains the origin of the myth. When you use your front brakes, the weight of the machine shifts forward, putting even more weight on the front tire, which increases traction, which increases the ability to stop. A rear brake has a single disc that usually isn't as big as the front disc or discs, so it has less stopping power. When only the rear brake is used, the weight of the motorcycle shifts to the front, which decreases the weight on the rear wheel, which decreases the traction.

Many motorcyclists don't even use the rear brake and instead rely on the front for all their stopping needs. The front has the most stopping power, and you can more precisely modulate the stopping power of the front through the front brake lever than you can modulate the rear brake through the rear brake pedal. Put another way, it's easy to lock up the rear wheel and make it slide by applying too much pressure on the rear brake pedal. That said, though, to stop as quickly as possible, you must use both the front and rear brakes.

To stop quickly, you don't grab a handful of front brake and stomp on the rear brake pedal. Doing so results in one of two outcomes: Either the front tire locks up and your handlebars twist, possibly tossing you to the road, or the rear wheel locks up and causes the rear end of the bike to fishtail, again probably resulting in your unexpectedly getting off the bike.

To stop quickly, smoothly but firmly squeeze the front brake lever and push down on the rear brake pedal. Again, don't just grab a lot of front brake and stomp on the rear pedal. Be smooth.

If the front wheel starts to lock up, let off on the brake lever slightly to get the wheel rolling again and then apply pressure to the lever again. If the rear wheel locks up, keep it locked. The problem with letting off on the rear brake after the rear wheel locks up is that the rear wheel can catch traction again and spit you off the bike. Practice quick stops repeatedly in an empty parking lot so that executing them is second nature when you need to do it on the road.

Now you know the technique for stopping in a straight line, but what if you have to make a quick stop while you're in a corner? For example, suppose you're coming around a curve on a mountain road and there's a pile of rocks smack dab where you want to go? In that case, you need to straighten up the bike and then apply the brakes. But suppose you don't have room to straighten up the bike before braking? In that case, you can slow the bike while in a turn by lightly and smoothly applying the brakes. As the brakes are applied, the bike will slow and straighten up, and then you can apply more brake. This takes practice, which can be done in a large, empty parking lot.

Swerving to avoid that pothole

Another valuable maneuver to practice in an empty parking lot is swerving. After all, swerving helps you avoid dangers like potholes, manhole covers, skunks, and even big cars — and swerving is also fun to do.

Okay, consider another weird thing about motorcycling. If you want to swerve left — that is, make a quick move to the left with your motorcycle — you need to push on the left handgrip. Yep, it's true. That's called *countersteering,* and if

The limits of traction

Whether you're accelerating, stopping, turning, or swerving, you must be aware of *traction,* or the grip between your tires and the road. Take a look at a motorcycle and at the area of the tire that touches the road. That's called the *contact patch,* and it's basically on a 4-inch by 4-inch square. That's not much rubber on the road. The reason you need your motorcycle as straight up and down as possible when you brake is because that's when you have the most available traction and can brake the hardest. When you're leaned over, there's less traction because an even smaller part of your contact patch is in contact with the road. So you need to be very careful how much brake you apply to slow down.

Besides the lean angle of your motorcycle, there are other things that affect traction. Consider these:

- Is there gravel on the road? What about oil?
- Is the road wet?
- Are you riding in an off-camber turn, where the road angles away from the inside of the turn?

In all these situations you have less traction than if you were on a clean road riding your bike straight up and down. Combine these situations with a leaned-over motorcycle, and even with being leaned over while accelerating, and you can get in trouble in no time. So you have to be smooth and gradual with your braking technique. Any careless actions will put you on your head quickly.

you've ridden a bicycle you know how it works. Even though the front tire is actually moving to point slightly to the right when you do this, the motorcycle will lean left and you will go left. Weird. The same is true for swerving right: You push on the right handlebar. Countersteering is a technique needed for all turns and curves, and becomes second nature quickly because otherwise your motorcycle will turn in the opposite direction that you want to go!

This swerving maneuver is a quick one, especially if you're making a quick left-right transition to get around something like a pothole. Don't even bother thinking about shifting your body position. Just make a quick but smooth push on the left handlebar and then the right one, to avoid the obstacle.

Suppose a big car is in front of you stopped right on the other side of the pothole or another obstacle. Hmmm, what to do, what to do? Either do a quick stop before you reach the pothole, or do a swerving maneuver and then make a quick stop after the pothole. Don't try to brake and swerve at the same time because you'll just end up on your head. It's very important when dealing with obstacles in the road to be aware of other possible dangers on the sides of the obstacles or on the other side in front.

Passing the safe way

Because of their power-to-weight ratio, motorcycles have great acceleration. Passing other vehicles is a snap, provided that you take steps first to do so safely. In this case, everything you learned in driver's ed for cars also applies for motorcycles.

Get in the left side of the traffic lane so you have a clear view of the road ahead and any oncoming traffic. When it's safe, signal your intentions and check your mirrors. Make a head check to be sure the car behind you hasn't decided to try to pass both you and the car in front of you at the same time. Then smoothly accelerate to get around the car in front of you; signal to get back into the lane, make a head check, and then do it. Simple.

If you aren't in the center of the lane when a car or truck decides to pass you, move over there. This way, the car won't accidentally clip you when it pulls out to make the pass. The rush of air from a passing car or truck also could disrupt your control of your bike a bit, so being in the center of the lane gives you a little more room to safely recover.

Skills for Taking Different Turns or Curves

Motorcycling is all about having fun, and where motorcyclists have a lot of fun (and most car drivers don't) is in corners and curves. Some motorcycles have blinding-fast acceleration that puts your heart in your throat and almost rips your arms out of their sockets, but all motorcycles lean over in turns. That's the nature of the machine. And that leaning is fun.

But those turns also spell danger if the motorcyclist goes into the turns too fast, leans over too far, or runs into something unexpected in the middle of the turn, like gravel or that pesky stray dog that's always hanging around.

Several different kinds of corners require different riding techniques, so a motorcyclist needs to be able to quickly judge the type of corner or curve coming up and plan accordingly. Turns vary from something simple, like a turn from one street onto another, to something more complicated, like a steep downhill decreasing-radius hairpin turn that's *off-camber*. By off-camber I mean that the asphalt tilts in the opposite direction of the turn, providing for less traction, which can be dangerous.

Simple street turn

The basics of turning are simple, whether you're turning off the street into your driveway, taking a constant-radius turn on a country road, coming up on an increasing-radius turn, finding yourself in a decreasing-radius turn, or tackling a bunch of different turns strung together. The basics are the same: slow, look, lean, roll.

- **Slow:** When you're approaching a turn, slow down. Depending on your speed, you can just roll off the throttle, roll off and tap your brakes, or roll off and apply steady pressure to your brakes. You want to have the proper approach speed for when you enter the corner.

- **Look:** Look through the turn, not at the apex. Looking where you want to go ensures that your motorcycle stays on course.

- **Lean:** Lean the motorcycle into the turn by countersteering. After all, that's how motorcycles turn. To turn left, gently press forward on the left handlebar. To turn right, gently press forward on the right handlebar.

- **Roll:** Roll on the throttle gently as you enter the turn and then continue to roll on gently, or hold the throttle steady, through the turn. This stabilizes the suspension so that the bike is steady as you go through the turn.

So to turn into your driveway or onto a street, you slow, look, lean, and roll. And, of course, you want to avoid any oncoming traffic or other dangers.

Simple constant-radius turn

Most turns or curves you'll encounter while riding are simple constant-radius turns, meaning the angle of the turn stays constant through the turn (see Figure 14-1). Besides applying your slow, look, lean, roll technique, you need to take other steps to get through this curve safely.

If the turn is a right turn, set yourself up for the turn by getting in the far-left portion of your lane. Then you slow, look, lean, roll, and ride your bike from the outside portion of your lane to the inside portion at the *apex,* or the midpoint of the turn. Finally, ride out again to the outside of the lane. Taking a constant-radius turn is simple, but it does take some time to master. Take it slow for a while until you feel comfortable.

Don't feel pressured by traffic behin_ _ou to take the turn faster than you're comfortable taking it. If you take a turn too fast, you may find yourself drifting across the center line into oncoming traffic. If you find yourself in that situation, either brake or countersteer to lean the bike over further to keep it on your side of the road. You'd be surprised at how far over you can lean a modern motorcycle without crashing.

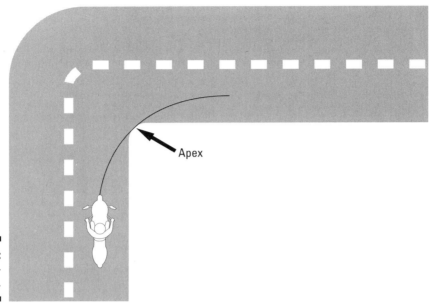

Apex

Increasing-radius turn

Things get a little more complicated when the radius of the turn changes. An increasing-radius turn is one in which the turn follows a line that opens up, or becomes wider, at the end of the turn (see Figure 14-2). This turn is an easy one to take but does require practice because it differs from other turns.

To take a right increasing-radius turn, you once again set up for the turn in the far-left portion of your lane. Slow, look, lean, and roll. To negotiate this turn safely, don't roll past the apex of the turn. Instead, take what's known as an *early apex,* making the tightest part of your turn at a point before the actual apex of the turn. Doing this keeps your bike safely heading in the proper direction of the turn, which is widening.

Decreasing-radius turn

A decreasing-radius turn is a tough one and takes a lot of practice to master. As in any turn, don't go faster than you feel comfortable going, even if that means you need to slow to a crawl. Going very slow is better than going off the road and crashing.

A decreasing-radius turn is one in which the turn tightens up on itself, like a hairpin turn (see Figure 14-3). These types of turns are commonly found on freeway off-ramps or on-ramps or in the mountains, so there's no avoiding them.

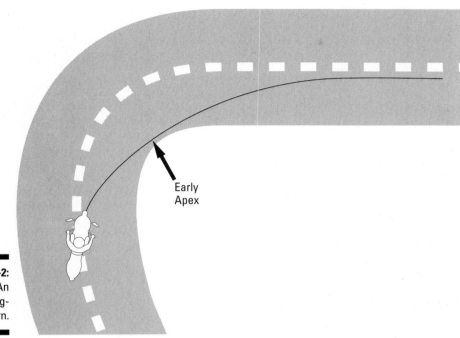

Early
Apex

Figure 14-2:
An
increasing-
radius turn.

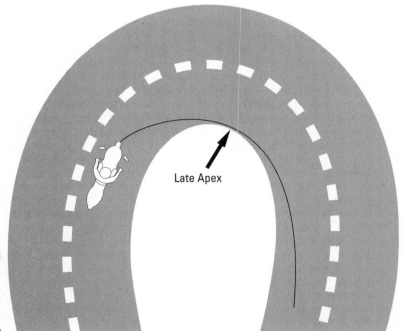

Late Apex

Figure 14-3:
A
decreasing-
radius turn.

To take a right-decreasing radius turn, set up for the turn in the far-left portion of your lane. Slow, look, lean, and roll on the throttle. This time, take what's known as a *late apex.* In other words, be on the far inside of your lane after the middle of the turn. This will enable you to stay in your lane as the turn tightens.

If you hit the apex of the turn or hit an early apex, you may end up crossing the center line and be in the path of oncoming traffic. Definitely take this turn slowly. A decreasing-radius turn gives even experienced motorcyclists trouble.

When you're approaching a blind corner or turn, treat it as if it's a decreasing-radius turn. That turn is the worse-case scenario, so you'll be prepared for the worst. If you then find yourself in a constant-radius or increasing-radius turn, you'll have no problem navigating successfully.

If you find yourself approaching a series of turns strung together, you can't necessarily use your common approach for the first type of turn to make it through. Look ahead and judge your line through the second turn (or even through the second and third turns), and plan your entry into the first accordingly. You have no easy answer here, so just take it slow.

Chapter 15

Advanced Riding Techniques: Staying Safer

*J*ust as when you're driving a car, you have to stay alert and keep track of the dangers around you when you're riding a motorcycle: traffic, bicyclists, kids playing near the road, potholes, road construction zones, and the like. But a motorcyclist also has to watch for dangers that pose no problem to car drivers but could seriously injure motorcyclists.

For example, car drivers probably never give much thought to road construction areas where workers have shaved down one lane of the freeway for repaving and have put a fresh coat of blacktop on the other. The height of the two lanes is a couple of inches or more different, and traffic is funneled from the low lane onto the high lane. If motorcyclists don't take care in this situation, they could end up lying on the side of the road.

Or consider railroad tracks that cross a road. Car drivers give them no thought. Motorcyclists must. If motorcyclists don't cross the tracks at the right angle, they, again, could end up crashing.

Road rage is another serious problem for motorcyclists. One car driver may get angry at another, and the two then exchange angry words and some animated gesturing. Maybe one driver gets aggressive with the other, pulls in front of the hapless victim, and puts on the brakes suddenly, or even swerves toward the other car to try to scare the driver. This situation can be deadly for a motorcyclist.

In this chapter, you discover how to handle the special dangers of city riding, uncover the problems that can crop up while riding in the country, and explore ways to handle various dangers, from a stuck throttle or a flat tire to finding yourself riding into a corner too fast.

Riding Safely in the City

If you think about it, the city can be a pretty dangerous place for a motorcyclist. After all, there's a lot of traffic, pedestrians, and even bicyclists who want to share space with you. While a motorcyclist should be attentive and cautious no matter where riding, he or she should be especially careful in the city.

As long as you're aware of some of the dangers you may face, you can deal with them. As a car driver you may not think much about intersections, but as a motorcyclist, you must take a good, hard look at what's happening at them when you approach. And you must always anticipate the actions of others. You can also face other potential dangers, such as street construction, so you must be ready to deal with those also.

Intersections mean special care

Intersections pose a danger to the inattentive rider. Why? Because car drivers, especially those who have been driving a long time and are on automatic pilot, simply aren't paying attention. Sure, they're looking for approaching traffic when they're at an intersection ready to pull out, but they're looking for cars and trucks. They aren't looking for motorcycles. Bicyclists also can appear at intersections. Or maybe a parked truck or a truck in traffic is blocking the view of a side street at an intersection. The bottom line is this: Approach intersections with caution.

The best way for motorcyclists to handle an intersection is to do what they should be doing while riding anywhere: Be aware of the surroundings. Look far ahead to see what the traffic situation is like, be aware of the surrounding traffic (even traffic that is behind), and look for potential dangers. Scan all around and evaluate the conditions and potential dangers, and have a plan to react.

Have a plan for what to do if that motorcyclist at the intersection on the right decides not to stop at the stop sign but, instead, rides into your path. Have a plan for what to do if that child on the side of the road darts in front of you. Be ready in case a driver in one of those parked cars suddenly decides to pull out into your path. Have a plan for what to do if you're approaching a stop sign at an intersection but the car behind you doesn't slow down. If you don't have a plan, you may become a pancake. Be ready for anything.

When approaching an intersection, position your bike in the traffic lane where it makes you the most visible to other traffic and leaves you a cushion in case you spot trouble. Normally, that means riding slightly left of the center of the lane, or, if you're riding by parked cars, riding in the far left of the lane.

The invisible gorilla

As I discuss in Chapter 14, most accidents between cars and motorcycles happen because car drivers violate a motorcyclist's right of way. The most common crash involves a car stopping to make a left turn at an intersection or a driveway and then pulling into the path of an approaching motorcycle. The car driver usually says he or she never saw the motorcycle, or didn't see it until it was too late. This happens even when motorcyclists believe they made eye contact with the driver and were seen. The fact is that the driver looked right through the rider.

The motorcyclist may have been completely legal in what he or she was doing, and the car driver may have been completely in the wrong, but the motorcyclist is the one who gets smashed up when this happens. It takes a conscious effort to look for a bike, and most car drivers aren't making that effort. They simply don't see motorcycles.

How can that be? In a study performed by Dr. Daniel Simons of the University of Illinois and Christopher Chabris of Harvard University, two teams of volunteers were asked to play basketball. Other students watched this on television, and they were asked to count how many times one team passed the ball. While the volunteers were tossing the ball, someone dressed in a gorilla suit ran into the middle of the players, jumped up and down a few times, and then ran off. The gorilla was in the scene for about nine seconds.

Later, when the professor questioned the students who were watching this on the television, he discovered that a lot of them had never seen the gorilla. Simply put, the student watchers were watching the people tossing the basketball; they were "looking for" the people tossing the basketball and weren't looking for or expecting to see a gorilla. They just never saw it. Scary.

Also, when approaching an intersection, slow down. Rest your fingers on your brake and clutch levers, and have your foot poised over your rear brake lever. Slowing down gives you more time to react to danger, and covering your brake levers and clutch lever reduces your reaction time if you need to brake quickly.

Dealing with railroad tracks

The Mr. Know-It-All in your motorcycling crowd may tell you he knows the best way to cross railroad tracks that run at an angle across the road, and he's willing to share his little secret with you. He'll tell you to swerve so that you cross the tracks head-on; then he'll smile smugly. But he's wrong.

The best way to cross the tracks is to simply keep riding straight. The swerving technique may be fun, but it also could be dangerous if you aren't able to stay in your own traffic lane.

On the other hand, suppose that you have to cross railroad tracks that run *parallel* to your path of travel, like streetcar tracks in a city. In this case, Mr. Know-It-All is right. But the difference here is that you want to get in the next lane. In this case, swerve so that you cross the tracks at a 45-degree angle.

Street construction and other uneven surfaces

A road construction zone has a lot going on: barriers, workers, heavy equipment, uneven road surfaces, metal plates, gravel, debris, and more. You have a lot to watch for and think about here. First, slow down to give yourself more reaction time. You may even want to cover your clutch and brake levers in case you need to make a quick stop.

If you're passing through a repaving project and must cross over an uneven surface, such as from a lane that hasn't been repaved yet to one that has, make the move at least at a 45-degree angle. If you try to make the move at a lesser angle, the uneven surface may catch your tire and kick it back, causing you to lose control. Also, raise yourself slightly off your seat and increase your speed a little just before you hit the uneven seam. Your best bet, if you have a choice, is to ride on the part of the lane that's higher than the other. It's easier to cross from high to low than from low to high.

Those big metal plates that are sometimes placed in the road over giant holes when work is being done can be very slippery for a motorcycle, especially in the rain. You handle these like you do any small obstacle, such as a board, in the road. Slow down when approaching it, lift yourself slightly off the seat, shift your weight back a little to lighten the front end, give the bike a little gas just before you hit the plate, and then hold the throttle steady until you pass it. If you twist the throttle a lot while you're on the plate, you're asking for trouble.

When you're on a metal plate or any other slippery surface, such as manhole covers or the painted markings on a road, be smooth in your actions. Any sudden accelerating, braking, or turning could cause you to lose traction and crash. In fact, as a motorcyclist, you should try to be smooth in all your actions all the time.

As long as you anticipate them, rain grooves and bridge gratings don't create any special hazards when riding over them. You may want to slow down as you approach them. Otherwise, just ride them straight with a steady throttle. The rain grooves may make the front of your bike twitch, but don't worry — it won't be enough to cause any problems.

The main thing to remember about bridge grates is that you don't have much traction on them, so you may want to leave a little extra room between your bike and the traffic ahead of you. And keep in mind that if there is any wind in the area where you're riding, the wind is likely to be stronger on a bridge and may push your bike around. Be prepared for wind on bridges by keeping a little firmer grip on the handgrips and being ready to make adjustments in your steering to compensate for the wind or wind gusts.

A stop sign at the top of a hill

Sooner or later, you'll be riding around a city or town and you'll come to a stop sign at the top of a hill. This can be tricky business even for experienced riders, especially if you're riding a big, heavy motorcycle.

To stop, approach the stop sign slowly and then pull in the clutch and use both your front and rear brakes to stop. When it comes time to start, leave your foot on the rear brake, release the front brake and slowly let out the clutch while turning the throttle. This takes practice to get the coordination right.

If you need to keep both feet on the road to keep your balance, you can keep the bike stopped with the front brake, and when it's time to go, you slowly release the clutch and brake levers while turning the throttle. Again, this technique takes coordination in manipulating the brake and clutch levers.

How to handle other (aggressive) drivers

You're riding down the street, minding your own business, when suddenly a car driver pulls up quickly on your tail. Then the driver pulls up alongside and shouts at you, pulls in front of you, and hits the brakes hard. "What the heck is going on?" you think. The driver may even try to run you off the road.

Road rage. For some reason, this driver is upset with you, and he or she has the advantage. That car weighs thousands of pounds, compared to the hundreds that your bike weighs, and that driver is surrounded by heavy metal protection. You're surrounded by, well, nothing.

Your first thought is to accelerate out of there. After all, that car is no match for your rocket ship of a motorcycle. Plus, you can weave in and out of traffic and squirt through small spaces a lot easier than a car can. Although all of this is true, it's a bad way to handle a case of road rage. Accelerating away could lead the angry motorist to speed off after you, and that high-speed chase could end in disaster. Weaving in and out of traffic is way too dangerous also. So don't speed off.

Don't stop, either. That could lead to a fist fight, or worse. Your best bet is to stay calm, don't react to the enraged driver, maintain your position in traffic, and try to get to a shopping center, store, gas station, or someplace else where people are around. Hopefully the enraged driver will leave you alone after you get to where people can help you, or where you can call the police.

Road rage is only one form of aggressive driving. Other aggressive drivers may not be targeting you, but they can be just as dangerous. These are the drivers who are speeding, weaving in and out of traffic, making dangerous lane changes too close to vehicles, making unsafe passes, and more. Be aware of traffic around you. Watch for signs of aggressive driving and stay out of the way of these drivers. Be prepared to shift lanes, accelerate, or slow quickly, depending on the danger the aggressive driver poses.

Distracted drivers pose a danger to everyone on the road. You've seen them: drivers talking on cellphones, eating fast-food, dealing with unruly kids in the back seat, fiddling with the radio or CD player, or even putting on makeup. Be aware of what drivers around you are doing in their vehicles and steer clear of those who don't appear to be paying attention to their driving.

Country Riding: Enjoy the Sights, But . . .

Little is more fun than exploring the countryside by motorcycle. You face little traffic and can enjoy the sights of cows and horses lazily grazing, wonderful old farm houses and barns, brightly colored wildflowers lining the road, and an occasional farmer on a tractor with a friendly wave.

Even though the scene and the riding are peaceful, you still have to stay alert. A study published by the U.S. Department of Transportation in 2001 showed that most fatal single-vehicle motorcycle crashes happen on rural roads. Some of the causes include drunken riding, failing to negotiate a curve, and speeding.

Country riding also sometimes serves up special challenges for motorcyclists. Remember those cows grazing lazily alongside the road? Well, sometimes they wander onto the road. Or imagine yourself cresting a hill only to find a slow-moving Amish buggy in your path. Motorcyclists who weren't paying attention have hit those cows and Amish buggies. This section gives you pointers for staying safe on your country ride.

Keep your head in the ride

With little or no traffic, it's easy to go on automatic pilot and not pay much attention to the road or the potential dangers around you. Just as when riding anywhere else, you need to scan the road both far ahead and immediately in front of you. And keep track of all activity around you, from tractors to animals.

You can still enjoy the countryside while remaining alert to possible dangers. In fact, you may enjoy the ride even more because you're noticing not only things that could pose a danger, but things that don't, such as the wildflowers or the pine trees and their smell, or the cows and their sme . . ., well, the cows.

Hopefully you gassed up before heading out in the country because gas stations can be nonexistent. But, on the flip side, if you run out of gas, the nearest farmer likely will have some around (and will probably give it to you and refuse to take any cash).

Be aware that if you crash or get into other kinds of trouble, you may be a long hike from the nearest farm house. So be sure to carry a cellphone so that you can call a buddy or family member for help or, in the worst case, 911. Having a riding buddy is best, just in case, but sometimes motorcyclists want to ride alone. Keep your cellphone in a jacket pocket so that it's within easy reach if you crash.

Watch for horse, um, surprises and other special concerns

Country roads can get pretty slippery sometimes. With cows and horses crossing the road, and sometimes leaving slippery presents for you to find, you have to be careful. You won't get a lot of traction in these piles, so try to avoid them.

Farm equipment also crosses the road and sometimes deposits mud or gravel there. Keep an eye out for this debris, and slow down before you reach it; then keep a steady throttle.

Motorcyclists also should slow down when taking a blind curve or cresting a hill. You may come across a slow-moving tractor, a cow, a pile of gravel, or an Amish buggy. If you end up behind a slow-moving Amish buggy on a straightaway, you can pass if it's safe, but consider pulling in your clutch to reduce your engine noise as you pass so you don't spook the horse, and give the buggy a wide berth. (Check out Chapter 14 for more on passing safely.)

Roadkill can be a problem in the country, so keep a lookout and swerve to avoid it. The same is true for small animals running on the road, such as rabbits or squirrels. If it's too dangerous for you to swerve, go ahead and hit it. Accelerate slightly and lift your weight off the seat to lighten the front end a bit. After all, hitting the animal is better than crashing. Of course, this works only with small animals. Don't try it with a cow. The old rule of thumb is this: If you can eat it in one sitting, hit it.

Watch for dogs alongside the road. If one runs out to chase you, slow down, shift down a gear, and then accelerate away. Easy. Also watch for deer alongside the road that may jump into your path. In the case of deer, it's better to slow down or even stop until the deer passes. And remember that deer are social, so if one crosses the road in front of you, you can be sure that one or more will follow.

Group Riding: Avoiding Disaster

Most motorcyclists are social creatures, and that makes group rides an important part of motorcycling. The group can consist of just a handful of your riding buddies, or hundreds (or even thousands) of riders for a big event like a parade or a toy run. No matter how big or how small, a group ride brings together riders of varying abilities. The most important part of any ride is staying safe.

Always arrive on time and with a full tank of gas for a group ride so that you don't keep the others waiting or make them stop early while you fill up. And before starting on the journey, be sure each group member knows the destination and the stopping points along the way, in case someone gets separated from the group. Also, all riders must know any hand signals that may be used during the ride, such as signals to speed up, slow down, close up the formation, turn around, avoid an obstacle in the road, and pull over.

It's also a good idea to have each rider keep an eye on the rider who follows and wait for that rider at intersections. That way when the group makes a turn at an intersection, a rider is waiting there for the rider who's catching up so that rider knows which way the group turned.

On the road, a staggered formation, preferably with a couple of seconds between you and the rider in front of you, leaves the most room for maneuvering to avoid danger. Riders also may need to follow single file sometimes, such as when going through a turn.

Sometimes on big group rides you'll see one rider get off at an intersection and block traffic to allow all the riders through, even if the intersection has a stop sign or a traffic signal. Don't do this — blocking traffic is illegal. If a light turns red and cuts a group in half, the trailing group knows where the first group is headed and will catch up.

If a group is riding faster than you like, don't push yourself. Let the last rider in the group, who is usually an experienced rider keeping watch on the rest of the group, know that you want to ride your own pace and are dropping back. Again, know where the group is going and you can catch up with the other riders there. Ride your own ride. Don't do anything unsafe. You'll be respected more for being a safe rider than you would be for riding over your abilities.

In fact, if the group is large, the riders may want to buddy up into minigroups of six or so. The riders in the mini group can watch out for each other, and if they get separated from the bigger pack, that's okay; they'll still have fun riding their own ride and riding in a group.

If a group has to pass a slow-moving vehicle, the motorcyclists should pass one at a time and only when safe to do so. Be sure to leave plenty of room between the bike and the passed vehicle, to allow other motorcyclists to make the pass.

Think Fast: Dealing with Dangers

Modern motorcycles are really marvelous machines. Unlike bikes in the old days, today's motorcycles are extremely reliable, so not every rider has to be a master mechanic as well. But even if you keep your machine in tip-top shape, you may find yourself in trouble, dealing with such things as a stuck throttle or a broken clutch cable. You need to know how to react to stay safe.

Think about these things before they happen so you don't have to try to figure out what to do when you're faced with a problem. And mechanical troubles aren't the only possible dangers you face. You may get yourself in trouble simply by not paying attention or by making a bad decision. For example, you may find yourself going into a curve too fast.

Motorcyclists before us have run into certain problems, and motorcyclists after us will run into the same problems. Fortunately, riders love to pass on their knowledge, so we know how to deal with just about any potential problem that could come up. I explain some of them in the following sections.

Coping with a flat tire

Eventually, anyone who puts any miles at all on a bike will get a flat tire. A nail may puncture a tire, the tire may not be fitted right on the rim, or the valve stem where you put in the air may leak. If you're lucky, the tire will go flat in your garage. If you're not lucky, it will go flat on the road far from home.

If you have a slow leak, you'll probably get some warning before the tire goes flat. If the front tire is losing air, the steering may get heavy or sluggish. If the rear wheel is losing air, the rear of the bike may start to feel a little soft or even squirmy. If you experience this, check your air pressure, fill the tire with air, and find the problem. Then correct it.

If your front tire suddenly goes flat while you're riding down the road, the front end will get very squirmy and you may have trouble steering. If the rear tire suddenly goes flat, it also will get very squirmy.

Keep a firm grip on the handlebars and slow down. Squeeze your knees into the tank to help control any potential oscillations. Use only the brake on the tire that isn't flat. Then safely get off the road.

Handling a stuck throttle

Throttles rarely stick, but it does happen. A stuck throttle can be disconcerting, especially if you're in a curve when it happens. When the throttle sticks, the speed of the motor stays constant or even speeds up — and that can mean big trouble.

Try twisting the throttle quickly fully open and fully closed a few times to see whether that unsticks the throttle cable. If that doesn't work, pull in the clutch lever so that the power of the motor isn't going to the rear wheel, and push your *kill switch*. This switch is a red on-off button on your handlebar that turns off the motor.

I recommend always stopping your engine with the kill switch instead of the key switch. That way, using the kill switch will be second nature when you need to shut off the engine.

Now you're coasting. Keep the throttle pulled in and carefully get off the road; then come to a stop. When you're stopped, examine the throttle cable carefully to see if it's binding somewhere. The cable may be routed wrong and may have become kinked; if so, give it a smoother bend between the throttle and the carburetor.

When the worst happens: Engine seizure

Engine seizure is extremely rare and is generally caused by a lack of oil in the motor. To keep your motor running correctly, check your engine oil regularly, and change it as scheduled in your owner's manual.

A seizing engine basically locks up the motor, which locks up your drive chain or belt or shaft drive, which locks up your tire, which makes you skid. Not good. If you don't react quickly, you may quickly find yourself lying alongside the road in a heap.

If your engine seizes, quickly pull in the clutch lever so that the motor isn't controlling your rear wheel. Then brake carefully and pull off to the side of the road. If you're lucky, no damage has been done and you can put in some oil and be on your way.

If you're not lucky, it's time to get a tow. When you call the tow company, make sure it has a flatbed tow truck rather than a truck that just lifts the front of the vehicle being towed. Otherwise, you could end up with a lot of expensive body damage to your motorcycle.

If you have a car towing service, check to see whether it also tows motorcycles. It probably doesn't. You may want to consider joining a motorcycle-specific towing service, such as MoTow, which is available to members of the American Motorcyclist Association (800-AMA-JOIN). This service handles your cars also. They know how to tow a bike without damaging it.

Have a wobble? Don't get on the gas!

A *wobble,* which is also known as a *headshake* or a *tankslapper,* happens when the handlebars shake violently from side to side. If you suddenly experience a wobble, the best thing to do is keep a firm grip on the handlebars but not fight the wobble. Instead of trying to apply force to one handlebar or the other to "catch" the wobble, apply forward pressure to both. Also, squeeze your knees into the tank to help dampen the oscillation. Slowly let off on the throttle to slow down, and pull off to the side of the road. Avoid braking, if possible.

What causes a wobble? Many times you hit something with your front tire that momentarily sends the tire off track. Maybe you hit the side of a bump or you leaned over and hit a bump. Or maybe you're carrying too much stuff in the rear, the weight isn't distributed evenly, or your cargo is riding too high. Rearrange that stuff.

Or maybe the bike has a problem, such as worn-out steering head bearings, a bent rim or an out-of-balance tire, or even a tire with low air pressure. Check for these problems. If you have a sportbike, consider adding a steering damper.

A locked-up rear wheel: It doesn't have to hurt

All motorcyclists have done it: In an attempt to stop quickly, we've locked up the rear wheel, making it skid. We may have even locked up the front wheel, or both. A skidding tire can be scary the first time it happens, but when you learn how to handle it, your heart won't be sent racing. The key to remember is that you handle rear-wheel skids and front-wheel skids differently.

A rear-wheel skid commonly occurs when you depress the rear brake pedal too hard. This makes the wheel stop spinning and likely causes the rear end to fishtail. In this situation, don't let off the rear brake pedal. If you do, the tire could regain traction and spit you off the bike. Instead, keep the wheel locked, keep a firm grip on the handlebars, and relax. The bike will straighten out and come to a stop.

If the front wheel starts to skid, it means you pulled in the front brake lever too hard too fast. In this case, quickly let off the front brake lever. Then reapply the front brake.

Dealing with a slippery road

Whether you're facing a rain-slick road, gravel, mud, wet metal plates, or anything else that may make your path slippery, remember to stay smooth. Don't accelerate, brake, or turn suddenly. And slow down.

Also keep your bike upright as much as possible. Sure, you have to lean to take turns or corners in the rain, but if you slow down, you can keep your lean angle to a minimum. When you're dealing with patches of mud, gravel, or a metal plate, you really don't want to be leaning when you hit them.

The most dangerous time when riding in the rain is just after the rain starts. Rain washes up gas, oil, and other vehicle drippings on the road and makes the road very slick. After a while, the rain washes that stuff off the road, but until then, be extra careful.

To get more traction, ride in the tire path of the car in front of you, not in the center of your lane where most oil drips. Remember that you can still get plenty of traction in the rain — you're not riding on ice — but you don't have the full traction of a dry day.

Handling going into a corner waaay too fast

Sometimes riders go into a corner or curve way too fast, which is known as *too hot*. Maybe the rider wasn't paying attention and was looking at something way off to the left. Maybe the rider misjudged how quickly the corner was coming up. Or maybe the rider was in a group following a much more skilled rider. Whatever the reason, getting into a corner or curve too hot doesn't necessarily mean that the motorcyclist will crash.

If this happens to you, straighten the bike and brake hard, using both brakes and making sure that you don't ride into the oncoming lane. You want to straighten the bike up so that you have as much traction as possible. The bike has less traction when it's leaned over. With hard braking, you may be able to slow enough to lean the bike over and make the turn. Skilled riders have a remarkable ability to slow or stop motorcycles in very short distances, so practice this skill often in an empty parking lot. Be smooth.

But suppose it's too late to brake. You're in the corner deep already, and fast. If you straighten the bike and brake, you definitely will end up in the oncoming lane. Well, if no traffic is coming, straighten the bike and use the other lane. But if there's any chance at all that traffic may be coming, or if for some other reason you can't brake, countersteer and lean the bike over a lot more. Have confidence in your tires. (They're in good shape, aren't they?) A motorcycle can lean surprisingly far at speed.

Looking where you want to go

Suppose you're riding down the road and you see a big rock in the middle of your lane. You stare at the rock thinking, "I don't want to hit that big sucker!" And then, bam! You smack it. You can thank target fixation for that. *Target fixation* is exactly what it sounds like. You fixate on a target, and that's where your motorcycle will go, despite the fact that the target is exactly what you wanted to avoid.

Motorcyclists need to be aware of the danger of fixating on a target. If a motorcyclist sees a big rock, boulder or even a pothole, the rider should immediately look to the side of it to avoid hitting it.

Chapter 16

Exploring by Motorcycle

*Y*ou're a motorcyclist, and you want to ride. But where? You're only limited by your imagination. Well, your imagination and how much time you can get off work. Okay, you're really limited by your imagination, how much time you can get off work, and how much extra cash you have laying around. But, in the end, if you want to take a motorcycle trip badly enough, you'll figure out a way to do it.

Imagine starting up your bike, clicking it into gear, and then heading out of the driveway to points unknown. You don't know where you're going — you're just going. Soon you're in the countryside riding on a gently curving ribbon of asphalt. You pass farm houses, pasture land, and grazing cows. Or maybe you're headed up a mountain on a winding road. The air gets cooler as you ascend, and you find yourself riding under a canopy of trees. Before you know it, the sun is setting and it's time to head home.

Just pointing your bike out of the driveway and heading off with no destination is a great way to ride, and something that a lot of motorcyclists do. But to get the most out of your motorcycling adventures, you need to do a little planning. After all, without planning you're relying on dumb luck to take you past scenic sites and through historic towns.

In this chapter, you find out about the different kinds of trips you can plan, how to plan them so that you see the scenic and historic sites that are out there, and discover some great destinations. Plus, you get tips on staying safe during your ride and, if they're your destination, at motorcycling events.

Planning a Trip the Way the Motorcycle Magazine Guys Do

A staple of motorcycle magazines that cater to touring riders is a story about a motorcycle *tour,* which is what motorcyclists call a long trip. In these magazines, readers will see stories with titles such as "Riding the Rockies," "Touring New Hampshire," "Discovering New Mexico," or "Riding in Amish Country." How do the writers of these stories (called *motojournalists*) plan their trips? I can say this for sure: It's a lot more complicated than pulling out a map of a state and running your finger along the squiggly lines that represent roads from Point A to Point B (although that's a perfectly good way to plan a trip, too).

Motojournalists usually have a limited amount of time to get the ride done, and a limited amount of company money to spend on the trip. (That situation sounds familiar, doesn't it?) So they do as much advanced planning as possible to get the most bang for their company's buck. After all, a motojournalist who takes a lot of time on a trip and spends a lot of company money will find that he or she won't get too many more assignments to go on a tour.

Fortunately, there are a lot of resources to help you plan a trip. You can request information from state tourism boards, and you can find tons of tourist-related guidebooks and scenic-drive books in the bookstores. And then there's the Internet, which is great for finding out about specific towns or attractions. The research can be quite time-consuming if you want to be sure to not miss a single scenic spot or historic attraction, but the research is well worth it.

If you read motorcycle magazines and their touring stories, there's usually enough detail for you to follow the same routes and see the same historic sites. Some stories even include road maps.

Deciding on a scenic or themed ride

You're a motorcycle rider, so, of course, you want a scenic trip. The question that remains is this: Do you want to tax your brain on this trip or just leave it at home? In other words, do you just want to ride and enjoy the scenery, or do you want to visit historic sites like Civil War battlefields and learn stuff? Either decision you make is fine, but what you decide will determine your research.

Planning a scenic ride can be just as difficult as mapping out a historic one. In fact, in many cases it may be even more difficult. Here's why: With a historic ride you have specific places you want to go, but with a scenic ride you have to try to find out where all the cool scenery is, and that, my friend, is more difficult.

For a scenic ride, certain things are easy to find out about. In fact, they're probably even located on road maps. For instance, waterfalls and high mountain lookouts are often found on maps. On the other hand, some things require more research, such as areas that have spectacular wild flowers in the spring. Scenic rides are a lot of fun because you're using your senses — you hear the waterfall, smell the wild flowers, and enjoy looking out over the vistas.

Themed rides, like exploring California ghost towns, discovering haunted Pennsylvania, or checking out historic Eastern Seaboard lighthouses are also great, but they take a lot longer to ride than scenic rides. After all, you'll be stopping a lot to explore your new discoveries.

If you don't have a lot of time, or you want to spend a lot of time on your bike, pick a scenic trip. But if you have more time to linger, and you don't mind spending almost as much time off your bike as on it, go for a themed, or historic, tour.

Researching great routes

Half the fun of a motorcycle trip is planning the journey. When armed with a lot of information you can let your imagination run wild. You'll envision yourself visiting all the great places and seeing all the great scenery. But, at some point you have to come back to reality and plan a trip that is doable with your amount of time and money. The following sections provide some tips on how to do that.

You can plan your trip as a loop or as a straight line. Loops are more fun because you get to see a lot more of the countryside and interesting sites. But if what you want to see doesn't lend itself to a loop, simply take your straight-line route and catch an interstate for the ride home. The interstate isn't scenic or twisty so it isn't much fun, but it will get you home quickly.

Gathering your research materials

To gather information about your scenic or themed trip, follow these simple steps:

1. **Contact the state tourism office of the state that you'll be riding in.**

   All the states have tourism Web sites you can visit. To find these sites simply type the state name, followed by the word "tourism," into your favorite Web browser. Or you can call the governor's office of the state you're interested in and they can direct you to the state tourism office.

2. **Request any brochures related to the area you plan to visit.**

   Some tourism offices even have recommended scenic driving trips on their Web sites or in their brochures. Be sure to get those. And don't forget to ask for a road map.

3. **Go to a bookstore and get a good tourist book related to the state you want to visit.**

There are a lot of books out there, and some are much better than others, so be very picky before you shell out your cash. You aren't looking for the book that tells you about cheap hotels and nightclubs in the cities. You want a book chock-full of information about scenic overlooks, waterfalls, flora and fauna, rivers and lakes, and the scenic drives around the state.

Figuring out what you want to see

After you have the info from the state tourism board and the bookstore, sit back, relax, and thumb through the stuff. See if there's anything that you really want to see — a spectacular waterfall or an abandoned insane asylum, for example. Write these locations down on a piece of paper. When you're done thumbing through your material, you'll have your list of must-see places.

Now pull out your state road map and locate those must-see spots. If they're all in one part of the state, you're in luck. In this case, your dream trip will be easy to plan. But if you find that some of the places you want to see are in the northern part of the state and the rest are in the southern, you need to make some choices. Unless you have an awful lot of time, it's difficult to cover an entire state in one trip. It can take days just to see what you want to see in one part of the state. (I cover how to figure out the amount of time to allot for a trip later in this chapter.)

Don't be wedded to the idea that you absolutely must find specific scenic sites to see, like waterfalls or mountain lookouts. You may want to plan your trip so that you're riding through forest, then through areas where colorful wild flowers are blooming, and then through farm country.

Mapping out the trip specifics

With the choice made of what part of the state to ride in, it's time to plan the specifics of the trip. You want to find good, scenic back roads that link the historic sites or scenic areas that you want to see. Look at your map, and look for very squiggly lines representing roads. Those roads are always fun to ride because they test your riding skills. After all, they're squiggly for a reason. Maybe they go up and down a mountain, for example.

Because mountain roads are usually a lot of fun and scenic, pick them out whenever you can. If you can choose a road that follows a river, do that too. These roads are almost always scenic, offering glimpses of the river and, if the river is big enough, barges and boats. Plus, there are usually riverside rest stops that are great for taking a break and contemplating life (or, if you prefer, not contemplating anything all). Something else to look for when finding paths that link your destinations are roads in areas where few towns exist. This is usually farm country and can be enjoyable even if the roads are straight.

After you've done all the paperwork, go online and look for scenic routes or drives in the areas you plan to travel in. You may find some alternate routes, or you may discover that a bridge is out on one of the isolated roads you planned to ride.

A good source for this kind of information is the American Motorcyclist Association's "Great Roads" database in the Members Only section of the AMA Web site at www.amadirectlink.com. There, thousands of AMA members have posted information on favorite roads in their states.

After you're done mapping out your route, take another hard look at it and at the map. Do you see any good back roads you missed that may be better than the ones you've chosen? If not, great! If so, consider revising your route, even if that includes (gasp!) a stretch of interstate to get from one great back road to another.

How long will the trip take?

A problem even motojournalists have when they plan trips is that they think they can fit in way more travel than they really can. It's surprising how a 100-mile ride can actually take eight hours or more.

Remember that if you take a lot of twisty, curvy roads on your trip, your ride will take more time. These types of roads can be slow-going. Why? There are several reasons, including the following:

- Even on straight country roads you shouldn't be doing freeway speeds.
- You may end up briefly behind slow-moving trucks, tractors, or even Amish buggies.
- You'll likely want to stop at scenic lookouts or even spend an hour or more touring historic sites.
- You need to eat and take breaks. When you do, you may end up bumping into other motorcyclists and chatting with them.

All of these things take up more time than you think, so be sure to figure in extra time for them as you plan for your trip.

If you're the type of rider who makes all his or her hotel reservations in advance (rather than just bunking wherever you can find a vacant hotel room when you get tired at the end of the day), it's critical that you plan a lot of extra time into your trip. Nothing is worse than being dog-tired after a long day of riding and still being 50 or 100 miles away from your hotel room.

After you have figured out how long your trip will take, double it. Once you make your first trip you'll have a better idea of how long a tour really takes. For your first trip, have a plan for hopping on the interstate and heading home halfway through the trip because you ran out of time.

Dream Rides: Some of America's Best

Talk to any experienced motorcyclist and he or she will share stories of great rides through scenic countryside with great sights, good food, and fun campgrounds or lodging. Motorcyclists tend to focus on great roads, but you can string a bunch of them together in an area to make a great trip.

In this section, I introduce you to some areas that make for great riding in the United States. If you live fairly close to any of these locations, suit up, get on your bike, and go for it. If you live quite a distance away, don't worry because you can still plan your dream ride. Consider flying to a location and renting a bike there. You can find motorcycle rental agencies by researching online, or if you call a dealer in the area that you want to visit, he or she should be able to hook you up with a rental company.

The Great Smoky Mountains

Every motorcyclist should have at least a short list of areas they want to visit, and the Great Smoky Mountains in Tennessee, North Carolina, and Georgia should be at the top of the list. After all, the area has everything a motorcyclist wants: great scenery, great roads, a giant motorcycle rally, motorcycle-friendly hotels and campgrounds, and a world-class motorcycle museum.

This area also has Deal's Gap. This road attracts riders from across the nation. Most motorcyclists just want to be able to say they've ridden it. Officially known as U.S. Route 129, Deal's Gap sits on the Tennessee/North Carolina border. Also known as "the Dragon," this road features 318 curves in 11 miles. Whew.

The Dragon is unforgiving for those who have more throttle hand than sense. Take it easy your first time riding it. And consider picking a good lookout spot near a tight turn and watch the carnage. People crash about every day at Deal's Gap. You'll see sportbike riders crouched down strafing the apex of the turn, touring riders leaned over so far that the hard parts on their bikes are touching the road and throwing sparks, and dual-sport riders leaned over further than you thought possible.

From Deal's Gap, you can make a loop on the scenic Cherohala Skyway. The skyway rises a mile high and features a lot of sweeping curves through the woodlands. After enjoying this road, make your way to Gatlinburg, which is a great tourist town. This town has everything, from fudge shops to a Ripley's Believe It or Not Museum.

From Gatlinburg, head to another one of the most famous motorcycling roads in America: the Blue Ridge Parkway. The parkway stretches 469 miles from the Shenandoah National Park in Virginia to the Great Smoky Mountains National Park near Cherokee, North Carolina. This road offers a great ride with sweeping turns and fantastic views.

While you're riding the Blue Ridge Parkway, don't forget to stop by the Wheels Through Time Museum in Maggie Valley, North Carolina. Owner Dale Walksler has put together a collection of rare motorcycles from the early 1900s through today. In fact, he has more than 250 motorcycles on display, and most of them still run. If you ask him, he may start up something for you to hear — nothing is quite like hearing the rev of a bike from the early 1900s.

From there, head to Ashville, North Carolina, and visit the Biltmore House. The house has nothing to do with motorcycling, but it's a great destination. Railroad tycoon George Vanderbilt built the 250-room mansion in 1895. Open for tours, the mansion is worth seeing for the artwork alone.

Do a little research and you're sure to find a lot more places you want to visit in the Great Smoky Mountain area.

Southern California

Southern California is considered a motorcycling mecca not only because major motorcycle manufacturers are based there (Honda, Kawasaki, Suzuki, and Yamaha), but also because of the great roads. Probably the most famous road in the area is the Pacific Coast Highway, which stretches up the state's Pacific coast. But other roads go inland and attract motorcyclists from all over the state.

The Angeles Crest Highway outside Los Angeles is a tight and twisty road that runs through the San Gabriel Mountains. The elevation changes from about 1,500 feet when you start to about 7,600 feet later in your 70-mile ride. The views from the lookouts are stunning as you gaze over the San Gabriel Valley, Pomona Valley, and Mojave Desert.

You can also hook up to the Angeles Forest Highway off the Angeles Crest Highway. It runs 25 miles north through forest land and provides a nice, relaxing ride with its long, sweeping turns and views of wildflowers. While the Angeles Crest Highway is a favorite of the sportbike crowd, the Angeles Forest Highway is the hot ticket for cruising riders.

The Rim of the World Drive actually is a connection of various roads — state Routes 138, 330, 18, and 38 — and takes you through forests, past lakes, and into valleys. The roads have long, sweeping turns, tight, blind corners, turns that turn back on themselves, and hairpin turns — all of which are a lot of fun. As with other rides through the mountains, elevation changes are a staple.

The Ortega Highway is another sportbiker favorite. For about 25 miles the road cuts through forest, drops into valleys, and twists and turns. Sportbike riders particularly enjoy this road, and sometimes at more-than-legal speeds. As a result, you can expect a police presence on the road. Obey those speed limit signs!

Texas Hill Country

The Texas Hill Country northwest of San Antonio is a great place to explore. The area features beautiful countryside, great views, and fantastic roads. Plus who doesn't love to see longhorn cattle in the pastures? The cowboy town of Bandera is a good place to start your ride.

Head up Highway 16 toward Kerrville and you get a taste of what's to come: gentle sweepers, sharp bends, and yellow and purple wildflowers. Then you start heading into the hills, and the turns get tight. Your journey takes you past working ranches, longhorn cattle, and spectacular vistas.

The historic town of Fredericksburg offers a taste of Germany in the middle of Texas. Luckenbach on Farm Road 1376 is a great place to stop and chat with other bikers. And, if you're lucky, you'll run into an impromptu bluegrass performance complete with banjos and washtub bass instruments.

The area around Llano, Texas, features some spectacular fields of yellow wildflowers. And Farm Road 1431 is a challenging roller-coaster ride through woods and past lakes, featuring sweeping curves and tight turns. Believe me when I say this road is a lot of fun.

Northern Pennsylvania

If you want to mix a little history with your scenic riding, the oil country around the Allegheny National Forest in northern Pennsylvania is a great place to go. Not only does the area feature some great roads, but it also has an interesting history as a major oil-producing area. In fact, the McClintock No. 1 Oil Well, between Rouseville and Oil City, has been producing oil continuously since August of 1861.

Oil City is rich in history, and a great place to start a trip. From there, you can take scenic roads through lush forest, including state Route 666, which is a fun road with a lot of tight twists and sweeping curves. You'll go through forests, farm lands, and small towns on your journey, and you'll spend some time going up and down mountains.

The 2,053-foot-long Kinzua Bridge — a railroad bridge first built in 1882 and rebuilt in 1900 — that spanned a valley near the mountain town of Mount Jewett was once a spectacular sight. It still is worth seeing, but a tornado in 2003 destroyed the middle part of it. And don't forget to drop by the Zippo lighter museum in Bradford, Pennsylvania. Be sure to pick up a cool lighter with a motorcycling design.

Louisiana Bayou Country

You can't go to Louisiana without going to New Orleans, and the French Quarter is the perfect place to start a ride through Louisiana's Bayou Country. Park, soak in the music, eat shrimp, and enjoy the street performers. Then hop on your bike and head west on U.S. Route 90.

Soon you'll be riding through swamps and past Spanish moss-covered trees. It's eerie, really. You won't want to miss state Route 307 with its tight turns, sweeping long curves, and short straights.

While you're in Bayou Country, try eating some alligator, or maybe take a swamp tour to see those critters poking their heads out of the swamps. Whatever you do, don't forget to sample some of the Cajun cuisine, and check out the antebellum homes.

Southern Arizona

For a glimpse of the Old West and for some great riding, head to southern Arizona near Tucson. In fact, a great place to start your trip is at Mt. Lemmon, an 8,000-foot-high peak just outside Tucson. This peak takes you on a 25-mile ride from the desert floor to the snowy tip.

Next, ride through the Saguaro National Park, one of Arizona's best scenic routes. Some of the giant cacti there rise 50 feet in the air. A can't-miss stop is the Old Tucson Studios, where Hollywood re-created the Old West. Some of the films shot here during the studios' heyday include *Gunfight at the OK Corral, Cimarron, Rio Bravo* and *Hombre*. In more recent days, *The Frisco Kid* was shot there.

After hitting the Old Tucson Studios, head south on Interstate 19 toward the town of Nogales. From Nogales, hop on state Route 80 and go to Tombstone. The ride features views of cattle ranches and wineries. And of course, you can't get more Old West than Tombstone.

Riding with an Organized Tour

Planning a trip takes a lot of effort and can be stressful. You have to figure out the routes, and you have to determine where to spend the night. And to top it all off, you may not be sure that you picked the best roads. (I explain how to take care of all this earlier in the chapter.) And who will help you out if you get hurt or wreck your bike?

One way to avoid all this hassle is to go on an organized motorcycle tour. The tour guides do all the work — ensuring you ride the best roads and have places to stay each night — and you have all the fun. It's a great way to take a vacation and share the camaraderie of like-minded riders.

These tours are usually one day to two weeks long and can cost up to $3,500 or more, depending on the length and locale. On some tours, you ride your own bike, but on others the tour company supplies the machine. In the following sections, I explain all you need to know about finding a tour for you, whether it's in the United States or across the pond.

Hooking up with an American tour

Tons of companies offer motorcycle tours in the United States. After all, who wouldn't want to combine their passion for motorcycling with travel? The tour companies range from outfits that offer different tours in various parts of the country to a couple of buddies who offer just one or two rides a year in a favorite area of their state. And remember that motorcycle tours aren't just for street riders. If you like dual-sport or dirt riding, there's a tour for you.

If you want to ride in a certain part of the United States, you can find a tour company to take you there. Check out motorcycle magazines for the ads of touring companies, and then call them up and have them fill your mailbox with brochures that describe the wonders you'll discover on a motorcycle tour. If you check out local or regional motorcycle publications, you may even find some tours in your state. And don't forget the Internet. It can be a great source for locating tour companies.

 Do a little research about the company before you sign up for a tour. Ask the company for the names and addresses or telephone numbers of some riders who have taken their tours. Check with the local Better Business Bureau to see whether any complaints have been lodged against the company. And be sure you understand the company's refund policy in case, for some reason, you can't go on the trip.

Some companies that specialize in American trips are

- ✔ **AMA Tours** (www.amadirectlink.com): An arm of the American Motorcyclist Association, AMA Tours offers tours along historic Route 66 from Chicago to California; through the Colorado Rocky Mountains; around Arizona and Nevada canyons; and in the Great Smoky Mountains.

- ✔ **Adventure Motorcycle Tours** (www.admo-tours.com): Although Adventure Motorcycle Tours also offers street tours, this is one of the few companies you can contact to take a dirt-riding tour. The company offers a ride from Los Angeles to Las Vegas on Suzuki DRZ400 dual sport-bikes (you can also ride your own bike if you want to). Other tours include a Grand Canyon Tour, a Sequoia Forest Tour, and more.

- ✔ **California Motorcycle Tours** (www.ca-motorcycletours.com): This company provides Harley-Davidson motorcycles to ride on its tours in California and the American Southwest. Tours include a Desert and Parks Tour, a Wine and Gold Country Tour, a Peaks and Passes Tour, and a Beach and Mountain Tour.

- ✔ **Eclipse Motorcycle Tours** (www.eclipsemotorcycletours.com): Eclipse Motorcycle Tours offers treks through the Great Smoky Mountains and New Mexico.

- ✔ **Elite Motorcycle Tours** (www.elitemotorcycletours.com): Elite Motorcycle Tours designs custom off-road adventures in Utah for riders. Utah is one of the best off-road riding locales on the planet.

- ✔ **New England Motorcycle Tours** (www.newenglandmotorcycletours.com): If Vermont, New Hampshire, and Maine are calling you, contact New England Motorcycle Tours. The company offers one- to four-day tours that start and end in Stowe, Vermont.

- ✔ **Rocky Mountain Motorcycle Tours** (www.rockymountainmotorcycletours.com): Rocky Mountain Motorcycle Tours offers organized and custom tours in Colorado.

Traveling overseas: Making your dream come true

What could be more fun for a motorcyclist than riding the Swiss Alps, trekking across Africa, or enjoying the paradise that is New Zealand? Not much. And you can easily make your overseas motorcycling adventure a reality by joining a tour group.

In fact, if you want to ride overseas, joining a tour is the way to go. When traveling abroad, you have to deal with different customs and legal requirements. Fortunately the tour companies have been dealing with these issues for years. So besides knowing the great roads and places to stay, they know all the documents you need to carry and all that other important stuff.

Overseas motorcycling tours can be pricey, but so are regular overseas vacations or cruises. And wouldn't you rather be on a motorcycle than on a boat?

Here are some specialists in foreign motorcycling tours:

- ✔ **Ayres Adventures** (`www.ronayres.com`): Ayres Adventures offers tours in Africa, Europe, and New Zealand on BMW motorcycles. It also offers tours in the United States and South America.

- ✔ **Beach's Motorcycle Adventures, Ltd.** (`www.bmca.com`): Beach's is a long-established tour company that offers rides in the European Alps, Italy, and New Zealand.

- ✔ **Edelweiss Bike Travel** (`www.edelweissbike.com`): If you want to ride overseas, Edelweiss Bike Travel probably has a tour for you. You want to ride the European Alps? No problem. Italy, Spain, and Greece? Sure. Africa or China? You bet. Edelweiss even offers American tours.

- ✔ **MotoDiscovery** (`www.motodiscovery.com`): Once known as Pancho Villa Moto-Tours, this company offers tours for all kinds of riders, from cruiser to dual-sport riders. You can take journeys to Mexico, Costa Rica, India, Mongolia, Vietnam, and other exotic places. Or, you can ride with MotoDiscovery in the good ol' U.S.A.

- ✔ **Costa Rica Motorcycle Tours** (`www.costaricamotorcycletours.com`): Costa Rica Motorcycle Tours and Rentals offers self-guided and guided tours on big adventure-touring bikes. Take a guided tour, or just rent a bike and go.

- ✔ **Coastline Motorcycle Adventure Tours** (`www.coastlinemc.com`): Coastline Motorcycle Adventure Tours offers tours of the Canadian Rockies and other Canadian places.

Motorcycling Happenings: You and Your 500,000 New Best Friends

It's always fun to have a destination when you ride. And what could be more fun than having a destination where hundreds, or maybe even thousands or tens of thousands, of other motorcyclists will be? Not much else, huh?

You can find thousands of motorcyclist events throughout the country year-round (yes, there's even a midnight ride in Michigan on January 1). So with that many to choose from, it's easy to find a rally or gathering that's right up your alley. (I cover ten must-see events in Chapter 18.) Whether you're a touring rider, sportbike rider, or a cruiser, there's bound to be an event where you will feel right at home.

Events range from Daytona Bike Week in Florida, which attracts 500,000 motorcyclists, to smaller local rides for charity. You're almost guaranteed to have a good time at any of them. After all, you're with your motorcycling brothers and sisters!

The easiest way to find these events is at the Web site of the American Motorcyclist Association (www.amadirectlink.com). The AMA sanctions thousands of events each year. The events also are listed each month in the association's magazine, American Motorcyclist. Call 800-AMA-JOIN (800-262-5646) to join the association and get the magazine.

Checking out the big events: Bike weeks and rallies

Some rallies are so big, popular, and historic that they're known by one name: Daytona, Sturgis, Laconia, Americade. These events are Daytona Bike Week in Florida, the Sturgis Motorcycle Rally in South Dakota, Laconia Bike Week in New Hampshire, and the Americade Rally in New York.

These events attract 25,000 to 500,000 motorcyclists, and every motorcyclist should attend one of them at least once. There are diehards who go to Daytona or Sturgis every year. What makes these special isn't just that you're with so many other bikers. The best part is that there's a real festival atmosphere with vendors, bike test rides, bands, custom bike shows, and sometimes even cole-slaw wrestling!

These events are so big that you have to plan far in advance or you won't even find a campground to pitch a tent (let alone a hotel room). Expect the hotel room prices to jump during the days of the event. Nobody said that having fun as a motorcyclist was cheap.

Satisfying your fix with the smaller events

Massive events like Daytona or Sturgis happen once a year and are a lot of fun. But you need your motorcycling fix year-round, right? That's where smaller events come in. With these you won't have to fight humungous crowds or pay jacked up hotel-room rates. In fact, you probably won't run into many expenses at all. Plus, these are events that you'll be able to find near your home. And you can probably find one every week.

Some regional rallies mimic the big ones but aren't as large in scale. They're a lot of fun and give you a taste of what the big ones are like. Also fun are state rallies and local rides. These are even smaller than the regional rallies but still satisfy your need to ride and be around other motorcyclists. All of these rides are sanctioned by the American Motorcyclist Association, so you can find out about them through the AMA Web site or magazine. Or ask at your local motorcycle dealership about rides in the area.

Here are some organized rides where you're always welcome:

- ✔ **Gypsy tours:** These are organized rides that usually lead to a scenic location. They have a long history that stretch back to the early 1900s.

- ✔ **Poker runs:** With these rides you stop at checkpoints along the way and pick a playing card or a number. Prizes are awarded at the end of the ride.

- ✔ **Toy runs:** These charity rides take place prior to Christmas. Each rider brings a toy and at the end of the ride all the toys are gathered up and given to needy children for Christmas.

- ✔ **Cruise-in or Bike night:** These events are gatherings of motorcycles at a restaurant or dealership. They're usually on a weeknight and were basically created so that bikers can have an excuse to ride there and share the camaraderie of other bikers.

You don't need to have a bunch of riding buddies to go for a ride. Organized rides happen all the time, and the organizers welcome strangers. These rides are a good way to meet people, maybe ride in an area you haven't ridden before, and just have fun for a day.

Riding on race day

Don't forget the races! While not all car drivers like car racing, almost all motorcyclists like bike racing. It's fun to ride to a race and then watch the race bikes in action. As an added bonus, you get to hang out with fellow motorcyclists.

There are a lot of different forms of motorcycle racing, but three offer the most excitement and most festive atmosphere. These three include the following:

- ✔ **Professional roadracing:** This type of racing takes place on asphalt courses. Professional motorcycle roadraces, where the bikes hit top speeds of close to 200 mph, are held on famous tracks such as the Daytona International Speedway in Florida, Mazda Raceway Laguna Seca in Monterey, California, and the Mid-Ohio Sports Car Course in Lexington, Ohio. International roadrace stars appear at races at Laguna Seca and the Indianapolis Motor Speedway in Indiana.

  These high-speed battles are always thrilling to watch. But there's also a lot of excitement off the track, particularly in the vendor area where you can shop for new riding gear like helmets, jackets and gloves. Of course, you can also gawk at the many bikes that spectators rode in on and eat some track food.

- ✔ **Flat-track or dirt-track racing:** Dirt-track races are usually held at fairgrounds on mile- or half-mile-long dirt ovals that are usually used for horse racing. Dirt track racers hit top speeds of 140 mph on the straights and throw their bikes sideways to slide around the corners. You can count on finding vendors and track food at these races. The Springfield Mile in Springfield, Illinois, and the Peoria race in Bartonville, Illinois, are a couple of the more famous ones.

- ✔ **Supercross:** Supercross racing, which is held in football stadiums, has grown to be extremely popular over the years, even among nonmotorcyclists. It's great entertainment, with loud music, flashing lights, and spectacular racing on tight dirt courses with hills and tight turns. Racers sometimes even do tricks when they take the big jump at the finish line. The season starts in Anaheim, California, and ends in Las Vegas, Nevada.

You can get complete racing schedules at www.amaproracing.com or in American Motorcyclist magazine. The AMA sanctions all the races.

Special Precautions for Attending Any Event

Attending a major biker rally, such as Daytona Bike Week or Sturgis, can be an overwhelming experience. Every street is packed with motorcycles, every sidewalk is filled with people, and every store has patrons elbow to elbow looking at jackets, chaps, vests, and other motorcycling goodies. Imagine Mardi Gras in New Orleans and you get the idea.

Unfortunately, not everyone attending a big motorcycling event, or even a smaller rally or a race, is a motorcyclist. Yep, like every other major event, bad guys are always around. Unlike other major events, though, you don't just have yourself to worry about. You also have to worry about your bike.

With so many motorcycles at an event, you have to worry about getting hit while riding. On the sidewalks, you're bound to come across pickpockets. But even if you're walking around and feel personally safe, what about your bike? After all, some goons could be lifting it up and throwing it into the back of a pickup truck at the same time you're wondering whether your bike is okay.

But never fear. You can take some precautions to help ensure your own safety and to keep your bike your own, whether you're at a major mega-event or a local rally. I explain everything in the following sections.

Staying away from danger

Daytona Bike Week and Sturgis are a couple of must-see biker events, and because of that they attract hundreds of thousands of motorcyclists. Plus, these events are week-long parties. And partying means booze and show offs doing burnouts, wheelies, or other stunts on their bikes. Then there are those folks who are simply riding too fast.

Having said all that, here's my advice: The first thing you need to do is not drink and ride. Even one drink can affect your ability to operate your motorcycle. It takes a lot of skill and coordination to ride a bike, and a lot is going on around you while you ride at a mega-event. So don't risk crashing by drinking.

So you're at Daytona Bike Week sipping your lemonade. But what about the other 499,999 bikers there? You can bet they aren't all as smart as you. That means you have to be aware of the motorcyclists around you. For instance, be sure to watch for the bikers making a little too much noise with their bikes, those having a difficult time operating their machines at slow speed, or those approaching intersections from side streets too quickly. These riders may not even be tipsy. They may just not be paying attention to the right things, such as that stop sign in front of them.

When you're on the road, use all the techniques you learned in your motorcycle safety training course. Scan the road ahead, watch for dangers on the side streets, expect the unexpected, keep a safe distance between bikes, and don't ride next to another biker. Be extra cautious on the road because you also have to worry about car drivers. And watch for pedestrians. (Check out Chapter 3 for more on bike safety and training.)

After you park your bike and head off on foot, you can stay safe by taking the same precautions you would in a major city or at an event such as a football game. Just stay alert, be aware of your surroundings, stay near people, and keep your wallet in your front pocket or your purse clutched tightly on the side that your friend, if you have one with you, is walking on.

I don't say all of this to scare you. I only want to prepare you. You can safely enjoy a major event like Daytona Bike Week or Sturgis even at the heart of the action, as long as you stay alert and are careful.

Keeping your bike from getting stolen

Dealing in stolen motorcycles is lucrative for thieves, whether it's shipping entire bikes overseas or stripping bikes and selling the parts. And major bike events, or even smaller ones, offer bike thieves the opportunity to take whatever kind of bike they want, because all kinds are there.

Law enforcement recently busted a multistate motorcycle theft ring that traveled to major motorcycle rallies to steal bikes. They would take an enclosed trailer to the rallies, steal bikes, and dismantle them right inside the trailer. In other words, don't think it can't happen to you, because obviously it can.

A determined thief will take your bike no matter what. But you can take some steps to help protect your machine. Here they are:

✔ **A motorcycle cover is a good idea.** You can get a cover at any bike shop. When you're at a rally or race, or anywhere, for that matter, just throw the cover over your bike. That way, a thief won't know whether there's a great machine under the cover, or a piece of junk. And believe me, a thief won't want to take the time to find out when there are easier pickings. A good cover will have metal rings or grommets on the bottom so you can padlock the cover. That way no one can easily walk off with it.

✔ **Get a lock for your motorcycle.** A good lock will make your bike difficult to roll away. Use either a motorcycle lock or a padlock through a hole in your brake rotor.

✔ **An alarm built specifically for motorcycles is helpful.** Some even come with remote pagers so that you know when someone's trying to move your machine.

✔ **Your motorcycle should have a built-in fork lock that locks the forks cocked to an angle.** Be sure to use that. Every little bit helps deter thieves.

✔ **Park in a place with a lot of people around, and try to position your bike so it's difficult for a truck or van to get close to it.** Thieves usually just roll up in a truck or van, lift and throw the machine in the vehicle — even if it's locked up — and take off.

Chapter 17

Travel Tips: What You Need to Know from Weather to Luggage

In This Chapter

▶ Discovering how to cope with bad weather

▶ Exploring how to carry stuff while traveling by bike

▶ Making sure you pack everything you need

*I*f you're like most motorcyclists, you like to travel. It's in your DNA. For you, a romantic notion is to hop on your bike and take off for points unknown. You may take a day trip to another part of the state or a two-week-long trip across the country. Maybe you have a destination. Maybe you don't. You just like to get out in the fresh air, enjoy the sounds of the motorcycle and the sights of the countryside, and be alone with your own thoughts. No cares. No worries. No cellphone. Well, okay, maybe you have a cellphone. But it's not turned on.

To get the most out of any trip, though, you must be prepared, especially for a cross-country jaunt. That doesn't mean you have to plan every hour of every day — arriving here at this time, eating there at that time, or sleeping in this hotel or at that campground in this town on a certain night. But you do need to be prepared for the speed bumps that inevitably will show up during your trip. You need to take essential items so that you don't find yourself contemplating life at a scenic lookout and suddenly slapping your head and saying, "Shoot, I wish I would have brought an (insert your particular essential item here)."

In this chapter, you explore how to deal with different weather conditions so that your dream ride doesn't turn into a nightmare. After all, violent thunderstorms can, and should, send you scurrying to the nearest hotel. But rain shouldn't stop you from enjoying your trip. Extreme heat can make you miserable on your ride, unless you're prepared. And cold? Cold weather can be dangerous, but motorcyclists who ride year-round attest that not only can it be done comfortably, but it can also be a lot of fun. I also give you tips on how to safely carry all the stuff you need to take, and I advise you as to which essential items you need to pack, whether you're going to be away from home for a day or a week.

Exposed to the Elements: Coping with Weather

Part of the fun of motorcycling is that you get to experience the weather. You aren't riding down the freeway or along great country roads locked up in a box with artificial climate control. Car drivers are likely to tell you that they would never ride a bike a long distance because they wouldn't want to get caught in the rain, the blazing heat, or the cold. But riding in different kinds of weather is part of the motorcycling experience.

Coping with weather is no problem as long as you remember a few important points. For instance, you need to do the following:

- Pack the right riding gear.
- Know and watch for the signs that indicate the weather may be affecting your ability to ride, not only because of the elements, but also because of what it may be doing to your body.
- Recognize when the weather affects your ability to think clearly and react to possible dangerous situations.

It's obviously important to think about the weather when you hop on your bike and take off, but you also need to anticipate what it will be like when you return, whether that's in six hours or six days. Unless you're taking a one-way trip, you'll be exposed to the elements both coming and going, and you need to plan accordingly.

Riding in the rain the safe way

Rain doesn't have to prohibit you from riding. In fact, you may find that some of your most enjoyable rides are on spring days in a light drizzle when the air is cool and the trees and flowers smell sweet. When the rain starts pounding a little harder, however, riding can get more challenging. You need to remember a few certain things when riding in the rain — whether it's a drizzle or a downpour.

If lightning is nearby or if it's raining so hard that you can hardly see, pull over. Stop under a freeway overpass (but do remember to climb up away from the road), go to a restaurant and have some coffee or a leisurely meal, or go into a gas station. Talk to some folks to see what they've heard about the weather. Or if you're one of those high-tech people, pull out your handy cellphone that allows you to download satellite weather images. Either way, determine whether the storm will pass quickly. If it appears that the storm isn't going to let up for quite a while, hole up in a hotel. In fact, if you're planning a long trip, add an extra day or two in case you need to kill a day in a hotel because of bad weather.

Tweaking your driving techniques

Riding in the rain changes the way you drive because

- ✔ Your tires have less traction on the road.

- ✔ Your brake discs are wet (meaning that you have less stopping power).

- ✔ Your vision may be impaired because of rain on the faceshield of your helmet.

- ✔ Car drivers may be even less likely to see you than they normally are because of poor visibility and their concentration on the weather.

Rain also can affect your ability to control your machine if you're uncomfortable because water soaked through your jacket, boots, and gloves.

The most dangerous time for a motorcyclist is just after it starts raining. Why? The rain mixes water with gas and oil on the road, making for a slick surface. It stays slick until the rain and cars force the dangerous mixture off the road. Road markings, railroad tracks, metal plates, and manhole covers are also all extremely slick when it rains, so be very careful if you need to ride over them.

Everything you do while riding in the rain must be smooth: shifting, accelerating, braking, changing lanes, leaning, and turning. With reduced tire traction in the rain, any jerky or fast movements are amplified, and you may not recover from them. Instead, you may find yourself sliding off a turn into a ditch. Following are some tips and tricks to stay safe:

- ✔ **When riding in the rain, remember that your brakes, for a split-second, initially won't have the stopping power you expect because of water on the brake discs.** This lack of stopping power will only be momentary, but it can mean the difference between hitting something and not hitting something if you don't anticipate that you won't have initial grip on your brake discs by your brake pads.

✔ **If it's absolutely pouring, ride your motorcycle in the path of the tires of the car in front of you.** This path offers more traction than the rain-covered road on either side of it. But if it's raining that hard, it's probably best to get off the road. Find a restaurant or hotel or pull over.

✔ **Wipe the rain from your faceshield occasionally to improve your vision.** You can wipe it with your gloved hand. Some gloves have a little squeegee on the finger made for clearing the rain off your faceshield. Another trick, if you don't want to take your hands off your handlebars, is to turn your head to the left or right briefly. The wind will push the rain off the side of your faceshield.

Suiting up in rainproof riding gear

To keep from getting soaked while riding in the rain, you need a good one- or two-piece rain suit. A *rain suit* is waterproof, of course, with sealed seams, a snug fit around the neck and ankles, and usually some big, waterproof pockets. *Note:* Be aware that some rain suits made out of a plastic material can make you very hot. And one-piece rain suits seem to work better than two-piece suits to keep you dry, but they're more of a hassle to get into and out of.

Make sure your rain suit is big enough to wear over your riding clothes. In fact, you should probably try on your rain suit over your riding clothes in the store before buying it. That way you make sure it fits properly. If it's too tight, the seams could split.

If you get caught in the rain without a rain suit, go to a store and buy a cheap raincoat or even a garbage bag. These options may not be very stylish, but at least they'll offer a little bit of protection.

Riding in the rain with sopping wet gloves can be uncomfortable, and even dangerous, because it affects your ability to control the clutch and brake levers. So, carry a pair of waterproof rain gloves or rain covers to go over your gloves, in case you get caught in a downpour. Similarly, if you think you may get caught in the rain, wear waterproof boots — or at least water-resistant boots — for the ride. Wet boots have the same affect on your feet as wet gloves do on your hands. Wearing soaking wet boots not only can make you uncomfortable, but it also affects your ability to manipulate the shift and brake levers with your feet.

Paying attention in extreme heat

Riders don't stop riding because it gets a little warm outside. Granted, 90- and 100-degree heat can get pretty darn uncomfortable. Luckily there are ways to cool down and keep the ride enjoyable. Just always remember that extreme heat can be dangerous.

Beating the heat and staying safe

While riding in heat, plan to take a lot of breaks so that you can drink some water and relax in the shade or in an air-conditioned building. The key to surviving hot-weather riding is lots and lots of water. Even if you aren't thirsty, you need to drink water to avoid dehydration and heat stroke. Sports drinks are also good.

If you plan a lot of hot-weather riding, consider buying a *backpack-style hydration system.* This type of system is essentially a bladder (which you fill with water) in a little backpack. A drinking tube runs from the bladder to the front of your jacket. Then you can take cool sips of water as you ride along. Taking a lot of cool sips while riding is a much better way to battle the heat than gulping down water every hour or so during stops.

Ride in the early morning and late afternoon, when it's cooler. Avoid the blazing midday sun. You should wear a bandanna around your neck to keep the area between your jacket collar and your helmet from getting sunburned. A bandanna can also make a great ice cube holder to help keep you comfortable. For example, during a rest stop, put some ice cubes in the bandanna and then tie it around your neck. This helps to cool your blood a bit as it circulates to your brain. If you're wearing a T-shirt, you can soak that with cool water too.

On warm days many times you see riders not wearing safety gear. They may tell you it's just too hot to wear a helmet, or jacket, or boots, or even gloves. Wear them. This is safety equipment, not I'll-only-wear-it-in-comfortable-weather equipment. Plus, not wearing a jacket makes you more prone to suffer from heat stroke during a ride and causes you to dry out faster, as the hot wind rushes by your upper torso.

You should have hot-weather riding gear: a ventilated jacket, pants, gloves, and boots. For a reasonable price, you can even get a mesh jacket with lots of protective armor to wear on really hot days. Open up your vents, including the ventilation in your helmet.

Watching out for signs of heat exhaustion or heat stroke

You know your body well. Listen to it. Watch for signs that you may be headed toward heat exhaustion or heat stroke. Signs of heat exhaustion include

- Clammy skin
- Dizziness
- Headache
- Muscle cramps
- Excessive sweating

- ✔ Weakness
- ✔ Slow thinking or getting foggy in the head.

Heat stroke is even worse, and can be debilitating. Signs of heat stroke include

- ✔ Hot, dry skin
- ✔ Increased heart rate
- ✔ Incoherent or slow, slurred speech
- ✔ High body temperature
- ✔ Difficulty concentrating

If you think you may be overheated, end your ride for the day. Check into a hotel and cool down. Relax. If you're near a fire station, pull in and ask for help. Firefighters know how to cool you down so you don't pose a danger to yourself and others.

It's really cold up in them thar hills: Traveling in winter

Winter isn't the only time that you can face riding in some really cold weather. Just getting up into the mountains can pose a danger unless you're prepared and recognize the signs of trouble. By anticipating and dealing with the cold, you can make cold-weather riding enjoyable.

When riding in the heat, you need to guard against your body temperature elevating. The opposite, of course, is that when riding in the cold, you need to guard against your body temperature dropping. Low body temperature can pose a real danger, clouding your ability to think and to properly control your motorcycle.

When riding in the cold, take breaks so you can warm up in a restaurant or gas station, and drink plenty of fluids. Dehydration is just as much of a danger in cold weather as it is in hot conditions. Watch for shivering, numbness, and clouded thinking. Try not to reach that stage, but if you do, go warm up.

Cold weather requires you to dress accordingly. Cold-weather gear includes a jacket and pants with a cold-weather lining, lined boots and gloves, and, of course, a full-face helmet. Dress in layers for the ride, and make sure all of your skin is covered. The wind chill from riding in the cold can make riding with exposed skin unbearable. Make sure your gloves have gauntlets that go over the wrists of your jacket so that your wrists aren't exposed, and wear a bandanna around your neck to protect the skin there. Close the ventilation in your helmet.

You know your body, so if it's too cold, don't ride. It's not worth the risk. If you aren't comfortable riding in 40-degree weather, don't do it. But if you're comfortable and clear-headed riding in 30-degree weather, go ahead. Remember, you're ultimately responsible for your own safety. Sure, there may be peer pressure to join a midnight winter ride, but don't do it if you're not comfortable. There's no shame in knowing your limits, and motorcyclists respect other motorcyclists who consider safety first.

I don't recommend riding in the snow. But if you feel you must, it's like riding in the rain but much, much more slippery. Ride slowly, turn slowly, stop slowly, and accelerate slowly. To me, the danger isn't worth it — not only because of the danger you face controlling your machine but also because of the difficulties that all the car drivers have controlling theirs. Besides, the salt and other chemicals that are laid down on the road to melt the ice can eat up parts on your motorcycle pretty quickly. In my humble opinion: Park your bike for the winter.

Consider buying an electric vest and gloves to keep you toasty while riding in cold weather. You can also do what hunters do: Get some disposable heat packs to stick in your gloves to help keep your hands warm.

Packin' Up: Carrying Your Gear

A long trip usually means that you need to carry a lot of stuff, including clothes, rain gear, and maybe a toothbrush. You can't just throw all your stuff into a bag or two, strap it on your bike, and take off. Well, you can, but if you don't put a little bit of thought into how you carry your stuff, it may end up falling off the bike during a trip. Worse yet, it can throw off the balance of your machine, which can make for some interesting riding the first time you toss your bike into a turn.

If you're one of those people who can pack everything you need for a week-long vacation into a carry-on bag, you're the perfect candidate for a motorcycle trip. But if you need four suitcases and one carry-on when you go to the Bahamas for a couple of days, you're going to have to do some serious whittling down of what you take before you hit the road on a bike.

A lot of stuff can be carried on your machine. Just be sure that you pack carefully, distribute the luggage on your machine evenly, and don't exceed the maximum weight limits that are found on the sidewalls of your tires and the combined passenger-and-luggage weight limit of your motorcycle, which is found in your owner's manual.

Special luggage you may need

If you have a touring bike, you already have some hard luggage built in, either permanently affixed to the bike or removable so that you can take it into a hotel room when you stop for the night. But if you don't have a touring machine that comes with luggage, you need to decide whether you want to add luggage to your machine.

Hard luggage

There are companies that make hard luggage, primarily saddlebags, for a variety of motorcycles (see Figure 17-1 for a look at a hard saddlebag). Adding hard luggage to your machine can be pricey, but you have the assurance of getting a quality product and knowing the bags will fit. Many times the luggage is integrated so well that the bike looks like it came from the factory with the bags.

Figure 17-1: Hard saddle-bags are expensive but worth the price.

Besides saddlebags, you can get a *top box* (shown in Figure 17-2) that attaches to the back of your motorcycle and provides room to carry more stuff. Many top boxes are big enough to fit a full-face helmet or two.

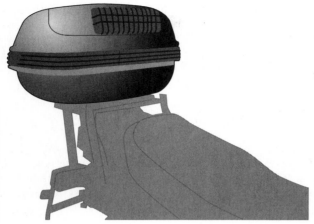

Figure 17-2:
A top box
gives you
extra
storage
space.

Soft luggage

If you don't want to go with hard luggage, soft luggage made of leather or a
synthetic material is the way to go. Check out Figure 17-3, which shows soft
saddlebags. This luggage is much cheaper, and attaching the bags to the bike
is simple. Soft saddlebags come in a variety of sizes to fit everything from
sportbikes to cruisers. Plus, they usually come with rain covers to keep everything dry if it rains. You also can put heavy-duty garbage or trash compactor
bags inside the saddlebags for another layer of protection against the rain.
However, you need to watch out for the following hazards:

- ✔ Make sure that the luggage doesn't touch your exhaust pipe because
  synthetic bags can catch on fire or melt.

- ✔ Don't have loose straps flapping around that could get caught in your
  rear wheel or drive chain.

Figure 17-3:
Soft
saddlebags
protect your
things but
are less
expensive
than hard
luggage.

If saddlebags don't give you enough room to carry the things you need, you can add a *tank bag*. Tank bags are synthetic and rest on the top of your gas tank. They're usually attached with either straps or magnets. You can get tank bags in various sizes to carry a little or a lot. However, be sure that it isn't so big that it gets in the way of your reaching the handlebars. This can be particularly bothersome on a sportbike, so sportbike riders need to look for smaller tank bags.

Need to carry even more stuff? You have the following three options:

✔ **You can get bags designed specifically to strap onto the rear seat of your motorcycle.** These bags, commonly called *duffel bags* (see Figure 17-4), give you more carrying capacity, but you need to make sure that they're attached securely and the straps don't hang down where they can get caught in your rear wheel.

✔ **You can purchase a backpack made specifically for motorcyclists (see Figure 17-5).** These include padding where the pack meets your back and crossed straps so that the pack stays snug and secure while you're cruising down the road at 50 mph. You don't want to weigh down a backpack with a lot of stuff, though, because the weight on your back can get tiresome and annoying.

✔ **You can use a courier bag (see Figure 17-6).** While they aren't made for long trips, *courier bags* for motorcyclists can be handy if you're just running down to the store to pick up a few items.

While soft luggage made for motorcycles comes with the straps you need to secure the luggage to the bike, it's always a good idea to have a few extra straps to help secure things, like that souvenir stuffed fish that you just had to buy on your trip. Forget those elastic bungee cords that you can buy almost anywhere. They're difficult to use on a motorcycle, and usually don't keep things snug enough. Buy straps with D-ring cinchers or other secure connecting hardware.

Figure 17-4:
You can strap a duffel bag to your rear seat.

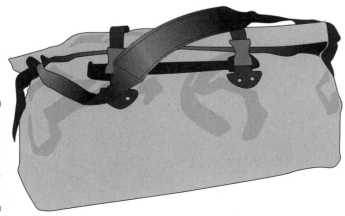

Suppose you're on the road and you find a mounted moose head in a store that would look great in your den. How are you going to fit *that* on your bike? You're not. Take it to the nearest pack-and-ship store and send it home. Keep that in mind for any items that are too bulky to carry, or even if you just want to unload some of the stuff that you brought along because you've decided you really won't need it.

Figure 17-5:
A backpack made for motor-cyclists.

Figure 17-6:
A courier bag for quick jaunts to town.

Weight distribution is critical

After you're ready to load up and hit the open road, you need to give a little thought to the weight distribution of the stuff on your motorcycle. After all, if you have all the heavy stuff on the left side of your bike and all the light stuff on the right side, you may find yourself leaning over as you go down the road, and taking turns may be quite interesting. Or if you put too much weight on the rear, your headlight may be pointed toward the sky. You may even have a skittish front end because it is so light.

Pack your saddlebags so that the right and left bags weigh about the same amount. Put lighter stuff in your top box, tank bag, and rear seat bag because those bags ride higher on the bike. You want to keep the weight as low as possible.

When you load up all your stuff, make sure you don't exceed the maximum carrying load that's stamped on the sidewall of your rear tire. Exceeding that limit could lead to catastrophic tire failure.

You also may want to adjust the *preload* on your rear shock — that is, how much the spring on your shock is compressed with no weight on the bike — so that it's compressed more to handle the extra weight in the rear. The added stiffness will improve the ride. Your owner's or service manual shows you how to adjust the preload.

Knowing How to Pack Successfully for a Long Trip

You really can carry everything you need for a long trip on your motorcycle. You just need to be smart about what you pack, and think carefully about what you really need.

When deciding on what clothes to take, keep in mind that you may run into different weather along the way, so be prepared for warm- and cold-weather riding. Think layers, so that you can start out with a T-shirt under your jacket if the weather is warm but then add another shirt or even a sweater later if the weather turns cool. And don't forget to pack your rain gear. Forgetting to take a rain suit almost guarantees that you'll get caught in a downpour.

Remember that the towns along your trip route have laundromats. There may even be a washer and dryer at the hotel where you stay. So don't think that you have to take enough clean clothes to last your entire trip.

Choosing the right clothes

Everybody is different, but you really can't go wrong taking three T-shirts and a couple pairs of blue jeans for when you're off the bike, plus maybe four pairs of underwear and socks for a trip. Add a long-sleeved T-shirt or sweatshirt that you can put on over a T-shirt and some long underwear if you think you may hit some cold weather, and your motorcycle trip wardrobe is complete.

Going a step further, you need to add a rain suit, rain gloves or rain covers for your gloves, a couple of bandannas, and a pair of tennis shoes if you don't want to walk around in your riding boots at the end of the day. You can also carry a spare set of gloves in case yours get wet.

It's a good idea to have a couple small towels or rags to wipe the dew off your bike in the morning. Hotel managers frown on the use of their towels for that purpose. Alternatively, you can bring along a light motorcycle cover to protect your bike overnight. A cover may also make the bike less attractive to thieves because they won't know exactly what's under it — a new machine or a 30-year-old junker.

Packing medicines, snacks, and other health-related items

The point of a motorcycle trip is to have fun and get away from it all. But you don't want to be 1,500 miles away from home when you discover that you don't have some critical item you need. To avoid such a scenario, make sure you pack the following:

- ✓ **Medicines:** If you take medication regularly, take it with you. And be sure you have enough to last through your entire trip plus a few extra days.

- ✓ **Spare glasses:** If you wear prescription glasses, take a spare pair. Otherwise, if you break your glasses, you may be stuck with the hassle and cost of finding an establishment that can replace them in about an hour.

- ✓ **Aspirin:** Getting a splitting headache in the middle of nowhere is not only no fun, but it can also be dangerous on a bike.

- ✓ **Granola bars or energy snacks:** Healthy snacks along the way can keep you feeling well.

- ✓ **Lip balm, sunglasses, and sunblock:** These are good to have on hand when you're spending many hours out in the sun.

- ✓ **Emergency information:** Be sure to carry the names and phone numbers of people who should be called in an emergency, either healthwise or in case of a crash. A lot of people wear dog tags with their name, phone number, and an emergency contact. Also be sure to note whether you're allergic to any medicines.

- ✓ **A first-aid kit:** A small first-aid kit helps to cover unforeseen contingencies.

Taking the necessities

Here are few last-minute (but important) items that you may want to have with you when you're traveling by bike:

- ✔ **A cellphone:** A cellphone can get you out of a jam or make it easier to make a hotel room reservation, so it's a good idea to carry one along. In fact, you generally get a better room rate if you call a hotel and make a reservation than if you walk in and ask for a room. If you don't have a cellphone, a telephone calling card can enable you to call someone to get out of a jam.

- ✔ **A tire-repair kit:** Know how to use this kit if you bring one. Practice on an old tire before you take your long ride. Also, be sure to take a tire pressure gauge.

- ✔ **A flashlight:** This item is critical if you have to check things out on your bike or fix a flat tire in the dark.

- ✔ **Fuses:** You should have extra fuses on hand, just in case.

- ✔ **An extra bike key:** What would you do if you lost your bike key a thousand miles from home? Well, it would be no problem if you kept a spare key in your wallet or hidden on your bike. Also, consider taking a disc lock or padlock to secure your machine when you settle into a hotel or tent for the night. And be sure your license and registration are up-to-date.

- ✔ **A siphon hose:** This hose is useful if you run out of gas and another motorcyclist stops to help you out.

- ✔ **Hand wipes:** These are always useful to help keep you feeling fresh.

- ✔ **A weather radio:** Check the radio from time to time to be sure that you aren't riding into a nasty storm.

- ✔ **A small cable lock:** If you plan to do some walking on your trip, such as visiting a museum, you may want to bring along a small cable lock that you can thread through the sleeve of your riding jacket and helmet to secure them to your bike. That way you don't need to carry them around.

Before you make your trip, do a detailed preride inspection of your machine. I cover how to do a preride inspection in Chapter 13. Consider the length of the trip and whether you should get new tires or perform an oil change before you go.

Part V
The Part of Tens

The 5th Wave By Rich Tennant

"Motorcycles have such a mystique to them. Like Six Sigma management techniques or the Forex."

In this part . . .

This part gives you some great information in bite-sized chunks. For instance, I introduce some cool stuff, such as the top-ten great biker events and valuable motorcycling organizations you can consider joining. And because motorcycling is full of colorful characters and people who have made important contributions to the sport, I give thumbnail sketches of the ten most important folks. I also pick some of my favorite motorcycle-related movies, from serious documentaries to drive-in movies. Enjoy!

Chapter 18

Ten (Plus One) Can't-Miss Events

In This Chapter

▶ Discovering different motorcycling events

▶ Finding out why each event is so special

*I*n the motorcycling world, certain events are so well known that you can just mention their names and everyone knows exactly what you're talking about. They're also the events that, inevitably, someone is going to ask if you've ever been to. It can be pretty embarrassing to admit that you have never been to at least one of these top events. If you go to one and don't like it (which is doubtful), at least you have the motorcycling cred to last you a lifetime.

While motorcyclists of all different stripes go to these events, some are known as "biker" gatherings, and others appeal more to the sportbike or touring crowd. After you've decided what kind of motorcycle you want to ride and what motorcycling lifestyle you want to pursue, it's pretty easy to decide what events you really want to attend. (Turn to Chapter 4 for more on choosing a bike that fits you and your lifestyle.)

No matter what event or events you decide to attend this year, as a motor-cyclist you're guaranteed to enjoy the camaraderie and have a ball. In fact, plan your trip now because hotel rooms can fill up fast — sometimes six months to almost a year before the event. And in some places, expect to pay a premium for a hotel room during the event.

Daytona Bike Week

Usually held in late-February to early-March in Daytona Beach, Florida, Daytona Bike Week has actually grown into "Daytona 10 days." It's impossible to cram all the Daytona events into one little week. In fact, Daytona Bike Week, which has a rich history dating back to January 1937, has truly proven its status as one giant party with 500,000 of your closest motorcycling friends.

Daytona, which is the shorthand name that motorcyclists use for this event, has it all. It's best known for attracting older cruiser riders, but more and more younger sportbike riders are beginning to show up as a result of its wide offerings of fun.

Each day of Daytona Bike Week is chock-full of events. You'll find everything from custom bike shows and bikini-clad ladies wrestling in cole slaw to self-guided rides around the Florida countryside. You'll also find new bike displays by the motorcycle makers and charity fundraising rides. Main Street is the place to be if you want to watch the custom motorcycles of event-goers roll by. And if you need to buy anything at all related to motorcycling, the vendors at Daytona Bike Week probably have it. And don't forget to get yourself a tattoo!

The crown-jewel event of the many activities going on during Bike Week is the Daytona 200 motorcycle race, where the top professional roadracers in the nation battle handlebar-to-handlebar at close to 200 mph on the famed high-banked Daytona International Speedway asphalt track. The racing is exciting, especially when riders make last-second passes just before the finish line to win the race by milliseconds (which has actually happened in several recent races).

A round of the AMA Supercross Series also takes place at Daytona International Speedway during Bike Week. This highly anticipated event always makes for great racing. The factory teams pull out all the stops to try to win this prestigious event and demoralize the competition to gain momentum for the rest of the season. And then, of course, there's the professional dirt-track racing and the variety of amateur racing events, both roadracing and off-roadracing.

For the hard-core motorcyclist, Daytona Bike Week has it all. Check out the official Daytona Bike Week Web site for even more information about events and accommodations (www.daytonachamber.com/enbw/bwhomenew3.htm).

In the eyes of your fellow motorcyclists, you get extra credibility points if you ride your bike to Daytona from the frozen northern states such as Michigan, Massachusetts, or New York. If you make that icy trek, you're guaranteed to have a story to tell about your trip.

Biketoberfest

Biketoberfest, a smaller version of Daytona Bike Week, is held in October in Daytona Beach, Florida. While Biketoberfest isn't as huge as Daytona Bike Week, it's gaining in popularity because some riders just don't want to deal with the massive Daytona Bike Week crowd. You can consider Biketoberfest "Daytona Bike Week Lite."

Even though Biketoberfest lasts only four days and doesn't have professional racing, it still offers the custom motorcycles, vendors, cole-slaw wrestling, and other events that hard-core bikers have come to know and love. Attending Biketoberfest is a great way to cap the riding season for motorcyclists in states where they'll have to soon put away their bikes for the winter. Go to www.biketoberfest.org for dates and other information.

Sturgis Motorcycle Rally

Like Daytona Bike Week, the Sturgis Motorcycle Rally, held in Sturgis, South Dakota, has a long history. The seven-day event, which is traditionally held in early August, began in 1938. While Sturgis is ground zero for the festivities, the event has grown so big that Sturgis Motorcycle Rally activities are also held in nearby cities.

The Sturgis Motorcycle Rally is like Daytona Bike Week with its cole-slaw wrestling, custom bikes, hundreds of vendors, and bike-watching on the main drag through town. Daytona Bike Week trumps Sturgis with professional racing, but Sturgis outdoes Daytona on the party scene with a number of concerts performed by well-known rock and roll bands.

The Sturgis area also offers some great riding and easy trips to historic sites, such as Mount Rushmore. Even though more and more sportbikes are showing up at Daytona Bike Week, there are still very few at Sturgis. Sturgis is heaven for the cruiser crowd, particularly those on Harley-Davidsons. You can get more information on the event at www.sturgismotorcycle rally.com.

Laconia Motorcycle Week

Laconia Motorcycle Week is held in Laconia, New Hampshire, in mid-June. This nine-day mega-event is another favorite of the Harley-Davidson and cruiser crowd. The event made its debut in 1923. Along with Daytona and Sturgis, Laconia holds a spot in the top three most famous motorcycling events in the country.

Custom bike shows, self-guided rides, vendors, demonstration rides by the major motorcycle manufacturers, and all the other standard fare of a week of motorcycling nirvana is on tap at Laconia. Several types of amateur racing are also standard at this event. You'll also find tattoo contests and motorcycle riding skills competitions. Visit www.laconiamcweek.com/index.htm for more information.

MotoGP at Laguna Seca

Let's face it, car racing is for wimps. If you want to see real racing action, you have to see Superbikes and MotoGP bikes screaming around asphalt tracks at speeds of up to 200 mph. While the Daytona 200 is the granddaddy of American Superbike racing, Mazda Raceway Laguna Seca in Monterey, California, is the location for races featuring international stars. These are the best motorcycle roadracers on the planet. This is one of two American rounds of the international MotoGP Championship. The second is in Indianapolis, Indiana, which I discuss later in this chapter.

Called the Red Bull U.S. Grand Prix, the Laguna Seca race features specially built racing motorcycles that spend most of their time racing the MotoGP circuit in Europe and a few other places around the world. MotoGP is an international motorcycle racing championship, and the top riders make millions of dollars a year. America's Nicky Hayden, known as "The Kentucky Kid," was the 2006 MotoGP world champion. The 800cc MotoGP bikes have top speeds of about 208 mph, their engines produce about 220 horsepower, and they weigh just 326 pounds.

There are a few Americans battling in the MotoGP championship, and the large crowd at Laguna Seca is always rooting for one of the U.S. riders to win the race on their home turf. The Americans have the advantage on the technical 2-mile-plus Laguna Seca track because they've ridden it for years on Superbikes before making the move to MotoGP. But the Europeans have raced at Laguna Seca for several years now and have figured out the track, and that means they're starting to win the race. The track is famed for its *corkscrew*, which is a quick left and then right turn going down a steep downhill. What makes the corkscrew so tricky is that the racer is speeding up a long straightaway with a slight curve in it heading into the corkscrew, and the entrance to the corkscrew is blind.

MotoGP races in Europe attract up to 180,000 spectators. While MotoGP racing hasn't gained that much popularity in the United States, Laguna Seca still attracts tens of thousands of spectators. The race, which is held in July, has a festival atmosphere with skydivers dropping onto the track, stunt-plane fliers, and other types of nonmotorcycling entertainment. Plus you'll see lots of vendors selling everything the high-performance motorcyclist needs — from one-piece leather racing suits to top-of-the-line helmets to gloves with the best protection you can get. The race definitely attracts the sportbike crowd. And what's great about Laguna Seca is that it's a spectator-friendly racetrack — it's easy to find a great place to sit and watch the race.

The rare opportunity to see the world's best roadracers in action is reason enough to go to Laguna Seca. But wait, there's more! A few American racers are allowed to test their skills against the MotoGP regulars in the race, giving American fans even more racers to cheer for. And the MotoGP is packaged with an AMA Superbike race at the same track that same weekend, meaning spectators can watch America's best racers in action as well. It's a race weekend that many motorcyclists try to attend each year.

Plus, the after-race activities at night in nearby downtown Monterey, California, particularly the Cannery district, is great. Sportbikes line the streets at night and make for some great viewing. And it's always fun to chat with the owners. You can find out more about the Red Bull U.S. Grand Prix at www.redbullus grandprix.com/#s=home.

MotoGP at Indianapolis

The Red Bull Indianapolis GP in Indiana, first scheduled in September 2008, gives race fans in the Midwest a chance to see the best roadracers in the world. Did you know that the first race ever held at the Indianapolis Motor Speedway was a motorcycle race? The race will be neutral ground for all the MotoGP riders because none of them has ever ridden on the track. To accommodate the motorcycle race, the Indianapolis Motor Speedway built a new 2.6-mile road course. This is the second of two American rounds of the International MotoGP Championship, with the other being at Mazda Raceway Laguna Seca in Monterey, California.

While the Red Bull Indianapolis GP won't feature AMA Superbike racing like Laguna Seca does, it will have something that will give American fans a true taste of what MotoGP racing is like in other parts of the world: a 250cc class and 125cc class as well as the premier MotoGP 800cc class, just like at all the MotoGP races around the world except Laguna Seca. Visit www.redbull indianapolisgp.com for more information on this MotoGP event.

Americade

Harley-Davidson and cruiser riders have their Daytona Bike Week, Sturgis Motorcycle Rally, and Laconia Motorcycle Week, but touring riders have Americade, which is held in June. This massive five-day event held in Lake George, New York, attracts more than 50,000 motorcyclists. While most of them are touring riders, you'll also find people on sport-touring machines and cruisers. All riders are welcome. Note that the event organizers don't like loud pipes on bikes, and neither do most of the participants.

What makes Americade so popular? Besides the large number of events, Americade is a wholesome rally that you wouldn't be embarrassed to tell your parents about. You won't find burn-out contests or bikini-clad women cole-slaw wrestling here. Activities include guided and self-guided riding tours in upstate New York, boat cruises, dinners, a rodeo, charity rides, fashion shows, motorcycling-related seminars, trade shows, and more than $100,000 in door prizes. Check out www.tourexpo.com/data/mos/Frontpage/ Itemid,1 for more details.

Honda Hoot

The Honda Hoot is a four-day event that's held in June in Knoxville, Tennessee, and, like Americade, it has a true family flavor. It's called the Honda Hoot and is put on by the American Honda Motor Company, but all brands and types of motorcycles are welcome. The Honda Hoot is a favorite of the touring and sport-touring crowd.

The event features scenic rides, riding demonstrations, movies, a riverboat cruise, bike shows, motorcycle test rides, vendors, an ice cream social, a fish fry, and more. Plus, there's great riding in the area, as I mention when I discuss Deal's Gap in Chapter 16. To find out dates and other information, visit www.hondahoot.com/index.aspx?bhcp=1.

Golden Aspen Rally

The Golden Aspen Rally, held for four days in mid-September in Ruidoso, New Mexico, is a friendly rally like Americade and the Honda Hoot. This rally is primarily for tourers but welcomes all motorcyclists. Events include a trade show, rider safety training, field events, a parade, area riding, and even the crowning of a king and queen. Go to www.motorcyclerally.com for more information.

The Springfield Mile

Dirt-track racing is a true American sport, and it was invented in the United States with racers on specially built motorcycles battling on a dirt oval. The Springfield Mile, held on a mile-long dirt oval at the Illinois State Fairgrounds in Springfield, Illinois, on Labor Day weekend, is considered one of the most famous races on the AMA Flat Track Championship circuit.

Speeds average 100 mph on the track, and racers slide their machines around the corners handlebar to handlebar with one foot on the track. Racers wear a specially made steel sole that straps on their racing boot so they can keep a foot down on the track. With the roar of the engines (most of the race machines are Harley-Davidsons) and the close racing, the Springfield Mile is a spectacle. And it's a favorite among Harley-Davidson riders. For more information, go to the Web site of the promoter, the Illinois Motorcycle Dealers Association, at www.illinoismda.com, or to the AMA Web site at www.amaflattrack.com.

Supercross

Some 17 rounds of the AMA Supercross Series are held around the nation each year, beginning in January in Anaheim, California, and wrapping up in May in Las Vegas. *Supercross* is racing on a dirt course that features high jumps, tight turns, and rows of small hills that racers stutter over. The Supercross track is built in a stadium using tons of dirt.

Supercross attracts the younger set, and, in fact, probably a lot of the people who attend Supercross events probably don't even ride dirt bikes. Motorcyclists and nonmotorcyclists alike can appreciate the skill it takes for these riders to navigate the tight Supercross track at speed. The whole Supercross experience is like attending a rock concert. It's complete with loud music, bright lights, and plenty of excitement. After you attend one Supercross race, you're hooked and will always want to go back for more. For schedules and other information, visit www.amamotocross.com.

Chapter 19

Ten Great Motorcycling Groups

In This Chapter

▶ Looking at motorcycling groups you can join

▶ Reviewing what makes each organization special

There's a lot of fun and excitement in motorcycling, but it's even more fun when you can share the excitement with like-minded riders. By joining an organization, you find out about events to attend that are related to your particular style of riding, you have knowledgeable people to turn to when you need technical help with your bike, and you have an enthusiastic group of guys and gals you can pal around with who are always happy to see you.

You should also consider joining other organizations that are for the good of the whole of motorcycling now and in the future. These are groups dedicated to protecting the rights of motorcyclists, keeping roads and trails open to motorcycles, and fighting discrimination against motorcyclists.

It's good to be a member of one group, and great to be a member of several. This chapter gives you a look at some of the best motorcycling organizations in the country.

The American Motorcyclist Association

The American Motorcyclist Association (AMA) is the one do-it-all motorcycling organization in the United States. Whether you're concerned about protecting your rights as a rider, you want to discover great places to ride, or you want to race, you need to be a member of the AMA. The AMA was formed in 1924 and now boasts more than 280,000 members. It's the largest motorcyclists' organization in the world.

The AMA has a strong government relations department that tackles issues important to motorcyclists, such as bike bans, land closures, and discrimination against motorcyclists. Motorcyclist discrimination involves such things as health insurance policies that don't pay for the treatment of injuries sustained in a motorcycle crash — even though those same policies will pay for injuries suffered by someone who crashes while driving a car drunk. (I cover insurance in more detail in Chapter 10.)

To satisfy your passion for riding, the AMA can point you to hundreds of AMA-sanctioned rallies and riding events each year. The organization has arranged for discounts for AMA members for all sorts of stuff ranging from motorcycle insurance to bike parts. And the organization produces a monthly magazine called *American Motorcyclist,* one of the largest in the nation, which covers the many facets of motorcycling.

The organization also oversees amateur and professional racing across the country. If you've seen a motorcycle race, it was probably sanctioned by the AMA. If you want to get involved in amateur racing or hope to one day become a pro, the AMA can show you how. To find out more about the AMA, visit www.amadirectlink.com.

The BlueRibbon Coalition

The BlueRibbon Coalition, formed in 1987, is a national organization that's best known for protecting the rights of dirt bike riders. But the group is also involved in other things, such as promoting the responsible use of public land by off-road riders, educating land-use decision makers about the need for recreational trails, and educating the news media about motorized recreation. Check out www.sharetrails.org for more information about this coalition and issues affecting motorcyclists. At the coalition's Web site, you can also find out the status of some of the major legal fights involving motorcyclists around the country.

The BMW Motorcycle Owners of America

The BMW Motorcycle Owners of America, or BMWOA, is a social club for BMW owners that was formed in 1972. This social club, which has more than 37,000 members, holds an international rally each year in the United States or Canada. This rally attracts more than 7,000 riders. The organization's local clubs also hold smaller rallies around the country. Like all social clubs, the BMWOA promotes camaraderie and friendship. It also offers information on touring overseas. You can find out more about events and membership at www.bmwmoa.org.

The Gold Wing Road Riders Association

The Gold Wing Road Riders Association, known as GWRRA, was formed in 1977 and is for the touring set. It's made up mainly of Honda Gold Wing riders. (See Chapter 4 for a description of the Gold Wing.) With more than

80,000 members worldwide, the club promotes rider safety training, camaraderie among motorcyclists of all stripes, a positive image of motorcycling, and, of course, fun.

And I mean it when I say that club members do have fun. The GWRRA, for instance, sponsors rallies of various sizes around the nation. The crown jewel is the organization's annual national rally called the Wing Ding, which attracts around 10,000 riders and is held around July 4 at various places in the country. Most of the organization's rallies include bike shows, skill events, seminars, vendors, and, of course, rides. Find out more about membership and events at www.gwrra.org.

The Harley Owners Group

The Harley-Davidson Motor Company established the Harley Owners Group, or H.O.G., in 1983, and it now boasts more than a million members worldwide. This is definitely *the* social club for the Harley-Davidson crowd. Like other social clubs, H.O.G. sponsors local and national rallies. It also holds what it calls "touring rallies," in which Harley-Davidson riders ride from town to town.

The group's rallies usually feature live bands, bike shows, parades, skill games, and more. The touring rallies usually take place over several days as riders ride to various destinations, and they don't usually involve the humongous crowds that can be found at national and state rallies. Visit www.harley-davidson.com for more information.

The Honda Sport Touring Association

With a reputation for being the club for riders who truly like to get out and do some riding, the Honda Sport Touring Association, or HSTA, welcomes riders on all brands of motorcycles. The organization sponsors more than a dozen rallies around the country and they do a lot of riding. These rallies include rider safety training, campouts, and even some off-road rides.

Founded in 1982, the HSTA is a social club dedicated to promoting camaraderie among bikers and learning about motorcycling. The riders in this group are a little more spirited than those in some other groups, meaning they like to ride a little faster and tackle roads that are a lot twistier than riders in some other groups. The association has strong ties to the American Honda Motor Co. For more information on the HSTA, visit www.ridehsta.com.

The National Off-Highway Vehicle Conservation Council

The National Off-Highway Vehicle Conservation Council, known as NOHVCC, is an off-highway group dedicated to protecting the rights of off-road riders and to promoting safe and responsible riding. The group has representatives in each state to provide information to riders, associations, government officials, and politicians in order to promote responsible motorized recreation. Check out www.nohvcc.org for more information.

The Riders of Kawasaki Club

The Riders of Kawasaki Club, also known as ROK, is a Kawasaki factory-sponsored club for riders of all styles of Kawasaki streetbikes. Riders of other brands of machines are also welcome. This social organization, which began in 1991, promotes friendship and good times. You can find out more at www.kawasaki.com.

The Riders Association of Triumph

The Riders Association of Triumph, or R.A.T., is the official factory-sponsored riding club for Triumph owners. This social organization puts together rides, track days to practice your skills at roadrace courses, and more. Visit www.triumph.co.uk/usa for more information on membership and events.

The STAR Touring & Riding Association

With more than 40,000 members, the STAR Touring & Riding Association is the official riding organization of Star motorcycles. This cruiser organization bills itself as a family organization that welcomes riders on all makes of machines. It stresses a family atmosphere at its gatherings. For example, there are games for kids to play and no scantily clad women walking around.

STAR rides and rallies are held throughout the United States, and the national rally is called STAR Days, which features bike shows, vendors, rides, and tons of fun. Find out more at www.startouring.org.

Chapter 20

Ten Great People in Motorcycling

In This Chapter

▶ Reviewing motorcycling legends

▶ Looking at the accomplishments that make these motorcyclists great

*M*illions of motorcyclists are on the road today, and millions have been on the road since the beginning of motorcycling in the late 1800s. These motorcyclists range from the guy you're sure to run into at a motorcycling rally wearing a furry helmet with Viking horns, to the women who have made their marks in professional motorcycle racing, to the designers and engineers who have tomorrow's motorcycles in their heads today.

Out of this mix of millions of riders with different skills and accomplishments riding various machines, how many are true legends? Lots. Here, I've picked ten folks who I believe deserve the honor. Bring up these names in discussions with motorcyclists and some will agree with the list and some won't, sparking a spirited debated about motorcycling (which, of course, is something that motorcyclists enjoy).

However, many other people won't have a clue who these people are. That's okay, too. After all, those who know some of the names will be impressed by how knowledgeable you are, and those who don't know these legends will be interested in hearing about them. And by reading about these legends, you'll get a feel for how truly special, and diverse, motorcycling is.

Giacomo "Ago" Agostini

Giacomo "Ago" Agostini is revered as one on the greatest motorcycle road-racers of all time, and it's easy to see why. This Italian racer, who was on the world roadracing scene from 1964 to 1976, won races, races, and more races.

A world grand prix racer riding the most exotic machines against the best racers on the planet, Ago had some classic battles against Britain's Mike "The Bike" Hailwood, who also is considered one of the greatest racers of all time. In fact, Ago just narrowly won the 1966 and 1967 world 500cc grand prix championships, edging out Hailwood.

Ago rode for the MV Agusta factory team most of his career, but then he moved to Yamaha in 1974. That year, he won the Daytona 200 as he raced against international and American motorcycle racing stars.

When his career ended in 1976, Ago had won 122 grand prix races. He earned 15 world grand prix titles and 12 titles at the famed Isle of Man race in Britain. He then became a grand prix team manager.

Erwin "Cannonball" Baker

Erwin "Cannonball" Baker is known for making some incredible transcontinental rides at speed back when motorcycling was still relatively new, men were men, and cross-country highways didn't exist. His record-setting runs were the stuff of legend.

In 1908, at the age 26, Cannonball began winning local races aboard an American-made Indian. In 1909, he won the very first race ever held at the Indianapolis Motor Speedway. But he's best known as an endurance racer, making long distance runs from town to town racing trains and setting records for crossing the United States. He also set endurance records overseas.

Cannonball, who got his nickname from a newspaper reporter who compared him to the Cannonball Express train, died in 1960.

Erik Buell

Erik Buell is a motorcyclist who made his dreams come true. He left the Harley-Davidson Motor Company to form his own American motorcycling firm, which Harley-Davidson eventually bought.

A motorcycle roadracer, Buell worked at Harley-Davidson as a chassis designer when he decided to head out on his own in 1982 to build racing machines. His dream quickly hit a roadblock when the American Motorcyclist Association, which sets the rules and sanctions professional motorcycle racing in America, eliminated the racing class that Buell built his bikes for. This wrinkle called for a new plan.

Capitalizing on his expertise as a chassis designer, Buell decided to make sportbikes using Harley-Davidson motors. He built his first Buell RR1000 in 1985, and then he built sportbikes with bigger motors starting in 1988. Buells gained a reputation as great-handling, American sportbikes. The Harley-Davidson Motor Company bought Buell Motorcycles in 2003, and Buell himself still heads the company.

William G. Davidson

Yep, William G. Davidson, or Willie G., as he's affectionately known to millions of motorcyclists around the world, is a member of *that* Davidson family. He's the grandson of William A. Davidson who, along with his brothers Arthur and Walter, and William Harley, formed the Harley-Davidson Motor Company in 1903. But Willie G.'s lineage isn't what elevates him to god-like status among Harley-Davidson riders; it's what he has done at the Harley-Davidson Motor Company that has earned him the respect of all motorcyclists — and not just Harley-Davidson fans.

Willie G. joined the Harley-Davidson design team in 1963 and rose to be the head of the styling department. He's credited with taking some risks at Harley-Davidson that have moved the company forward with new designs. For example, Willie G. saw what was happening in the motorcycling world in the late 1960s when riders were buying Harleys and then customizing them into choppers. Willie G. decided that it was time to give riders an opportunity to get a custom bike straight from the factory.

The result? The 1971 Super Glide, which essentially was the company's Electra Glide with a chopper, or extended, front end. He also designed an integrated, fiberglass seat and tail section, splashed on some bright colors, and rolled out a new bike with styling unlike anything anyone had ever seen from Harley-Davidson.

Unfortunately, sales of the new Super Glide were, well, less than stellar. It seemed that the integrated seat and tail wasn't the look Harley riders wanted. But riders did like the low, lean aspects of this 74 cubic-inch (1,208cc), 560-pound cruiser. So when Harley-Davidson decided to drop-kick the seat-tail section in favor of a more conventional seat and rear fender, sales picked up. The Super Glide quickly became a favorite among riders. In fact, the Super Glide is still popular today. It is generally accepted as the first *factory custom*, a motorcycle built by the factory to appeal to the crowd that would normally buy a custom. The Japanese manufacturers later followed suit.

Willie G. is obviously well known for his styling efforts, but newer riders may not know the critical role he played in preventing the demise of the Harley-Davidson Motor Company. In the early 1970s, he and a dozen other Harley-Davidson executives joined together and bought the ailing company from owner AMF (the guys who make bowling equipment) just when it looked like Harley-Davidson might be forced into bankruptcy. Under the guidance of Willie G. and the other executives, the Harley-Davidson Motor Company was saved and has become a successful, profitable company.

Watch for Willie G. and his trademark beret at big Harley-Davidson rallies around the nation. He enjoys attending rallies and hanging around with riders. He's the most visible, and most recognizable, face of Harley-Davidson today.

Dick "Bugsy" Mann

A few motorcycle racers weren't happy doing just one type of racing over the span of their careers. These racers did whatever kind of racing they could, whenever they could. Few excelled in the various disciplines. But Dick "Bugsy" Mann did.

During his long professional racing career, which stretched from 1959 to 1974, Bugsy competed in dirt track, motocross, and roadracing championships. One of his biggest victories came in 1970 when, after 15 years of trying, he won the Daytona 200 roadrace. He won aboard a Honda 750, showing that the Japanese factories were up to the task of building premier race-winning machines.

On the dirt-track scene, he won his first professional race in Peoria, Illinois, in 1959. He won his first dirt-track championship in 1963 and his second in 1971. Bugsy also successfully raced in the then-fledgling sport of motocross professionally in the 1960s and 1970s. He retired from professional racing in 1974, and represented the United States on the International Six Day Trial team overseas in 1975.

In the old days, racers were also their own mechanics, and Bugsy became famous for wearing straw hats while working on his bikes. These hats were inexpensive and could be picked up just about anywhere, because they were popularly worn by women while they did gardening.

Jeremy "Showtime" McGrath

Jeremy "Showtime" McGrath is certainly one of the greatest Supercross racers of all time. He brought showmanship to the sport in the 1990s that wowed not only motorcycle enthusiasts but the general public as well. Crowds were packing stadiums across the nation to see the country's best Supercross racers in action, especially McGrath.

Before getting into Supercross, which involves racing on small tracks with tight turns and high jumps, McGrath raced BMX bicycles. One day he decided to bring some of his BMX tricks to the motorcycle scene. He invented the *Nac Nac,* a trick where he takes a jump and then hangs off the side of the bike while high in the air. McGrath's antics aboard his bike helped create a sport now known as *freestyle motocross,* in which competitors don't race, but instead do tricks on motocross machines.

McGrath began his professional Supercross career in 1989 and went on to become the winningest Supercross rider in the history of the sport, with 72 wins. He earned seven Supercross titles before retiring in 2003. Although retired, he still does test riding for Honda.

He also raced as part of the American Motocross of Nations team in 1993 and 1996. As a part of this team, McGrath competed in Motocross against other teams from around the world on outdoor natural terrain tracks. Those tracks are much longer than Supercross tracks but with the same challenging turns and jumps. The American team won both those years.

"King" Kenny Roberts

You can't be a sportbike or motorcycle racing enthusiast and not know the name "King" Kenny Roberts. This motorcycle roadracer from Modesto, California, raced in the United States before heading off to Europe to show the European riders and fans, who at that time sneered at American road-racers, that they could get beat by American upstarts. Roberts wasn't afraid of risks.

Roberts began his professional racing career at the age of 16 on American dirt tracks, sliding his racing machines around corners handlebar to handle-bar with the best racers in the nation. Remarkably, he won the very first race he entered as a professional in 1972. And he won the national No. 1 plates in 1973 and 1974. Roberts is probably best remembered as a dirt-track racer, though, and for racing a machine that had a Yamaha TZ750 roadracing motor stuffed in a dirt-track race bike frame in 1975. Most riders in his day were on Harley-Davidson motorcycles.

Roberts showed up with his unique bike for the race at the Indy Mile in Indianapolis in 1975. While the Harley-Davidson bikes probably topped out at around 120 mph on the long straights at the Indy Mile, Kenny's bike could hit 150 mph. He truly had a dirt-track weapon. The only problem was that he had a difficult time controlling the power of the monster Yamaha motor. Traction in the corners is the name of the game on dirt tracks, and it took all of Kenny's skill to keep the rear wheel of his machine from spinning so that he could maintain traction.

Roberts rode the bucking beast in the main event and found himself in fourth place in the last corner on the last lap. Somehow, he managed to get by the leading trio of Harley-Davidsons with just feet to spare at the finish line. It's considered one of the greatest achievements in American racing history.

Besides riding dirt track, Roberts was also a roadracer. He won the American Formula One roadracing title in 1977, and then he set off to challenge Europe's best roadracers in 1978 in the world championships. He stunned the European roadracing world in 1978 by winning the FIM World 500cc Grand Prix Championship in his rookie season, making him the first American to ever win the 500cc World title. He went on to win the No. 1 plate again in 1979 and 1980.

After the 1983 season Roberts retired as a racer. He has been running his own World 500cc Championship teams ever since.

Malcolm Smith

A great off-road rider, Malcolm Smith came to national prominence with the release of the 1971 feature film documentary *On Any Sunday*. This documentary examined motorcycle racing in America, and Smith was one of the featured racers. Probably the most memorable scene in the movie shows Smith, actor Steve McQueen, and dirt-track racer Mert Lawill having a ball while riding dirt bikes on a beach near the ocean.

In the early days of his racing career, Smith rode a 1953 matchless and then later a Greeves machine in hare scrambles races (which involved two-hour races over rugged terrain). Smith likes to tell the story about how Edison Dye, who promoted and built up in America the European sport of motocross, approached him in 1966 and asked him to race a Swedish machine that he was importing — the Husqvarna.

Smith was skeptical, but Dye told him if he liked the machine he would send Smith to the prestigious International Six Day Trails in Sweden. Smith liked the machine, and so he went to Sweden where he earned a silver medal. He attended the International Six Day Trials the next year in Poland and earned a gold medal. Over the years, he earned a total of eight gold medals.

Smith is also well known for his great racing in the Baja 1000, a 1,000-mile race in Mexico. Off-road riding gear called "MSR" is made by the company he founded, Malcolm Smith Racing.

Bessie Stringfield

Bessie Stringfield was a strong woman, and she rode a motorcycle back when women just didn't do that. During her 60 years of riding, she didn't just ride around town either; she made cross-country treks alone at a time when it was rare for a woman to do so — and downright dangerous for an African-American to do it. She died in 1993 at the age of 82.

Stringfield was 16 when she rode her first bike. During her riding career, she rode in every state in the mainland United States, and served during World War II as a civilian motorcycle dispatch rider. She also raced flat track, and won, disguised as a man. She became known as the "Motorcycling Queen of Miami."

Theresa Wallach

An early motorcycling pioneer, Theresa Wallach is probably best known for her grueling trek across Africa in the 1930s. But she also was involved in other aspects of motorcycling; she served, for example, as a military dispatch rider, mechanic, and safety-school instructor.

Born in 1909 in London, England, Wallach rode and raced motorcycles as a young lady. In 1935, she and friend Florence Blenkiron loaded up a motorcycle equipped with a sidecar and trailer and set off on an incredible journey from London to Capetown, South Africa. Imagine crossing the Sahara with no roads and all the dangers. Wallach and her friend did it, earning respect from the British motorcycling community.

She served in the British army as a mechanic and motorcycle dispatch rider. She also toured the United States, Canada, and Mexico, moving to live in the U.S. in 1952. While in the U.S., she started a motorcycle safety training school. Wallach rode until she was 88, and died in 1999 on her 90th birthday.

Chapter 21

Ten Must-See Motorcycling Movies

In This Chapter

▶ Exploring motorcycling through the movies

▶ Getting to know some of the best and worst biker movies

*F*ilmmakers had a fascination with bikers from the early 1950s to the late 1960s, and even beyond. But, as you can imagine, filmmakers weren't interested in making documentaries about the motorcycling lifestyle. Nope. They were interested in making movies that would make cash.

It's no surprise then that a lot of the biker movies made in the 1950s and 1960s followed popular Western movie formulas, including good versus evil, barroom brawls, love interests, and rivaling gangs. These movies made for entertainment even though they didn't exactly match reality.

In this chapter, I clue you in on some of these fabulously entertaining motor-cycle movies. So rent a few, grab the popcorn, turn down the lights, and have a ball.

The Wild One (1954)

Considered by most to be the movie that started the wave of motorcycle gang movies out of Hollywood, *The Wild One* stars Marlon Brando and Lee Marvin as rival gang leaders. The movie portrays bike gangs as young hood-lums rebelling against society. They just wanted to ride, fight, and party. This is the theme of most of the biker movies to follow. However, this movie is actually quite tame compared to the later biker movies.

This movie is based on a real-life incident shortly after World War II; this inci-dent was actually blown out of proportion by the news media. It was a gather-ing of about 4,000 motorcyclists in Hollister, California, in 1947. Some of the motorcyclists rode their bikes into bars, a few were drunk in the streets, and the media reported that bikers terrorized the town. I discuss the so-called Hollister riot in Chapter 2.

The Wild Angels (1966)

With stars like Peter Fonda, Nancy Sinatra, and Bruce Dern, what more could you want in a movie? In *The Wild Angels,* Fonda is named Heavenly Blues; his devoted girlfriend, Sinatra, is named Mike; and Dern is called Loser. Together Blues and Loser lead an attack on another gang. During the melee, Loser steals a motorcycle cop's bike and ends up getting hurt and going to the hospital (and his buds decide to bust him out). The gang ransacks a church and fights in a cemetery. These dudes have no morals and are just plain mean. At a funeral, Heavenly Blues says, "We want to be free to ride our machines without being hassled by The Man," which has become one of the most famous movie lines in motorcycling.

Hell's Angels on Wheels (1967)

In *Hell's Angels on Wheels,* Jack Nicholson is a gas station attendant who gets into a spat with a customer and, as a result, loses his job. But lucky for him, he already has a biker nickname, Poet, and runs into a gang of bikers who invite him to hang around with them.

The movie features a lot of brawls, a lot of riding, and a lot of partying. And to make things even more exciting, love-struck Poet falls for the gang leader's girl, Shill, who's played by actress Sabrina Scharf. Sigh. He has morals, doesn't believe the gang life is for Shill, and tries to talk her into leaving the gang with him.

Hell's Belles (1969)

In *Hell's Belles,* a dirt bike racer named Dan, played by actor Jeremy Slate, gets his bike stolen by a motorcycle gang. When he tries to get it back, he ends up being given a biker chick named Cathy (Jocelyn Lane) in exchange for it. Hmmm. But he still wants his bike back. So, with Cathy in tow, he hunts down gang members individually and in pairs. I still have no idea why they named the movie *Hell's Belles.* After all, the movie revolves around the dirt bike rider and his lady friend.

Easy Rider (1969)

In *Easy Rider,* Peter Fonda and Dennis Hopper are a couple of hippie bikers named Wyatt and Billy who hop on their machines and take off in search of adventure in the American South and Southwest. They're just modern-day cowboys looking for the freedom to be themselves and have a good time. Fonda and Hopper link up with Jack Nicholson, who plays a lawyer, along the way. What do they find on their journey? The freedom of the open road, drugs, communes, and rednecks. *Easy Rider* isn't really a biker gang movie. Instead, it's a movie about riding, exploring, discovering, and understanding the counterculture of the late 1960s.

Little Fauss and Big Halsy (1970)

In the movie *Little Fauss and Big Halsy,* Robert Redford stars as Big Halsy, a motorcycle racer. Michael Pollard, who's referred to as Little Fauss, is Redford's mechanic and team owner in their unsuccessful efforts to win various forms of motorcycle races. Redford is a cocky womanizer while Fauss is talented but unsure of himself. The movie revolves around their strained relationship, with a love interest for Redford thrown in for kicks.

On Any Sunday (1972)

More than 30 years later, many riders still consider *On Any Sunday* the best motorcycle movie ever made. Filmmaker Bruce Brown made the surfing documentary *The Endless Summer* in 1966, and then followed up with *On Any Sunday,* a motorcycling documentary. Why that title? Because the movie focuses on racing, both amateur and professional, and on any given Sunday across the United States you can find racers in the dirt and on the racetracks.

On Any Sunday looks at various forms of motorcycle sport from cross-country racing and hillclimbing to dirt-track racing and more. The film also shows regular people just having fun riding their motorcycles. Well, that is, if you consider actor Steve McQueen and racers Mert Lawwill and Malcolm Smith regular people.

This documentary showed America that motorcyclists aren't thugs out to pillage towns, but are simply regular folks with a passion for their sport. It also showed how fun motorcycling truly is.

Take It to the Limit (1980)

Take It to the Limit is a documentary that gives the viewer a good idea of the excitement of racing motorcycles on asphalt and dirt ovals. In fact, this movie has some incredible footage that's astounding to everyone, even longtime motorcyclists. Racer Kenny Roberts' come-from-behind win at the Indianapolis Mile in 1975 aboard a dirt-track machine with a powerful Yamaha TZ750 road-racing motor shoehorned into it is legendary. "They don't pay me enough to ride that thing," Roberts said afterward.

Various roadracing stars show what it's like to take on the world on asphalt racetracks at 180 mph. Russ Collins shows what it's like to rocket down the quarter-mile drag strip, and Mick Andrews and Debbie Evans slow things down by doing tricks on their dirt machines. Also significant is footage of the legendary Mike "the Bike" Hailwood racing on the streets at the Isle of Man in Great Britain.

Chopper Chicks in Zombietown (1991)

I warn you now: *Chopper Chicks in Zombietown* is a pretty bad movie. Unless, of course, you like this kind of bad-acting entertainment (and a lot of people out there do!). A female biker gang rides into the town of Zariah in search of well, men, only to discover (gasp) a zombie horde on a rampage. This movie has it all: biker chicks, midgets, zombies, blind orphans, and more. Jamie Rose plays Dede, Catherine Carlen plays Rox, and Lycia Naff is T.C.

Beyond the Law (1992)

In *Beyond the Law,* Charlie Sheen plays an undercover cop who infiltrates a motorcycle gang. As you can imagine, mayhem follows. The gang is made up of tough guys who are into drugs and guns, and Sheen has to prove himself a bad guy to keep in the good graces of the gang. The movie surveys how far he can go in committing crimes without crossing the line from cop to criminal. Believe it or not, this is a pretty good movie.

Part VI
Appendixes

In this part . . .

Part of what separates motorcycle riders from car drivers is that bike riders speak a totally different language. In fact, that's part of the fun of motorcycling. In this part, I introduce you to some of the jargon you need to know as well as a rundown on key laws affecting motorcycles and motorcyclists in all 50 states. That way when you plan your trips across state lines you know you'll be riding legally. I also give you a sampling of some great motorcycling resources; check these out for info and tips on everything from gear to events to the latest government research on motorcycle safety.

Appendix A

A Motorcycling Glossary: Talking the Talk

M otorcyclists have their own unique language, and to fit in you need to know at least some of the stuff that they're talking about. Once you become a motorcyclist, you'll catch on to the special language quickly. Until then, however, take a glance through some of the key words and phrases in this glossary. That way you don't feel like an outsider when you're hanging around your fellow motorcyclists. This glossary is just a taste of the words you'll hear while hanging around, and talking to motorcyclists. It is by no means a complete dictionary of the motorcycling language. It simply gives you a good start.

ABS: The shorthand way to refer to an anti-lock braking system. This system prevents your motorcycle's brakes from locking up. This system pulses the brakes rapidly instead of fully locking the wheel, allowing the rider to keep control under extreme braking instead of sliding a wheel.

aftermarket: The industry that makes parts for bikes. An aftermarket part is one that's bought for your bike from a maker other than your bike's manufacturer. An example is an aftermarket exhaust system.

air-cooled motor: An engine that's cooled by air flowing over it (rather than one that's cooled with a radiator).

AMA: The American Motorcyclist Association, which is the largest motorcyclists association in the world. The AMA concentrates on rights, riding, and racing.

American cruiser: Normally means a Harley-Davidson motorcycle, but also can mean a Victory motorcycle. Both are made in America. American cruiser is used to distinguish the machine from a metric cruiser, which is made in Japan.

ape hangers: Handlebars on custom bikes that are higher than a rider's shoulders. They're illegal in some states.

apex: The tightest point, or center, of a turn or curve. This is a point in a turn or curve that a motorcyclist should ride through to take a normal turn or curve correctly.

auger in: When riders crash their dirt bikes and land head first in the dirt.

bagger: A big touring machine with saddlebags or luggage. Also known as a dresser.

Beemer: A BMW motorcycle.

belt drive: A belt final drive that connects the motor to the rear wheel. Used mostly on Harley-Davidsons, some cruisers, and Buell sportbikes. See *final drive.*

blip the throttle: A quick back-and-forward twist of the throttle to quickly raise and lower the engine's rpms.

BMW MOA: The BMW Motorcycle Owners of America, which is a nationwide club.

camber: A term referring to the tilt of the road surface or racetrack. For example, a positive camber turn is a turn where the asphalt tilts inward, providing for more traction around the turn so you can lean your motorcycle further. An off-camber turn, on the other hand, means the asphalt tilts in the opposite direction of the turn, providing for less traction (which can be dangerous) so you shouldn't lean your motorcycle over as far as you would in a positive camber turn.

chain drive: A drive that uses a chain to transfer power from a front sprocket connected to the motor to a rear sprocket connected to the rear wheel. See *final drive.*

chicane: An S-turn that's put on the straightaway of a racetrack to slow the bikes down.

chopper: A bike with many items removed to make it faster and lighter. These machines usually have long front forks, wild paint jobs, and special handlebars. Choppers can be built from a bike that was bought from the factory or can be built from the ground up.

colors: The patch on the back of a motorcycle club member's jacket that identifies the club.

contact patch: The part of the tire that touches the road.

The Corkscrew: Probably the most famous racetrack corner in all of motorcycle racing. It's at Mazda Raceway Laguna Seca in Monterey, California, and it consists of a sharp left, right turn that drops down a steep hill.

countershaft: The front sprocket attached to the motor that a chain rolls on to transfer power to the rear wheel.

countersteering: A steering technique in which you push the left handlebar (rather than pull) to turn left and push the right handlebar to turn right.

cross up: A classic motorcycle trick. It can be in reference to when a dirt bike is in the air after taking a jump or when a streetbike's front wheel is in the air and the rider turns the handlebars fully to the left or the right.

crotch rocket: A sportbike. This term is considered somewhat derogatory.

cruiser: A motorcycle made for cruising. This bike is characterized by low seat height, high weight, and a torquey motor.

custom: A bike, with the characteristics of a chopper, which was built from the ground up. Show customs are usually very flashy and very expensive.

displacement: The size of a motorcycle engine, given in cubic inches or cubic centimeters. It's a measurement of the volume of the cylinders. Generally, the bigger the displacement the more powerful the motor.

DOT: Federal Department of Transportation. All helmets sold in the United States must be approved by the Department of Transportation and have a DOT sticker.

dual-purpose bike: A motorcycle designed for both road and off-road use. Generally it's a dirt-focused bike with equipment added to make it street legal. Also known as a dual-sport.

Duck: A Ducati motorcycle.

Enduro: A dirt-oriented bike with a headlight and taillight but that isn't street legal.

Engine braking: Using the engine, rather than the brakes, to slow down by downshifting, letting off on the throttle, and letting out the clutch.

engine cutoff switch: This switch, which is normally on the right handlebar, allows the rider to turn off the engine without taking a hand off the handlebars. Also known as a kill switch.

ergonomics: The relationship of the components on a bike to the rider. Good ergonomics means that the bike fits a rider well. Bad ergonomics means that a rider may have to really stretch to reach the handlebars, for example, or could have an uncomfortable seating position because of the location of the footpegs.

face plant: When riders crash their dirt bikes and land face first in the dirt.

fairing: The bodywork on the front or sides of a motorcycle. The front fairing and windscreen normally deflect air, while the side fairings improve aerodynamics.

final drive: The system for transferring power from the engine to the rear wheel. A chain drive is the most common type of final drive, but others include belt and shaft drives.

floorboards: Flat panels for placement of the feet instead of footpegs. These are found on some baggers and cruisers.

forks: The metal tubes on the front of a motorcycle that connect the front wheel to the chassis of the bike.

gauntlet: The part of a motorcycle glove that extends beyond the wrist.

gearbox: Another name for a motorcycle's transmission.

Gixxer: A Suzuki GSX-R motorcycle.

hairpin: A tight bend in the road that turns back toward the direction it started. Generally this is a 180-degree turn.

heel-toe shifter: A shift lever that allows the rider to shift gears with either the heel or the toe of a boot.

highside: When a rider is flipped over the high side of a motorcycle. This usually happens when the rider loses traction while leaned over in a turn and then abruptly catches traction again. A highside is the opposite of a lowside.

Hog: The trademarked nickname for a big Harley-Davidson motorcycle.

H.O.G.: The Harley Owners Group, which is a national club of Harley-Davidson owners.

horsepower: A way to measure energy. One horsepower equals lifting 33,000 pounds up one foot over one minute. It's used to illustrate the power of motors.

Husky: A Husqvarna motorcycle.

line: The path taken by a motorcycle, especially around a turn. This term is commonly used when discussing racing lines around a racetrack. For instance, you may hear someone referring to the inside line when a racer passes another racer on the inside of a corner, or the outside line when the racer goes around the outside of the other racer.

locked up: When a tire stops spinning. This can also refer to a motor where the pistons have seized and are stuck, which is also called a frozen motor.

lowside: When a motorcycle slides out in a turn because of a lack of traction, causing the rider to fall off the motorcycle on the low side of the bike.

lugging the motor: When a rider operates the motorcycle at very low rpms and the motor jerks. Lugging the motor isn't considered a good thing.

metric cruiser: A cruiser made in Japan.

MotoGP: An international motorcycling roadracing championship. The MotoGP class of the MotoGP championship features specialized 800cc, four-stroke bikes. These roadracers are considered the best in the world. It's considered the top rank of motorcycle roadracing competition.

MRF: The Motorcycle Riders Foundation, which is a motorcyclist rights group.

MSF: The Motorcycle Safety Foundation, which is best known for offering internationally respected rider safety training.

OEM: The original equipment manufacturer of a bike. These are the motorcycle factories as opposed to the aftermarket industry.

off-road motorcycle: A motorcycle built for riding off road.

one-piece: A one-piece riding suit; usually a roadracing suit made of leather.

panniers: Saddlebags or luggage that mounts on the side rear of a motorcycle.

pin it: When a rider twists a motorcycle's throttle all the way open.

poser: Someone who pretends to be a motorcyclist, either by rarely riding his or her motorcycle and just showing up at events for the lifestyle or by wearing motorcyclist garb without owning a motorcycle.

powerband: The rpm range in which an engine makes the most power.

Power cruiser: Cruisers with more powerful motors and usually beefed-up suspension and braking components compared to regular cruisers.

redline: The maximum rpms at which an engine can operate without damage. The redline is usually marked on an analog tachometer. Or, to avoid damaging the motor, a bike also may have a rev limiter that cuts out the engine momentarily when the redline is reached.

RPMs: The abbreviation for revolutions per minute. This is in reference to the revolutions per minute of the motor's piston or pistons.

seizure: When the piston or pistons in an engine stop moving up and down after getting too hot (due to a lack of lubrication) and expanding to the point that they won't move in their cylinders. This stoppage locks up the drivetrain and rear wheel. A seizure can be temporary, but if it isn't, and the motor can't be unstuck, such an engine is considered "frozen." A seizure can happen when you exceed the redline for too long.

short shift: When you shift into a higher gear at lower rpms rather than waiting until you get near heart of the powerband as you normally would. Short shifting is normally done when roads are slick (so you don't spin the rear wheel) or when you want to keep the noise of your exhaust system quiet while riding through a neighborhood.

six-speed: A transmission with six gears.

slick: A super sticky, treadless racing tire. These tires are dangerous, and illegal, for street use.

spark arrester: A device that goes on the end of an exhaust pipe of an off-road motorcycle so that no sparks come out of the pipe, which could possibly cause a forest fire.

specs: Shorthand for specifications for a motorcycle, such as horsepower, seat height, wheelbase, weight, and how many gallons of gas the tank holds.

squid: A new or reckless rider who rides over his or her abilities. It's a commonly used but derogatory term.

stoppie: When a rider lifts a motorcycle's rear wheel off the ground by quickly and forcefully applying the front brakes. This is an illegal maneuver on the street.

straight pipes: Exhaust pipes with no baffles; these pipes are extremely loud.

sweeper: A long, gentle curve or turn in the road.

torque: This is a measurement of force, usually in foot-pounds or inch-pounds.

tourer: Long-distance motorcycles built for comfort. They're big, heavy, and able to click off thousands of miles on the road easily.

traction: The grip between the tire and the road.

two-piece: A two-piece riding suit in which the jacket and pants zip together at the waist.

wheelbase: The distance between the axles of the front wheel and the rear wheel. A shorter wheelbase usually means that a bike will turn more quickly, while a longer wheelbase gives a bike more straight-line stability.

wheelie: Using the power of the motor to pull the front wheel off the ground. This is an illegal maneuver on the street.

Willie G.: Nickname for Willie G. Davidson, who's the styling guru at the Harley-Davidson Motor Company and grandson of William A. Davidson, one of the company's original founders.

Appendix B

State Motorcycling Laws

• •

*A*s a motorcyclist, you may decide to take a trip to another state or even to several states. If you do, you better know the laws for those states. (I guarantee the police officer won't be lenient if you plead ignorance.) For example, some states require you to wear a helmet, and some states don't (though you should always wear one regardless of the law).

The following is some basic information on the motorcycling laws in all 50 states, courtesy of the American Motorcyclist Association (AMA). Before making your trip, check to see whether any of these laws have changed by going to the AMA Web site at www.amadirectlink.com. Once you're at the Web site, click on the State Laws tab to see the full list.

Alabama

Helmet required; riding two abreast in the same lane allowed; mirror required

Alaska

Helmet required for those under age 18 and for passengers; eye protection required unless you have a tall windscreen; riding two abreast in the same lane allowed; left-side and right-side mirrors required

Arizona

Helmet required for those under age 18; eye protection required unless you have a windscreen; riding two abreast in the same lane allowed

Arkansas

Helmet required for those under age 21; eye protection required; no passengers under age 8; mirror required.

California

Helmet required; mirror required; turn signals required

Colorado

Helmet required for those under age 18 and for passengers; riding two abreast in the same lane allowed; mirror required

Connecticut

Helmet required for those under age 18 and for instructional permit holders; eye protection required unless you have a windscreen; riding two abreast in the same lane allowed; mirror required

Delaware

Helmet must have reflective stickers, must be in your possession, must be worn under age 20, and must be worn if you have an instructional permit; eye protection required unless you have a windscreen; mirror required

Florida

Helmet not required for those over age 21 who have a minimum $10,000 in medical insurance; eye protection required; riding two abreast in the same lane allowed; mirror required; turn signals required

Georgia

Helmet required; eye protection required unless you have a windscreen; riding two abreast in the same lane allowed; mirror required

Hawaii

Helmet must have reflective stickers and is required for those under age 18; eye protection required unless you have a windscreen; riding two abreast in the same lane allowed; no passengers under age 7; mirror required

Idaho

Helmet required for those under age 18

Illinois

Eye protection required unless you have a windscreen; mirror required

Indiana

Helmet required for those under age 18 and for instructional permit holders; eye protection required for those under age 18; riding two abreast in the same lane allowed; mirrors required for bikes built after January 1, 1956

Iowa

Riding two abreast in the same lane allowed; mirror required

Kansas

Helmet required for those under age 18; eye protection required unless you have a windscreen; riding two abreast in the same lane allowed; left-side mirror required; turn signals required for bikes built after 1973

Kentucky

Helmet required for novice riders, for those under age 21, and for instructional permit holders; eye protection required; mirror required

Louisiana

Helmet required; eye protection required unless you have a windscreen; riding two abreast in the same lane allowed; no passengers under age 5; left-side mirror required; turn signals required

Maine

Helmet required for those under age 15, for those operating under a learner's permit, for those operating with less than one year of experience with a motorcycle license, or as a passenger of an operator required to wear a helmet; riding two abreast in the same lane allowed; mirror required; turn signals required for bikes built after 1974

Maryland

Helmet required and it must have reflective stickers; eye protection required unless you have a windscreen; riding two abreast in the same lane allowed; left-side and right-side mirrors required; turn signals required

Massachusetts

Helmet required; eye protection required for instructional permit holders and required unless you have a windscreen; riding two abreast in the same lane allowed; mirror required; turn signals required

Michigan

Helmet required; eye protection required unless you have a windscreen; eye protection required at speeds over 35 mph; riding two abreast in the same lane allowed; mirror required

Minnesota

Helmet required for those under age 18 and for instructional permit holders; eye protection required; riding two abreast in the same lane allowed; mirror required

Mississippi

Helmet required

Missouri

Helmet required

Montana

Helmet required for those under age 18; riding two abreast in the same lane allowed; mirror required

Nebraska

Helmet required; riding two abreast in the same lane allowed

Nevada

Helmet required; eye protection required unless you have a windscreen; riding two abreast in the same lane allowed; right-side and left-side mirrors required; turn signals required for bikes built after 1973

New Hampshire

Helmet required for those under age 18; eye protection required unless you have a windscreen; riding two abreast in the same lane allowed; mirror required

New Jersey

Helmet with reflective stickers required; eye protection required for instructional permit holders and unless you have a windscreen; mirror required

New Mexico

Helmet with reflective stickers required; eye protection required unless you have a windscreen; mirror required; turn signals required

New York

Helmet with reflective stickers required; eye protection required; riding two abreast in the same lane allowed; mirror required

North Carolina

Helmet required; riding two abreast in the same lane allowed; mirror required

North Dakota

Helmet with reflective stickers required for those under age 18; riding two abreast in the same lane allowed; mirror required

Ohio

Helmet required for novice riders and those under age 18; eye protection required unless you have a windscreen; riding two abreast in the same lane allowed; mirror required; turn signals required for bikes built after 1968

Oklahoma

Helmet required for those under age 18; eye protection required unless you have a windscreen; right-side and left-side mirrors required

Oregon

Helmet required; riding two abreast in the same lane allowed; mirror required; turn signals required

Pennsylvania

Helmet not required over age 21 with successful completion of rider training or two full years of riding experience; eye protection required; riding two abreast in the same lane allowed; mirror required for bikes built after April 1, 1977

Rhode Island

Helmet required for novice riders, for those under age 21, and for passengers; eye protection required; riding two abreast in the same lane allowed; mirror required

South Carolina

Helmet with reflective stickers required for those under age 21; eye protection required under age 21 and unless bike has a windscreen; riding two abreast in the same lane allowed; mirror required

South Dakota

Helmet required for those under age 18; eye protection required unless you have a windscreen; riding two abreast in the same lane allowed; mirror required; turn signals required

Tennessee

Helmet required; eye protection required unless you have a windscreen; riding two abreast in the same lane allowed; mirror required

Texas

Helmet required for those under age 21; helmet not required for those over age 21 with successful completion of rider training or $10,000 in medical insurance; mirror required

Utah

Helmet required for those under age 18; riding two abreast in the same lane allowed; mirror required

Vermont

Helmet with reflective stickers required; eye protection required unless you have a windscreen; riding two abreast in the same lane illegal; mirror required; turn signals required

Virginia

Helmet required; eye protection required unless you have a windscreen; riding two abreast in the same lane illegal; mirror required

Washington

Helmet required; eye protection required unless you have a windscreen; riding two abreast in the same lane allowed; no passengers under age 5; left-side and right-side mirrors required

West Virginia

Helmet required; eye protection required; mirror required; turn signals required

Wisconsin

Helmet required for those under age 18 and for instructional permit holders; eye protection required for instructional permit holders and required unless you have a windscreen that is 15 inches or higher above the handlebars; riding two abreast in the same lane allowed; mirror required; turn signals required

Wyoming

Helmet required for those under age 18; riding two abreast in the same lane allowed; mirror required

District of Columbia

Helmet with reflective stickers required; eye protection required unless you have a windscreen; mirror required

Appendix C

A Motorcyclist's Resource Guide

• •

*T*here's a lot of information available in the motorcycling world for both beginning motorcyclists and long-time, hard-core riders. It's impossible to put together a list of all the great motorcycling organizations, brand-specific Internet forums, motorcycle makers, performance parts manufacturers, engine builders, and motorcycle rider safety training outfits in the country. But hey, I can try, can't I?

This appendix provides a look at a variety of resources available to motorcyclists today. Take a little time to check them out. You may discover new safety tips, fun roads, products you've just got to have for your machine. Or maybe you'll make some new, motorcycle-savvy friends. It's not a comprehensive list, but it provides a rich taste of the many facets of motorcycling. Enjoy the journey.

Aerostich/RiderWearHouse (www.aerostich.com): This company offers everything a touring rider needs and more, from its famed Aerostich riding suits to tire repair kits. Aerostich isn't just for touring riders, however. There are hard-to-find items that are useful for all motorcyclists. Do you need saddlebags, seat bags, tank bags, or even a special bag to carry your laptop? Aerostich has them. What about titanium tire irons? Yep, Aerostich has those also.

American Historic Racing Motorcycle Association (www.ahrma.org): If you want to get into vintage motorcycle racing, you need to join AHRMA. Check out the organization's Web site to see what fun you can have on older machines on asphalt racetracks and in the dirt.

American Honda Motor Company (www.powersports.honda.com): The official Honda motorcycle Web site.

American Motorcyclist Association (www.AMADirectlink.com): This Web site is overwhelming. It's chock-full of information about everything from riding tips for new riders to touring tips for experienced riders. Plus, you can find out about government attacks on motorcycling, get the latest info on professional racing, check out some of the association's outstanding tours, and read new bike reviews.

American Suzuki Motor Corporation (www.suzukicycles.com): The official Suzuki motorcycle Web site.

Antique Motorcycle Club of America (www.antiquemotorcycle.org): This club is the recognized expert organization in the United States on antique motorcycles.

Biker Billy (www.bikerbilly.com): Motorcycling's favorite cook serves up some hot dishes and advice on eating on the road.

BMW Motorrad USA (www.bmwmotorcycles.com): The official BMW motorcycle Web site.

Buell (www.buell.com): The official Buell motorcycle Web site.

Chaparral (www.chaparral-racing.com): Chaparral bills itself as "the Destination for Riders" and has just about anything a street or dirt motorcyclist needs, from helmets and jackets to tires and wheels. Check out Chaparral's "Closeout" section where you can find stuff for as much as 60 percent off, including women's riding gear.

Christian Motorcyclists Association (www.cmausa.org): You'll find the Christian Motorcyclists Association at most of the major motorcycling rallies and a lot of other events, giving riders free water and doing other good deeds.

Competition Accessories (www.compacc.com): Competition Accessories is a motorcycle and accessories store that does a lot of business online. Check out this site for special deals on helmets, jackets, gloves, and more.

Cycle Trader (www.cycletrader.com): This site is a good place to look if you want to buy or sell a motorcycle.

Cycle World International Motorcycle Shows (www.motorcycleshows.com): The winters can be long and lonely in some states when you can't ride your motorcycle because of the cold and snow. But you can get your motorcycling fix by attending one of the Cycle World International Motorcycle Shows around the country. The shows showcase new bikes and products and are a lot of fun.

Cycle World magazine (www.cycleworld.com): The largest motorcycle magazine in America, *Cycle World* does new bike reviews, motorcycle comparison tests, personality features, stories on interesting bikes, and more.

Daytona Bike Week (www.daytonachamber.com/bwhome.html): The official Web site for Daytona Bike Week, you can learn everything you need to know before you head to sunny Florida for the festivities.

Dennis Kirk (www.denniskirk.com): A mail-order outfit that boasts having more than 125,000 items in stock and ready to send. No matter what kind of riding you do, whether it's street or dirt, cruising, or touring, this company probably has the part you need. Be sure to check out the company's "outlet store" for special bargains.

Dirt Rider magazine (www.dirtrider.com): This magazine is for riders who love to play in the dirt. It serves up new bike tests, offers riding and training tips, and reviews gear.

Fox Racing (www.foxracing.com): One of the most famous names in off-road riding gear, Fox Racing is a good place to go for jerseys, pants, boots, and even T-shirts. The Fox head logo is something that motorcyclists see and recognize, and nonmotorcyclists don't.

Harley-Davidson Motor Corporation (www.harley-davidson.com): The official Harley-Davidson motorcycle Web site.

Iron Pony (www.ironpony.com): This motorcycling megastore that does mail order offers some great deals for both street and dirt riders. You can get leather motorcycling jackets for $110, Fox off-road jerseys and pants starting at $12.99 each, and off-road boots for $60.

International Journal of Motorcycle Studies (www.ijms.nova.edu): This journal includes interesting research related to motorcycling.

Kawasaki Motors Corporation USA (www.kawasaki.com): The official Kawasaki site.

Laconia Motorcycle Week (www.laconiamcweek.com): The official Web site of Laconia Motorcycle Week in New Hampshire. You can find out about lodging, vendors, and more.

Legend of the Motorcycle (www.legendofthemotorcycle.com): This annual motorcycle show in California features some fantastic machines every year. Check out the photos.

Let's Ride (www.lets-ride.com): Contains great listings of motorcycling events around the nation. Look up your own state and you're sure to find dozens to attend.

Mad Maps (www.madmaps.com): If you need maps of great back roads for motorcycles, Mad Maps is the place to go.

Motorcycle Cruiser magazine (www.motorcyclecruiser.com): If you ride a cruiser, you need to check out *Motorcycle Cruiser*. It reviews bikes and products, and offers a lot of motorcycle riding tips.

Motorcycle Consumer News (www.mcnews.com): *Motorcycle Consumer News* is a monthly motorcycling magazine that does product evaluations and new bike reviews, gets into the technical aspects of motorcycles, and does stories on how to be a safe rider. This magazine is unique in that it accepts no advertising — definitely worth checking out.

Motorcycle Forum (www.motorcycleforum.com): Forums for all brands of motorcycles.

Motorcycle Hall of Fame Museum (www.motorcyclemuseum.org): The Motorcycle Hall of Fame Museum at the headquarters of the American Motorcyclist Association in Pickerington, Ohio, isn't a stodgy old museum with a bunch of old bikes sitting around. Its exhibits are full of excitement, like its "Motocross America" exhibit that chronicles the rise of motocross and Supercross in America, and its "MotoStars: Celebrities + Motorcycles" exhibit that showcases the stories of movie and other stars and their motorcycles. Plus, you can learn a lot about the history of motorcycling from the Web site.

Motorcycle News (www.motorcyclenews.com): A British motorcycling magazine that gets a lot of world scoops on new bikes. It's also interesting to see the legal issues that European riders face.

Motorcycle Tourer's Forum (www.mctourer.com): Chat with your touring buds about great trips, tips, and destinations.

Motorcycle Riders Foundation (www.mrf.org): A national motorcyclists' rights organization that focuses on street riding issues.

Motorcycle Roads (www.motorcycleroads.com): A great source for guidance on great motorcycling roads in the United States. If you're planning a trip to another state, or even just want to explore some nice roads in your own state, check out this Web site.

Motorcycle Safety Foundation (www.msf-usa.org): Whether you're a beginning rider or have a lot of years of riding under your belt, the MSF site is worth checking out. You can get riding tips, find out how to sign up for a motorcycle safety training class for beginner or experienced riders, and even discover how to become a motorcycle safety trainer instructor so you can share your love of the sport.

MotorcycleUSA.com (www.motorcycle-usa.com): An online motorcycle magazine that features bike tests, riding stories, new products, and more.

Motorcyclist magazine (www.motorcyclistonline.com): The second largest motorcycle magazine in the nation, *Motorcyclist* covers new bikes, does features on personalities, and does some great work comparing motorcycles.

National Highway Traffic Safety Administration (www.nhtsa.dot.gov): The official government site where you can get the latest information on motorcycle crash and fatality statistics, what the U.S. government is doing to reduce motorcycle crashes, and what's up with motorcycling research.

Skull rings (www.skullrings.net): Okay, what self-respecting biker doesn't have a skull ring? Get one here.

Skunkworx Custom Cycle (www.skunkworxcc.com): Award-winning custom bike builder Bruce Mullin's Web site.

SPEED (www.speedtv.com): If you want to watch some of the fastest motorcycle racing action on the planet, SPEED is the place to go. Besides giving you the TV schedule for motorcycle races, SPEED offers news on the motorcycling industry, and previews new motorcycles.

Star (www.starmotorcycles.com): The official Star motorcycles Web site.

Sturgis Motorcycle Museum & Hall of Fame (www.sturgismuseum.com): If you're planning a trip to Sturgis, South Dakota, you won't want to miss this museum.

Sturgis Motorcycle Rally (www.sturgismotorcyclerally.com): If you want to get the scoop on all the excitement surrounding the Sturgis Motorcycle Rally, one of the biggest rallies on the planet, check out this official Web site. There are photos from past rallies, information on lodging, a schedule of events, and more.

THOR (www.thormx.com): A famous name in off-road riding gear.

Touratech-USA (www.touratech-usa.com): If you want to go adventure touring, then Touratech-USA should be your first stop on the Internet before you go anywhere else. You can get luggage, camping gear (including an outdoor toilet paper holder), titanium chopsticks, global positioning system receivers and mounts, and even a large gas tank for certain BMW models so you can extend your adventure-touring ride.

Victory (www.polarisindustries.com): The official Victory motorcycles Web site.

Whitehorse Gear (www.whitehorsegear.com): Great riding gear like jackets and lots of tools like specialized pliers are just some of the items sold at Whitehorse gear. Take a look at their vast array of stuff and start making your Christmas list now.

Yamaha Motor Corporation USA (www.yamaha-motor.com): The official Yamaha motorcycle Web site.

Yoshimura R & D (www.yoshimura-rd.com): One of the best companies in America for performance products such as exhaust systems. This company has been heavily involved in motorcycle racing for decades.

Index

• *N* •

• *O* •

• *P* •

• T •

• V •

BUSINESS, CAREERS & PERSONAL FINANCE

0-7645-9847-3

0-7645-2431-3

Also available:
- Business Plans Kit For Dummies
  0-7645-9794-9
- Economics For Dummies
  0-7645-5726-2
- Grant Writing For Dummies
  0-7645-8416-2
- Home Buying For Dummies
  0-7645-5331-3
- Managing For Dummies
  0-7645-1771-6
- Marketing For Dummies
  0-7645-5600-2

- Personal Finance For Dummies
  0-7645-2590-5*
- Resumes For Dummies
  0-7645-5471-9
- Selling For Dummies
  0-7645-5363-1
- Six Sigma For Dummies
  0-7645-6798-5
- Small Business Kit For Dummies
  0-7645-5984-2
- Starting an eBay Business For Dummies
  0-7645-6924-4
- Your Dream Career For Dummies
  0-7645-9795-7

HOME & BUSINESS COMPUTER BASICS

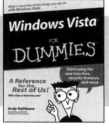

0-470-05432-8

0-471-75421-8

Also available:
- Cleaning Windows Vista For Dummies
  0-471-78293-9
- Excel 2007 For Dummies
  0-470-03737-7
- Mac OS X Tiger For Dummies
  0-7645-7675-5
- MacBook For Dummies
  0-470-04859-X
- Macs For Dummies
  0-470-04849-2
- Office 2007 For Dummies
  0-470-00923-3

- Outlook 2007 For Dummies
  0-470-03830-6
- PCs For Dummies
  0-7645-8958-X
- Salesforce.com For Dummies
  0-470-04893-X
- Upgrading & Fixing Laptops For Dummies
  0-7645-8959-8
- Word 2007 For Dummies
  0-470-03658-3
- Quicken 2007 For Dummies
  0-470-04600-7

FOOD, HOME, GARDEN, HOBBIES, MUSIC & PETS

0-7645-8404-9

0-7645-9904-6

Also available:
- Candy Making For Dummies
  0-7645-9734-5
- Card Games For Dummies
  0-7645-9910-0
- Crocheting For Dummies
  0-7645-4151-X
- Dog Training For Dummies
  0-7645-8418-9
- Healthy Carb Cookbook For Dummies
  0-7645-8476-6
- Home Maintenance For Dummies
  0-7645-5215-5

- Horses For Dummies
  0-7645-9797-3
- Jewelry Making & Beading For Dummies
  0-7645-2571-9
- Orchids For Dummies
  0-7645-6759-4
- Puppies For Dummies
  0-7645-5255-4
- Rock Guitar For Dummies
  0-7645-5356-9
- Sewing For Dummies
  0-7645-6847-7
- Singing For Dummies
  0-7645-2475-5

INTERNET & DIGITAL MEDIA

0-470-04529-9

0-470-04894-8

Also available:
- Blogging For Dummies
  0-471-77084-1
- Digital Photography For Dummies
  0-7645-9802-3
- Digital Photography All-in-One Desk Reference For Dummies
  0-470-03743-1
- Digital SLR Cameras and Photography For Dummies
  0-7645-9803-1
- eBay Business All-in-One Desk Reference For Dummies
  0-7645-8438-3
- HDTV For Dummies
  0-470-09673-X

- Home Entertainment PCs For Dummies
  0-470-05523-5
- MySpace For Dummies
  0-470-09529-6
- Search Engine Optimization For Dummies
  0-471-97998-8
- Skype For Dummies
  0-470-04891-3
- The Internet For Dummies
  0-7645-8996-2
- Wiring Your Digital Home For Dummies
  0-471-91830-X

* Separate Canadian edition also available
† Separate U.K. edition also available

Available wherever books are sold. For more information or to order direct: U.S. customers visit www.dummies.com or call 1-877-762-2974.
U.K. customers visit www.wileyeurope.com or call 0800 243407. Canadian customers visit www.wiley.ca or call 1-800-567-4797.

 WILEY

SPORTS, FITNESS, PARENTING, RELIGION & SPIRITUALITY

0-471-76871-5   0-7645-7841-3

Also available:

- Catholicism For Dummies
  0-7645-5391-7
- Exercise Balls For Dummies
  0-7645-5623-1
- Fitness For Dummies
  0-7645-7851-0
- Football For Dummies
  0-7645-3936-1
- Judaism For Dummies
  0-7645-5299-6
- Potty Training For Dummies
  0-7645-5417-4
- Buddhism For Dummies
  0-7645-5359-3

- Pregnancy For Dummies
  0-7645-4483-7 †
- Ten Minute Tone-Ups For Dummies
  0-7645-7207-5
- NASCAR For Dummies
  0-7645-7681-X
- Religion For Dummies
  0-7645-5264-3
- Soccer For Dummies
  0-7645-5229-5
- Women in the Bible For Dummies
  0-7645-8475-8

TRAVEL

0-7645-7749-2   0-7645-6945-7

Also available:

- Alaska For Dummies
  0-7645-7746-8
- Cruise Vacations For Dummies
  0-7645-6941-4
- England For Dummies
  0-7645-4276-1
- Europe For Dummies
  0-7645-7529-5
- Germany For Dummies
  0-7645-7823-5
- Hawaii For Dummies
  0-7645-7402-7

- Italy For Dummies
  0-7645-7386-1
- Las Vegas For Dummies
  0-7645-7382-9
- London For Dummies
  0-7645-4277-X
- Paris For Dummies
  0-7645-7630-5
- RV Vacations For Dummies
  0-7645-4442-X
- Walt Disney World & Orlando
  For Dummies
  0-7645-9660-8

GRAPHICS, DESIGN & WEB DEVELOPMENT

0-7645-8815-X   0-7645-9571-7

Also available:

- 3D Game Animation For Dummies
  0-7645-8789-7
- AutoCAD 2006 For Dummies
  0-7645-8925-3
- Building a Web Site For Dummies
  0-7645-7144-3
- Creating Web Pages For Dummies
  0-470-08030-2
- Creating Web Pages All-in-One Desk
  Reference For Dummies
  0-7645-4345-8
- Dreamweaver 8 For Dummies
  0-7645-9649-7

- InDesign CS2 For Dummies
  0-7645-9572-5
- Macromedia Flash 8 For Dummies
  0-7645-9691-8
- Photoshop CS2 and Digital
  Photography For Dummies
  0-7645-9580-6
- Photoshop Elements 4 For Dummies
  0-471-77483-9
- Syndicating Web Sites with RSS Feeds
  For Dummies
  0-7645-8848-6
- Yahoo! SiteBuilder For Dummies
  0-7645-9800-7

NETWORKING, SECURITY, PROGRAMMING & DATABASES

0-7645-7728-X   0-471-74940-0

Also available:

- Access 2007 For Dummies
  0-470-04612-0
- ASP.NET 2 For Dummies
  0-7645-7907-X
- C# 2005 For Dummies
  0-7645-9704-3
- Hacking For Dummies
  0-470-05235-X
- Hacking Wireless Networks
  For Dummies
  0-7645-9730-2
- Java For Dummies
  0-470-08716-1

- Microsoft SQL Server 2005 For Dummies
  0-7645-7755-7
- Networking All-in-One Desk Reference
  For Dummies
  0-7645-9939-9
- Preventing Identity Theft For Dummies
  0-7645-7336-5
- Telecom For Dummies
  0-471-77085-X
- Visual Studio 2005 All-in-One Desk
  Reference For Dummies
  0-7645-9775-2
- XML For Dummies
  0-7645-8845-1